THEATRE IN PRISON
THEORY AND PRACTICE

Edited by Michael Balfour

intellect™
Bristol, UK
Portland, OR, USA

First Published in the UK in 2004 by
Intellect Books, PO Box 862, Bristol BS99 1DE, UK

First Published in the USA in 2004 by
Intellect Books, ISBS, 920 NE 58th Ave. Suite 300, Portland, Oregon 97213-3786, USA

A catalogue record for this book is available from the British Library

ISBN 1-84150-066-6

Cover Design: Patricia Emery (www.patriciaemery.com)
All photos reproduced with kind permission from Jack Webb, ©Jack Webb.
Copy Editor: Julie Strudwick

Printed and bound in Great Britain by Antony Rowe Ltd.

CONTENTS

Acknowledgements

I would like to thank all the authors for their hard work and determination to turn in their chapters. Particularly for those outside the luxurious confines of academia (!), as finding the time to think and write is not always easy.

My grateful thanks also to King Alfred's, Winchester for allowing me the time to edit this book. And to my colleagues and especially the students on the BA Drama, Theatre and Television course who have inspired, challenged and surprised me with their ideas over the last four years.

I would also like to thank Ginny for her support, advice and editorial guidance, and for knowing when to drag me away from my computer.

The Prison Poem by 'Ali' and the screenplay *One Hour in the Semi Open* were given to me by people involved in prison theatre projects. I have tried in vain to track down the writers of these pieces to credit their work. I hope seeing the work in print will be of some consolation.

The biggest inspiration for the book has been the people in prison I have worked with over the last ten years. Their stories have provoked insight, depression, self-analysis, politicisation, anger, fear, laughter and a million other forms of emotion I never knew I had. Their willingness (and sometimes the opposite) has forced me to consider and re-consider this thing we call theatre. And if there is one thing prison work teaches you it is humility. Because the only thing I am certain of is that I never taught anyone in prison anything, but I learnt a hell of a lot in the process of failing.

The Contributors

Michael Balfour is a Senior Lecturer and Director of the BA Drama, Theatre and Television course at King Alfred's, Winchester. He is a former Director of the Theatre in Prisons and Probation (TIPP) Centre, where he worked from 1994-1997.
He has extensive experience as a theatre practitioner and consultant in community-based arts projects, including work for the British Council in Nigeria, Youth Offending Programmes in the UK, and cross-community work in Northern Ireland. He is the author of *Theatre and War: Performance in Extremis, 1933-1945* (Berghahn Books, 2001), and *The Use of Drama in the Rehabilitation of Violent Male Offenders* (Edwin Mellen Press, 2004).

Centre for Conflict Resolution:
Christopher Glen Malgas is a correctional officer at Pollsmoor Prison in the Western Cape; Joanna Flanders-Thomas is a former Co-ordinator of CCR's Prison Transformation Project; Chris Giffard is a CCR Research Associate; Stan Henkeman is a Senior Trainer with CCR; Roshila Nair is Editor of Track Two at the Centre for Conflict Resolution; Paul is a prisoner at Pollsmoor Prison, and participated in conflict resolution programmes run by the Centre for Conflict Resolution at the prison.

Clark Baim established Geese Theatre UK after touring in the mid-1980s with Geese Theatre USA. He was the UK company's first Director and is now an independent psychodrama psychotherapist, supervisor and theatre director/teacher. He continues to specialise in work with offenders and among his other responsibilities he is a lead national trainer on accredited programmes for the National Probation Service.

Imogen Blood is a qualified social worker who has worked with drug users in prisons, supported accommodation and probation. She is now Senior Research and Evaluation Officer at NACRO (National Association for the Care and Resettlement of Offenders) where she has responsibility for evaluating criminal justice based interventions with drug users.

Maud Clarke co-founded Somebody's Daughter Theatre, in the early 1980s, and has since developed it into a unique Australian company of women who have experienced imprisonment and drug addiction. As well as numerous prison projects, there has been a series of professional shows at venues such as the Malthouse Theatre between 1991 and 1999 in Melbourne; a sell-out season at the 1995 National Festival of Australian Theatre in Canberra; and in 2000, an art exhibition and performances at the Victorian Arts Centre. The company has also made a number of tours to rural and regional centres in Victoria, the Australian Capital Territory and New South Wales. Clarke has made presentations at a wide range of state, national and international conferences, as well as sessions for health professionals, magistrates, community organisations, university students and academics.

Arnold Goldstein has written more than sixty books and published over a hundred articles on such subjects as aggression, social training, and juvenile delinquency. He pioneered the intervention method of structured learning and developed model programmes such as Skillstreaming, PREPARE and Aggression Replacement Training. These programmes are being implemented across the United States and in many different countries throughout the world. Dr. Goldstein was the initiator for The Center for Research on Aggression at the University of Syracuse and received numerous academic awards. Together with some twenty art experts, academics and practitioners he founded The International Center for Aggression Replacement Training (ICART) in 2001. The chapter in this book was co-written with Douglas A. Blancero, Wilma Carthan, and Barry Glick.

Paul Heritage is Professor of Drama and Performance at Queen Mary, University of London and Director of People's Palace Projects, a research centre in applied performance with offices in London and Rio de Janeiro. He set up the Theatre in Prisons and Probation (TIPP) Centre with James Thompson at Manchester University in 1992. Since 1991, he has been working in Brazil where, in collaboration with Augusto Boal and the Centre for the Theatre of the Oppressed, he has established the Staging Human Rights programme. He has organised two international conferences on theatre and development for The British Council entitled Changing the Scene 1 & 2, and edited the two publications which followed (1999 and 2000). A former director of Gay Sweatshop, he has published a variety of articles and chapters on sexuality and performance. In Brazil he has directed Shakespeare productions with university students, young people in conflict with the law and some of Brazil's most famous soap-opera stars. He has a studio theatre named after him inside the prison complex of the Federal District of Brasília. For further information: www.peoplespalace.org

Dr. Emman Frank Idoko, is a Senior Lecturer at the University of Maiduguri, Borno State, Nigeria. He has been a teacher of drama and theatre for ten years. He won the DAAD (German Academic Exchange Service) in 1999-2000 and the Alexander von Humboldt Foundation AvH (Georg Forster) 2001-2002.

Chris Johnston is a writer, director and performer. He is particularly interested in the theatricalisation of the social dynamics of community, either through a closed drama process or through interactions with an audience. He is currently co-director of Rideout (Creative Arts for Rehabilitation) and director of Fluxx, which creates improvised performances in a range of theatre and non-theatre settings. He is also Fellow in Creative and Performing Arts at Warwick University. He is the author of *House of Games* (*Making Theatre from Everyday Life*), published by Nick Hern Books.

Baz Kershaw trained and worked as a design engineer before reading English and Philosophy at Manchester University. He has extensive experience as a director, devisor and writer in experimental, radical and community-based theatre, including productions at the legendary Drury Lane Arts Lab in London. He has published many articles in international journals, and is the author of *The Politics of Performance: Radical Theatre as Cultural Intervention* (Routledge, 1992) and *The Radical in Performance: Between Brecht and Baudrillard* (Routledge, 1999); and co-author of *Engineers of the Imagination: the Welfare State Handbook* (Methuen 1990). He is currently Chair of Drama at the University of Bristol, and Director of PARIP (Practice as Research in Performance).

Kate McCoy is Theatre in Prisons and Probation's (TiPP) senior practitioner and Projects Director. She works as an arts trainer and facilitator in the Criminal Justice System particularly enjoying work with drug users, women and projects exploring conflict. She teaches Applied Theatre in the Drama Department at Manchester University where she is an Honorary Research Associate. Current interests include NVC (non-violent communication) and learning to play Bridge.

Ken Saro-Wiwa was one of Nigeria's most beloved writers. Poet, novelist and screenplay writer, his work won both critical and popular acclaim. He was executed by hanging in Nigeria on 10 November 1995. He was arrested the previous year and charged with incitement to murder. He was an outspoken critic of successive military governments and a defendant of the Ogoni tribe, of which he was a member.
James Thompson is a Senior Lecturer in the Drama Department, Manchester University and Director of the Centre for Applied Theatre Research. He was a founder of the Theatre in Prisons and Probation Centre and Director until 1999. He has devised and run theatre programmes in Brazil, Burkina Faso, Sri Lanka, the UK and the US. He is author of *Drama Workshops for Anger Management and Offending Behaviour* (1999) and *Applied Theatre: Bewilderment and Beyond* (2003) and editor of *Prison Theatre: Perspectives and Practices*.

Philip G. Zimbardo has been Professor of Psychology at Stanford University for over thirty years. He has authored more than two hundred articles and has received numerous awards for writing, teaching, and research. The most recent of these awards include the Phi Beta Kappa Distinguished Teaching Award for Northern California (1998), the Robert Daniels Teaching Excellence Award, APA Division 2, Society for the Teaching of Psychology (1999), and an APA Presidential Citation for outstanding contributions to psychology for the Discovering Psychology video series (1994). The chapter in this book was co-written with Craig Haney and Curtis Banks.

For my mother

INTRODUCTION

> In a respectable practical society, where everybody is useful, the poetic imagination in man is an anachronism, an irritant which disturbs the chemical sleep of habits of such a system by making it conscious of the degradation of its mechanisation, by the appearance of extraordinary desires; by overshadowing it with the super-reality of theatre, by unsettling it with a thirst and a hunger for external beauty (Collins, 1944, p. 9).

This is a collection of international essays describing the rich diversity of theatre and drama work in prison-related contexts. From role-plays with street gangs in the USA, to comedic cabaret with drug users in Manchester; from staging Human Rights performances in Brazilian penitentiaries, to psychodrama with violent and sexually abusive offenders in therapeutic communities, the book will discuss, analyse and reflect on theoretical notions and practical applications of theatre for, with and by the incarcerated.

The writers are theatre practitioners, academics, prisoners and guards, all with considerable experience in the field. They explore key aspects of their practice – problemitising, theorising, describing and questioning specific approaches to working in prisons. I have also included poems and plays written by prisoners, which will, I hope, help to add additional insight into prison life.

This book follows on from *Prison Theatre, Practices and Perspectives* (Thompson, 1998). As such it seeks to record the developments in the field during the interim years, but also to extend and enrich its insights into how theatre and drama practice engage with criminal justice systems by looking at examples from different cultural contexts. What are the paradigms of working in gang-run wings in South Africa? How can theatre be dialogic in a country with four hundred languages (Nigeria)? The theme remains the same. How do theatre makers negotiate the territory, what compromises are made, what 'truths' are revealed by the work, and what theories are generated by these experiences?

Some History

It is probable that soon after the first prison was built, the first unrecorded moment of prison theatre/art occurred. In 1870 there is evidence of drawings by plains Indians imprisoned in US Army forts (Berlo et al., 1996). The drawings were done on pages ripped from 'ledger books' and stolen from the army, who used them to record numbers of prisoners and descriptions of appropriated possessions. It is difficult to say what the Indians might have felt about their art at the time, but the image of the transformation of bureaucratic forms into autobiographical art resonates as an act of self-affirmation.

There is also considerable evidence of prison theatre and art work during the Second World War, of performances in concentration camps, in ghettos, in internment camps and in the communist Gulags (Balfour, 2001; Berghaus and Wolff, 1989; Berghaus 1996; Jelavich, 1993; Solzhenitsyn, 1975).

1

Theatre or art in these prison camps did not save anyone from their ultimate fate. No piece of artwork, no performance, no poetry was lasting protection against the orders onto a transport to 'the East'. What might be said, in a context where surviving one more day was no small achievement, was that 'individual identity could be reclaimed – albeit momentarily – through art. Art, music and performance transformed fear into freedom. The act of making art suspended the collective nightmare...it helped to sustain hope, a sense of the self, and the will to live' (Dutlinger, 2001, p. 5).

As the Collins quote at the start of this introduction observes, in a land governed by the useful (Arbeit Macht Frei?), the presence of the 'poetic imagination' tends to act as an 'irritant', whose power to resist lies in the inversion of being purposeful. There was no hope of an opening night, or an exhibition, the impulse came from a strong desire to create. In some people this need was as important as food, shelter and personal safety. Because in creating art and performances they were putting these basic needs at risk. This may appear at first a rather romanticised view, but the evidence of countless art and performances, made under the murderous conditions of prison camps in the Second World War, provide graphic testimony that the creative impulse is more fundamental to humans that might be expected. What is of importance here is not the 'the product' for, like the original values of Aboriginal art, the product is the residue of an impulse to express something, to represent an experience about the nature of being human. And it is this impulse that needs to be valued.

These traces of prison theatre history are important, because like contemporary practice, they raise questions about the nature and reason of the creative process for the incarcerated. Why would an Indian risk being killed in order to steal paper to draw on? Why would a starving person in a concentration camp hold back food to use it as colour pigment on an elicit painting? These questions point to a need for creativity that goes beyond the basic perception of art as entertainment, leisure or even education. In these extreme contexts, where it was far easier to give up than it was to have a spark of hope and humanity, people took the risk to create and find a temporary escape, a moment of resistance, against formalised and pervasive systems of power.

Where theatre (and art) is born out of a need for the creative impulse, or it respects the integrity of the creative process, it may serve out its ultimate purpose – to be useless. But theatre, in particular, can be made to be useful. It can be fashioned into a tool designed to re-educate, re-socialise, and 'rehabilitate' people. Or it can try. Solzhenitsyn's (1975) wry observations of the cultural life in the Soviet Gulag prison camps were that as soon as theatre served a political purpose it became burdened by inept 'messages' of moral propaganda (right or left wing), as soon as it became useful to 'the authorities', it becomes heavy with 'the mechanisation...of dead ideas' (p. 118). Solzhenitsyn points his finger critically at theatre that allies itself too closely with the systems of power, when it becomes drenched in ideological morality that convinces few and undermines any potential efficacy of the medium.

These early stories of theatre in prison also point to the danger of aligning art too closely with 'the system' (even one that attempts to be benign). In the context of prison, this humanising process will never be a fundamental priority. It exists in contradiction to the administrative task of the institution. Prison is in the business of containment, observation, punishment, categorisation, restriction, separation, and on occasion rehabilitation. And even the rehabilitation is generally framed within the paradigm of the useful (re-socialisation into a life full of purpose). So prison theatre, theatre in prisons, is a term in eternal contradiction with itself. A living, breathing, noisy, chaotic, confusing and compelling paradox.

The more recent history of prison theatre is one in which these contradictions have been encountered, questioned, challenged and explored in a variety of ways. There is a continuing need for the field to walk a tightrope between incorporation into and resistance to the criminal justice system it seeks to exist in. Unlike the example of the war years, where the prisoners created illicit art, contemporary artists have been successful in breaking into prisons and persuading institutions to legitimise artistic activity. But as Heritage notes in his chapter in this book, sometimes the price one pays for the visa into the borderlands of the prison, is a high one. In gaining entry to the institution, one enters a building that echoes with a confusion of criminological discourses. One needs to quickly learn the language in order to negotiate and haggle with the gatekeeper. But in this fraught, complex negotiation, one also needs to hold onto the language of the useless, to not forget that the performance for the gatekeeper is but one performance that gives way to further performances. It is therefore critical that the contemporary prison theatre field needs to be approached with both an understanding of criminological discourse, and an awareness of the paradox of creative work within a system orientated as much to punishment as to rehabilitation. To not understand this uneven landscape, is to blunder around it without a compass, map and a healthy sense of direction.

In the next section I will outline some key elements of criminology, and will use specific examples drawn from a UK context. This is a conscious bias, but a bias that needs to be explained in a book dealing with international contexts. It does not imply a uniqueness or superiority (that would be foolish) it simply reflects my own familiarity with the context of the criminal justice system in Britain. The following therefore, is meant as an overview that, I hope, will help the reader to identify and recognise some of the complexities of criminological discourse.

Brief Encounters with Criminology

Criminology's history is not one of steady progress and refinement because, as in other academic fields, it does not exist in a social or political vacuum: the dominant ideas of a period (whether establishment or radical), the social problems of a particular society, the government in power and shifting political pressures – all shape its discourse. This is not to suggest a relativism of theory, rather it points to a reflexivity. Young's clarification is useful here: 'theory emerges out of a certain social and political conjuncture: this generates points of sensitivity and areas of blindness which inhibit the development of a general theory...'(Young, 1994, p. 71).

Where then might a theatre practitioner fit into this multi-agency field? As soon as s/he enters the confines of a criminal justice institution, s/he will be judged as operating from a particular theoretical viewpoint. For example, the combination of cognitive-behavioural methodologies with theatrical techniques in a short educational programme addressing offending behaviour implies a belief in the agency and free will of the individual. This is an assumption that cannot be taken for granted. Indeed it would be foolish to deny the existence of other influential factors that can act on individuals and lead to them breaking the law e.g. political reasons, economic hardship, biological determinants.

Two different images of the criminal actor have persisted during the last hundred years of criminology. The first is of a wilful hedonist who takes deliberate decisions to break the rules of a consensus. The second is of one who has been predisposed to crime by forces within or external to him/her (possessed by demons, psychologically 'sick', hereditary criminal personality). It is notable that the most diverse theories converge with these two images in the most unlikely of pairings; for example the conservative and the anarchist hold that an offender operates with free will (for one it is a lapse in moral reasoning, for the other the criminal is a hero); whilst the Lombrosian and the social reformer believe that the actor's behaviour is determined (one argues for biological factors, the other for the influence of poor socio-economic environments). These two equally abstract images of the wilful and the 'propelled' actor reverberate throughout the history of criminology, despite their tenuous link to social reality.

Voluntarism

At one end of the theoretical continuum there are paradigms which are characterised by a belief in the wilful offender (or individual voluntarism) such as classicism, conservatism and humanist reformism. Whilst it is misleading to indiscriminately use these generic terms to denote absolute paradigms of thinking, they provide a useful framework of different forms of inquiry. For example, classicism, although referring to such different thinkers as Beccaria and Bentham and eighteenth-century thought more generally, maintain similar views of a rational, free-will offender.[1] Classicism holds that the social order is maintained by a contractual legal consensus and that the definition of crime is a violation of the consensus; the extent of crime is marginal and is the result of individual irrationality which can be corrected through punishment and deterrence.

Conservatism differs from classicism in a number of small, but important points (Haag, 1975). Conservatism maintains that the social order is essentially a moral and traditional consensus (class system, family values) and that threats to the social order may be considered a crime. Conservatism sees the cause of crime as the result of deviance (as a result of personal gratification), and correspondingly believes punishment must be rigorously enforced, to teach a lesson to individuals, and to act as a general deterrence to the rest of society.

The classical and conservative picture of the wilful law violator lies behind endeavours to punish the criminal and protect society. The fundamental argument is that the proper amount of legal punishment is enough to deter crime. Those who are not deterred by the threat of punishment should, upon proof of guilt and conviction, be punished severely so that they will never violate the law again. The weapon used to enforce this view is harsh and long sentences or, in some countries, capital punishment. Classicism and conservatism tend to a retributive view of policy, advocating that the focus of justice should be on the victim of crime rather than the criminal. The role of the justice agency should be to protect the innocent from criminal acts. The main aim of the justice system is to take criminals out of the community, until they are fit to return.

Like classicism, humanist reformism maintains that an act of crime breaks a social contract, and that as a result society has the right to redress the wrong-doing. However, emerging out of the 'excess of violence' in the eighteenth-century, reformism proposed that the limit of punishment was 'the humanity of each subject'; punishment should be transparent to the crime and as non-arbitrary as possible; punishment should be a deterrent, a recompense, and a lesson (Dreyfus and Rabinow, 1982, p. 147-148). The influence of reformism on the current system has meant that although a greater proportion of people are going to prison, the sentences they receive for similar crimes are less likely to vary widely than in previous years (Siegal and Senna, 1990). The emphasis is on the examination of penal codes in an effort to simplify the classification of offences and create a more rational approach to sentencing.

Positivism

At the other end of the theoretical continuum is the image of an individual whose behaviour is more or less determined by internal or external factors. Positivism is traditionally the antithesis of classicism. Essentially positivism holds that behaviour is governed by biological, physiological and psychological factors. The criminal actor is one who violates the behavioural consensus, due to genetic/physiological incapacity or ineffective inculcation.

Positivism is a diverse theoretical approach that describes a range of criminological work which has been carried out within an empiricist framework. However it emerged from quite specific claims of Lombroso and his *scuola positiva* in the late nineteenth century (the born criminal, the constitutional and hereditary roots of criminal conduct, criminal types, etc.) (Smith, 1968). Lombroso put forward the view that the criminal is born and not made, and that each criminal could be distinguished from non-criminal people by the 'stigmate' (Young, 1994, p. 71): in other words, certain physical abnormalities which would be found only in criminals. Lombroso although not the first to 'discover' the 'criminal type' is now often used as a reference point to identify theories which seek to locate criminality as a naturally occurring entity. For example, Thompson wrote in 1867 about 'the criminal class' describing these individuals as 'morally insane' and 'defective in physical organisation ...from hereditary causes' in a way that appeared altogether 'Lombrosian' before Lombroso. Thompson (1867, p. 341):

> All who have seen much of criminals agree that they have a singular family likeness or caste...Their physique is coarse and repulsive; their complexion dingy, almost atrabilious; their face, figure, and mien, disagreeable. The women are painfully ugly; and the men look stolid, and many of them brutal, indicating physical and moral deterioration. In fact there is a stamp on them in form and expression which seems to me the heritage of the class.

Although Lombroso's theories have been largely discredited, the general proposition that heredity plays a part in the causation of crime has continued to develop. The contemporary view is that what each of us inherits is a biological system that may provide an orientation or tendency to respond in a certain way to our environment (Rowe, 1990). However, positivism also tends to acknowledge the influence of other factors. For example Erikson's position is expressed in his idea of 'triple book-keeping'; that in order to understand identity we need to look at its biological basis, at a person's development and at the social context in which he or she lives, each in relation to the others – and on the understanding that none of these are fixed (Stevens, 1991, p. 29). From a rational point of view, positivists do not regard criminals as being separate from the rest of the population. Instead, criminals are seen as representing the extreme end of a continuous distribution, 'very much as a mental defective represents the extreme end of...intelligence' (Eysenck, 1970, p. 74).

Social democratic positivism also holds a determinist view of behaviour, but prefers to see crime as the result of external and environmental factors (Young, 1994, p. 73). Social democratic positivism was part of a widespread post-war consensus that one of the causes of crime was impoverished social conditions. It was part of a more general conviction that through political interventions anti-social conditions could be improved resulting in a consequent reduction in anti-social behaviour. During the post-war period in Britain much work was done to demolish slums, increase educational standards, create full employment, and introduce comprehensive welfare reforms. The root cause of crime, the social democratic positivism argument holds, is poverty, deprivation, lack of education. The general theory holds that criminals themselves are victims of poverty, lack of hope, alienation, family disorganisation, racism and other social problems. Crime can be controlled by enabling people to cope with their life situations, and helping them to lead law-abiding lifestyles. The social democratic view believes that it is far cheaper, more efficient and humane to help offenders establish themselves in the community rather than punish them with a prison sentence and lock them into a life of crime. In its most basic form social democratic positivism merely argues that when affluence rises, crime will decrease (Young, 1994, p. 72).

A Double Crisis

The swing between the traditional arguments of classicism and positivism has been a constant feature of criminology and policy implementation in post-war Europe. However in the last ten years, policies drawn from any one theoretical paradigm have proven questionable in their effectiveness to explain and prevent crime. For example, what Young refers to as the 'etiological crisis' came about as a result of most 'advanced' industrial countries in the post-war period experiencing rising affluence and increased welfare spending, combined with huge increases in crime and delinquency (Young, 1994, p. 72). Although all sorts of justifications were made about this, including denying the crime wave existed, the situation very much undermined the social democratic argument. For example, between 1951-71 in Britain there was a sixty-four per cent increase in disposable income, whilst crime in that period rose by 172 per cent (Young, 1994, p. 72).

Although social democratic theories are still a major component of contemporary social thought, the changed prospects for policy based on social intervention gave way to a corresponding growth in neo-classical methods of intervention. An increased police force, the building of more prisons, and a 'more effective' justice system began to inform British policy. For example Rab Butler's 1959 White Paper introduced the biggest prison building programme for young adult offenders, with sixteen new institutions 'designed to administer a "short, sharp, shock" to the evidently more recalcitrant young offenders of the new age' (Fyvel, 1963, p. 17).

This is the neo-classical response to the criminal who wilfully breaks the law; to impose increasingly stiff prison sentences, and in harsher settings. The 'short, sharp, shock' regimented prison programmes aim to reduce subsequent criminal activity by 'hard punishment' and deterrence. Criminals are processed through a militaristic-style 'boot camp' approach to punishment intended to be both physically and psychologically gruelling (see Thompson's chapter in this book). The argument being that when criminals are forced to conform to rules or are compelled to work regularly, they learn 'good habits' which are transferable to their lives on release. Foucault writes with great insight on this method, describing how the human body of the criminal is objectified in order to be manipulated and controlled (Foucault, 1979). The type of procedure used in 'boot camps' is what Foucault refers to as 'technologies'; the joining of knowledge and power, with the aim of 'forging a docile body that may be subjected, used, transformed and improved' (in Rabinow, 1984, p. 17). This is done in several related ways: through drills and training of the body, through standardisation of actions over time, and through the control of space. The link to military tactics of discipline is clear and overt; the focus is on the formal organisation and disciplined response of the constituent parts of the body, the automatic reflex of hands, legs and eyes. The 'boot camp' programmes also emphasise, more than other prison regimes, the allocation of time. The theory is that prisoners are made to 'sweat' for their crimes, to be 'exhausted, and worked hard' as a punishment for their delinquency. Control of a prisoner's time is not applied sporadically or even at regular intervals. There is a constant, regular physical and mental application.

The effect of these neo-classical practices on the arts and education in prisons is a concern to appear 'useful' or 'effective'. The language used to justify artistic activities in prison becomes functional, for example drama may become 'social skills'; performance may become 'life-skill rehearsals'; the arts are justified as tools of the prison to increase self-esteem and team building – everything must be justified in pragmatic, physical terms.

The discrediting of both positivism and classicism in the last fifty years is not always evident in political rhetoric or contemporary policy. But most current theories have by now reacted to the double-barrelled crisis in aetiology and penalty with the tendency to identify multiple causes of crime; each individual criminal act is seen as a function of a varied number of social, psychological, or environmental factors, with no two sets of factors necessarily being exactly alike. Thus most recent theories don the Emperor's new clothes in their attempts to solve old problems, wearing cloth woven together by old criminological discourses from the 1960s and 1970s. Young points out that, surprisingly, they share some common ground: 'they all play down the role of the police in the control of crime; they are all critical of the existing prison system; and they all reject traditional positivism and classicism' (Young, 1994, p. 80).

The Rehabilitation Perspective

Alongside the development of explanatory theories about criminal behaviour there has been a corresponding concern with forms of treating and/or preventing criminals from committing further offences. The image of the voluntaristic or determined actor has influenced the way in which criminals are treated once incarcerated.

The notion of rehabilitation for offenders tends to be linked to the image of the determined actor, who whilst having some degree of agency, is propelled by social misfortune or biological deficiency. Rehabilitation programmes consist of some explicit activity designed to alter or remove conditions operating on offenders which are deemed responsible for their illegal behaviour. One positivistic approach to rehabilitation work is to view the criminal on a parallel with the neurotic or psychotic individual, except his personality pathology is expressed in an illegal fashion. This view holds that offenders need to be 'rewired' by a psychiatrist or some other psychotherapeutic technician who can delve inside their psyches. In general this approach focuses more on the individual and less on his social circumstances. The criminal is a person whose (Johnson, 1996, p. 6):

> ...behaviour is a function of cognitive elements buried deep within the 'layers of personality'. These deep-seated tensions are dimly perceived by the individual, or may be unperceived by him, but can be made apparent by a skilled psychiatrist.

Once the 'patient' becomes sufficiently aware of his dysfunctions then, with the psychiatrist's help, he is back on the road to mental health. Undoubtedly there are some people who will fit the psychiatric picture of the abnormal offender, so these forms of psychotherapeutic activities may be useful. For example the Parkhurst Special Prison Unit (now closed) succeeded in reducing violent assaults by ninety per cent (Johnson, 1996, p. 6). This was not achieved by swapping DNA or lowering testosterone levels, but by helping these extremely violent men to 'escape from their childhood prison' (Johnson, 1996, p. 6):

> ...the stark fact is, inside every man, there is a violent infant...Violence is a disease. Disease, however, can be cured.

Probation and prison rehabilitative programmes deal with an offender's belief systems and the interpretative frameworks by which they 'make sense' out of sensory perception and direct their behaviour. If offenders are to be directed away from unlawful acts they must learn to recognise and change certain self images, attitudes and beliefs.

The emphasis in rehabilitation programmes focuses on the idea that offenders are characterised by various definitions, rather than a uniform set of attitudes and beliefs, which separate them from non-offenders (McGuire and Priestly, 1985). The key principle in this area of work is to look at the offender's explanation of a criminal situation, and particularly at the set of justifications and rationalisations that are made.

The rehabilitation perspective links an offender's perceived deficit of social skills to offending behaviour, and explores alternative ways of social functioning that are legitimate. For example participants on an anger management programme have a lack of self-control, there may be a deficit in empathy for victims and an insufficient notion of consequences (for self and other people). This notion of social skills deficits suggests that a process of social education has not transpired 'properly' in an individual, and that rehabilitation seeks to redress the balance and enable an offender to adapt or re-adapt more successfully to society. This is a central theoretical and practical premise of rehabilitative work, and one that informs the way in which role-play and social skills training is developed in this context. It acknowledges socio-economic and political pressures, but focuses on an individual's efficacy to change behaviour. The function of the aesthetic experience is therefore to re-engage with the decisions of a criminal act and highlight consequences of actions in order to encourage greater degrees of social responsibility and moral maturation. This brings us to a rather threatening concept: that society engages the science of criminology as a 'disciplinary technology', with the aim of socialising deviant citizens into behaving according to moral (or legal) 'norms' (Dreyfus and Rabinow, 1982, p. 152). Whether or not this process is indeed a threatening one, depends on one's perception of how socialisation connects with the 'culture' and ideologies of a society.

Organisation of the Book

The eleven chapters in this book are designed to provoke thought and insight into theatre in prison practice. The authors range from theatre practitioners, academics, ex-prisoners, psychologists, psycho-dramatists, and prison guards. The authors question, doubt, critique, reflect and celebrate the absurdities and paradoxes of working in prisons. And it is these multiple perspectives and histories that make the book so rich and diverse in its analysis. In selecting these essays I have not attempted to create a vision of the field that is complete and harmonious. The nature of prisons would not allow such delusions. But I hope that the cross currents of arguments, perspectives, theories and practical experiences serve the purpose of illuminating some of the contradictions and paradoxes that are necessary to a field that is still very much in development.

The inclusion and rare re-publication of Zimbardo's original research on the famous Stanford University Prison Experiment needs to be contextualised in a book about Prison Theatre. Despite the widespread knowledge about the experiment (a familiar reference for any foundation psychology student, several documentaries, an excellent German-language movie, a recent BBC reality television show, and even a Los Angeles punk-rock band), it is rare to read the original transcriptions and published outcomes in full. It is remarkable that these six days in the summer of 1971 continue to provoke and inspire endless ethical debate about the human condition and the way the prison environment constructs symbiotic, destructive relationships between guards and prisoners. This should be of enough interest to anyone working or about to work in prisons. But an added dimension to Zimbardo's experiment was the role of performance as a form of 'simulating' the realities of the prison experience. The volunteers were asked to adopt roles as 'guards' or 'prisoners', and it is fascinating to hear, first-hand, how deftly these identities were internalised through the basic outlining of their duties and the issuing of some representational 'uniforms' (for both guards and prisoners). The regime that was created resulted in a brutality and inhumanity that the experimenters were not expecting, and the simulation was closed down early to prevent things getting further out of control.

One of the many questions that arise from the Stanford experiment, for theatre makers at least, is where art fits into this dehumanising paradigm, and why and how should it engage with these types of environments? I would like to suggest that the answers do not lie in certainties and 'best' practices that can be copied and replicated. But that each artist who engages with a prison environment finds their own small indices of hope. Some of the writers in this book write not just about the practice, but about the paradoxes of engaging with 'systems of formalised power', as if negotiating rocky and, at times, treacherous, criminal justice terrain. I think this is critical. Theatre has potential in prisons, but theatre practitioners need to engage theoretically with the ideological cross currents, if they are to make it to the other side. To not do so is to risk naïve incorporation into the very 'systems' that theatre attempts to resist.

Baz Kershaw's chapter deals directly with this issue, by asking the question 'how do the practices of drama and theatre best engage with systems of formalised power to create a space of radical freedom?' Kershaw argues that radicalism is likely to provide the most contagious type of ideological bug, and so searches for the communal and individual sources of radicalism in theatre and drama practices. Framing the question in the context of a post-modern world, Kershaw suggests that the most interesting examples might be drawn from places where it is most under threat, e.g. prisons. He uses three examples (two prison workshops and a street procession) of practice to explore his argument that it is necessary for theatre, if it is to radically transcend its environment, to engage with the discourses of power of the immediate context directly and critically. Kershaw also underlines the importance of using the drama or theatre representations to analyse *itself* as the key 'object' of study, and of the potentialities of the project. This is quite useful, because so often project evaluations are drawn into the grammar of the useful, prioritising learning outcomes, objectives and transferable skills, while ignoring the potential rich analysis that can be drawn from the performance or workshop activities.

James Thompson develops this idea of performance analysis by extending the notion that prison and punishment are forms of performance texts in themselves and consequently need to be read with great care. Much of the chapter concerns itself with the US criminal justice context, drawing on vivid examples from the Texas Youth Commission. In particular, there is a strong resonance here between Zimbardo's simulated prison that quickly developed into a brutal, numbing system and the descriptions of Marlin Orientation and Assessment Center where new juvenile offenders are told that:

...they now have to do as they are told and not question. All have their heads shaved, crew cut army style. All are given bright orange smock top and loose fitting orange trousers. They all have to march in single file everywhere they go, with their hands tied behind their backs and their chins touching their chests.

This is symptomatic of the system that Thompson observes. The mechanisation of the system that de-individualises the criminal, in order to break the mind and body down, to strip the 'self' into its component parts, and then reconstruct it, re-socialise it (these terms are still common currency), with a new role and a learnt script, to the satisfaction of the panopticon and its baying tax paying audience. What Thompson is keen to highlight is the way that theatre and drama practices have been put to use in the service of this performance of punishment. It is not the techniques of psychodrama, role-play, image work that are problematic, but the ideological and institutional frames that surround their intended use, that need to be viewed with deep scepticism. In the context of 're-socialisation' programmes in Texas, the 'tools' of drama, are identified, recognised and utilised to limit the self-censorship and ability of juveniles to 'edit, distort and desensitize their offences by relying on verbal reports'(TYC, 1995, p.1). The practices of drama and theatre therefore become scalpel-like tools that are used to dissect the self, and scrape out the cancer of criminality and immorality, but performed by a surgeon also intent on demonstrating political retribution on the patient. Is this the price for the orthodox acceptance of Prison Theatre within the criminal justice field? I remember an incident during a drama-based training programme I ran for Prison Officers in Lancashire several years ago. After the usual shock and reluctance about using drama, the group of officers participated with great enthusiasm. One of the officers looked particularly pleased with himself, and during the feedback sat back in his chair and said: 'You know, I can see how I can use this. It's a great technique for finding out exactly what these buggers have been up to'.

Despite this questioning of the limitations of cognitive behavioural naturalistic social skills work, the discourse in the criminal justice field is far from being marginalised, and role-play continues to be an important, if not central, element of delivery methodology. There are numerous cognitive-based programmes (Ross, Novaco, McGuire, Goldstein to mention a few) that focus on a range of specific crime based issues, anger management, offending behaviour, drug addiction, car theft, street crime, burglary, etc.

Goldstein et al.'s work with what he called 'pro-social gangs' provides a particularly interesting example of this cognitive approach to working with criminality. It is grounded in a form of psychological skill training developed in the early 1970s (Bandura, 1973), that views the 'helpee' as an individual lacking or deficient in the skills necessary for 'effective and satisfying interpersonal and intrapersonal functioning' (Goldstein, 1988). Rather than intervention based on psychotherapy, e.g. interpretation, reflection, reinforcement, the purpose of the skill training was to focus on the deliberate teaching and demonstration of specific pro-social behaviours.

Goldstein combined skill training with moral reasoning education to create a programme directed at young adolescents with a propensity for violence and antisocial behaviour in the US. Goldstein became particularly interested in applying these ideas to working with gangs. They recognised that the gangs, though often anti-social in behaviour, were also healthy, legitimate and even desirable social groupings that were akin to extended family support networks. And in many cases, due to the breakdown of conventional family networks, the gangs became the chosen replacement and resource for social support. So, building on the work of the Detached Worker Programmes, Goldstein made an effort to work with a series of intact gangs, as gangs, in order to 'move their members in more constructive directions and begin creating a series of pro-social gangs'. (Goldstein, 1988, p. 48)

Like Zimbardo's work, I think Goldstein's chapter needs contextualising in relation to prison theatre. It is not strictly theatre. It simply uses role-play as an appropriate and accessible method of delivery. However, the chapter offers a challenging example of the ways in which theatre methodology, education and psychology can become intensely entwined in the pursuit of a criminological goal. There are other examples of this from a more theatrical perspective (Baim, 2002; Thompson, 1999), but I thought it more provoking to see theatre through the lens of an educational psychologist developing what is still a highly innovative programme, if one that needs to be approached critically and with a good deal of suspicion. Here is an example of how theatre is used as a pragmatic and useful tool to rehearse new life skills as part of the rehabilitative industry. It promotes a view of 'anti-social' behaviour that is governed by improving rational cognitive thinking skills, and of rehearsing 'correct' behaviour through the learning of a proscribed pro-social script. This type of practical skills based intervention can be extremely attractive to criminal justice agencies, it does not involve in-depth psychotherapy, it can be packaged as a repeatable programme and staff can be accredited to 'teach' these skills to a wide range of offenders. It is clean, clinical and on paper looks like an accessible interactive course with serious rehabilitative outcomes. However, as Thompson notes, in a more retributive context this type of programme can be used as a performance of punishment – or at least a badly mouthed form of karaoke rehabilitation – where the cognitive language is learned to serve the interests of the system rather than the individual.

Maud Clarke has been working with women prisoners and ex-prisoners in Australia for over twenty years. In her chapter she charts her personal journey through a self realisation that equality is a basic concept that practitioners often pay lip service to, but more rarely feel. The concept of (women) prisoners as 'different' from 'normal' women, or the way that drama might be referred to as 'therapy' (setting up polarities of power – the therapist and the patient), allows practitioners to create a separateness from the experiences of women. Even a benign 'them' and 'us' construct creates distance and provides a form of protection for art workers and a way to say 'that what happens in the prison world is OK'. Clarke argues for a practice that takes equality as a vital starting point for creative work. And that practitioners need to critique their positions within a group and a system that is dominated by labelling and alienation, because the understandings that unite women in prisons derive from their shared experiences of separation and disempowerment.

On the basis of some of the writing in this book, one of the significant shifts in the last five years of prison theatre work is a growing desire to escape the confines of a purely cognitive behavioural approach to the work. In both Chris Johnston's chapter and Kate McCoy and Imogen Blood's contribution, the escape has been achieved through experimenting with non-naturalistic forms and styles of theatre making. In 'The Role of the Camshaft in Offender Rehabilitation', Johnston, while acknowledging the usefulness of a 'cognitive skills' approach, gently mocks the mechanistic limitations that 'strips down his (the offender's) thinking and examines patterns, as one might strip down a car and lay it out in a garage'. Instead, the author discusses his experiments with trying to locate the 'dreaming self', and argues for work that engages with, and does not deny, the illogical and fantastical imagination within individuals. Usefully, he shares the somewhat painful realities of trying out these ideas in practice, in a project that worked with adult male offenders, women, and young offenders to develop kinetic sculptures. The practical work also challenges the perceived role of the facilitator in the process of creativity:

> Sometimes it's a good idea to raise the issue of the alternative perception – what a more psychotherapeutic pair of eyes might see in a piece of work – but also, sometimes, it isn't. Sometimes to do this may be seen as taking the piss, or as a kind of damning judgement on the creator's work – especially since it accesses terms of reference unfamiliar to the creator. So it was a matter of taking each situation separately on this project, and often we kept quiet.

This links strongly with Maud Clarke's argument that equality needs to be the cornerstone of working creatively with groups in prison. In moving to a freer and less inhibited practice, an approach less confined by the cognitive-behavioural model, practitioners need also to redefine their relationship with people in prisoners and the system. Not being an educator, or a therapist, or someone who speaks the orthodox language of rehabilitation, de-professionalises a practitioner, and makes them vulnerable once again. Because creative work without a purpose or a probation-orientated learning objective is not useful and does not appear to serve the aims of the 'correctional industries'. In rejecting the language of the 'cognitive gods' (Thompson, 2001), in favour of finding a more localised and creative form of communication, practitioners potentially risk the 'irritation' of those that most supported them in the first place – the educators and probation workers – their natural allies. But it is clear that both in Chris Johnston's case, and more specifically in Kate McCoy and Imogen Blood's example, that a degree of trust and mutual respect has built up between theatre makers and those in the probation and educational sectors of the system. The work in establishing prison and probation work over the years, into what may now with some confidence be referred to as a field, has generated in most cases strong partnerships that have enabled theatre practitioners to test out and develop new approaches to old problems. And it is this new ownership, or at least partial freedom to experiment with different creative practices, that has generated the most interesting indices of hope for the field.

Generally prisons and laughter are not common cell mates, and the narrative of heroin use is rarely the basis of comedy routines. But in Dealing with Drugs, Kate McCoy and Imogen Blood explore how a long term project in a male prison in Greater Manchester developed from a cognitive behavioural orientated project using naturalistic representations of addictions into a series of devised comedy routines using surrealism and metaphor to explore the internalised world of the drug addict. This fascinating work was driven by the group's need to find new ways to translate and represent their experiences, and a desire to create performances that were as much about learning the language of theatre as focussing on the issue of drugs. McCoy and Blood refer to this as a 'cycle of creativity', in which the group began with looking at an issue (drugs) using the unfamiliar methodology of theatre, then began to lose interest in the issue and focussed on experimenting with creative skills, which in turn led them to striving for ways of using this creativity to express the complexities and pain associated with drug use.

The project, it seems to me, had great integrity because it responded dialogically to the group's needs. Both McCoy and Blood allowed themselves to be surprised by the group and the projects direction. What that seemed to enable was a greater creative freedom that helped the group of men to genuinely explore and experiment with rational and irrational forces that governed their addiction. Not limited by cognitive-naturalism, they revelled in experimenting with different forms and styles, and found an approach that suited them. That this form should be comedy and stand-up cabaret is all the more intriguing.

While this type of cognitive skills course dominates current criminal justice thinking, and in some cases seems to have produced some credible results (Goldstein, 1988; McGuire and Priestly, 1985), it also implies a machine like model of human behaviour, one that perceives the mind as 'an internal combustion engine, or as a battery-driven machine' (Helman, 1994, p. 26). At best this is a pragmatic approach to human behaviour, at worst a mechanistic model that reduces thinking and feeling to a series of cogs and switches. A different approach is illustrated in Clark Baim's chapter about the use of psychodrama with offenders who have committed sexually abusive and violent offences. In 'If all the world's a stage, why did I get the worst parts?' he describes his thoughts and experiences about using psychodrama as an underlying framework for drama-based interventions and the ways in which it might contribute to an understanding of the roots of violence. If in the most basic of terms, cognitive behavioural work emphasis the need to identify and intervene in negative thinking patterns 'in the now' 'in the present tense', then psychodrama is predicated on the fact the crimes of violent offenders may be partially understood as 'a distortion of early traumatic experience that remains unprocessed in the mind of the individual, too painful to look at or work through (Greenberg and Paivio, 1998; Jefferies, 1996; de Zulueta, 1998; Schwartz et al., 1993)'. Unlike some of the psychodrama examples in Texas that seem to be framed within a retributive context (Thompson), Baim's work is carefully placed in institutional situations that are orientated towards the psychotherapeutic needs of the individual. Baim's work is also, as evidenced in the chapter, meticulous in its integrity of trying to help and support individuals in their own self development.

Even the most interactive, creative and imaginative programmes will be diluted, if the ideas and skills learnt can not be directly tried out and applied – and felt to work – in the immediate context outside of the programme environment. The idea of including the 'total institution' in the change culture have had some notable precedents, Kohlberg's Just Communities, Barlinnie Special Unit (Boyle, 1977), Parkhurst Special Unit, Tihar Prison, Delhi, India (http://tiharprisons.nic.in/vstiharprisons/html/reform.htm), as well as more therapeutic orientated prisons such as HMP Grendon. Prison Transformation in South Africa documents the extraordinary work of the Centre for Conflict Resolution, based in Cape Town, and already the subject of two BBC documentaries (Correspondent). The chapter presents multiple perspectives of the prison transformation process from a repressive system, dominated by gang violence and a harsh brutal regime, to a prison that gradually began to change from the inside out. The commentators include CCR staff, who ran a range of programmes at all levels in the prison, as well as a prisoner and a prison officer who share their own stories about how these changes affected them. Theatre and interactive exercises were a small but important part of the transformation process, in that they helped to build trust at an inter-personal level, but also were important signals of the intentions of the institution to commit themselves to a more positive and progressive future. The CCR were the human face of the policy that the prison was trying to implement.

What can be drawn from the examples of CCR and the Prison Transformation project, or the other experiments in institutional change mentioned earlier, is that positive prison environments where individual development and growth are valued (surely the real goal of rehabilitation) are governed by the human attributes of the system. Boyle, a then convicted murderer, on the Barlinnie Special Unit:

> Out of everything that makes up this Unit, the thing that costs nothing in terms of money is staff and prisoners getting together and talking; it is the one thing that has brought about results. The emphasis is placed on seeing the individual as a person in his own right without relying on labelling or categorisation in order to identify. It is unique in the sense that two opposing factions have come together and worked towards building a Community with a remarkable degree of success. An important lesson is that no professional psychiatric or psychological experience was needed to make it so. Our basic ingredients have been some people, goodwill from all sides and with those we became the architects of a model that could be used anywhere.

Emman Frank Idoko's chapter about a prison theatre project in Nigeria also sets out the difficulties of undertaking work within a criminal justice context that is at best interfering, at worst liable to ban the work at the slightest suspicion. The chapter also problematises a recurrent situation in some prison theatre practice, of what action to take if the creative process highlights contradictions or even injustices inherent within the structures of the criminal justice system. As Kidd notes, 'it is not enough to rehearse struggle if it does not lead to struggle' (1980, p. 11). Idoko poses the question of where theatre stands in relation to the people it is working with, and to the State bureaucracy, and wonders if theatre is not sometimes engaged in 'popular forms of statement for purposes of cultural·underdevelopment' (Abah, 1993, p. 9).

Similar questions are raised in the Brazilian prison context, where Paul Heritage has been developing an impressive range of work from HIV/AIDS programmes to Staging Human Rights performances, via Shakespeare with juvenile prisoners. After considerable bureaucratic scepticism, Heritage has seen projects develop in 'thirty-seven prisons across the state the size of Spain, with the involvement of over 10,000 prisoners, guards, prison staff and families'. From his first visit to a Brazilian prison where he was asked to adjudicate a prison samba competition, Heritage has revelled in the surprises and complexities of the cultural border lands that intersect between prison and society. The chapter traces his entrances and exits, the ins and outs of making theatre in Brazilian prisons, while continually questioning how to judge the efficacy of the work in a system that is as much concerned with quelling the next riot as it is with the concerns of individual human rights or rehabilitation. Heritage is also cautious of the process involved in applying for a 'visa' into the prison world – the emphasis on results based work that reduces risk, increases safety, constructs responsible citizenship. Is this a tie that binds or a way of smuggling in creative and humanitarian processes? During the evaluation of a four-day workshop on AIDS/HIV, Heritage (in this book) was asking a group if the workshops might have changed their behaviour in the future, one of the young men exploded with emotion:

> I have just taken part in a workshop where I have cried, hugged, laughed, played in ways that I have never done in the past. I have changed totally. Perhaps next week I will have unsafe sex. I don't know. Why are you so obsessed with the future? What has happened now is most important.

The justification for working in prisons; the 'visa' that allows one to enter the space, is often defined by its use to the system. But it can also constrain and restrict the creative potential of theatre and performance work. Therefore, the theatre practitioner is often forced into a duplicitous position, caught on 'a knife's edge between resistance to, and incorporation into, the status quo' of the criminal justice system (Kershaw, p. 8). Or does one end up making different promises to different people, but lying to both as a way to survive the contradictions of the system? Heritage's chapter does not offer secure solutions, but allows the questioning to come through the practice, and describes his passions for the work, the many surprises he encounters and the deeply-felt doubts he suffers in reflecting on his work in this context.

It seems to me that these are essential faculties for working in any prison context in any country. Passion, surprise and doubt. Without passion we would not enter the gates again and again, without surprise we would not be responsive to what we meet, without doubt we would not stop to analyse the paradox of creative work in these systems of formalised power called a prison.

Conclusion

'Theatre' – 'Prison', are two ideas that are destined to circle round each other in mutual distrust, until one gives up or the other is forgotten. The theatre practice described in this book is a fragmented picture of a longer contested history. But if there is a common thread running through the chapters, it is of a growing awareness of the possibilities of theatre in prison. A developing confidence in articulating theatre and art based aims as the foundation for work, rather than simply as a vehicle – a delivery style – for cognitive rehabilitation. As the Collins quote argues, the poetic imagination needs to be an irritant that makes the 'system' conscious of 'the degradation of its mechanisation' (Collins, 1945, p. 9). Otherwise it risks being incorporated into the culture of the 'useful' and the realms of the facile morality and 're-education' plays that Solzhenitsyn (1975) so vividly scorned. But some of the chapters point to other solutions, that theatre can make interventions into the system directly by working with prison authorities, staff and prisoners to create negotiated spaces that are, at least, in theory, more egalitarian, democratic and humanitarian (see Prison Transformation chapter). These are all significant developments for the field, and ones to cherish, but it is important to keep reminding ourselves that no matter how the system is developed, it remains a 'detestable solution' to a much broader and complex question about the nature of crime, the politics of power and the type of society in which we choose to exist (Foucault, 1984, p. 215).

Notes

1. There are a number of influential textbooks which discuss the history of criminology, and identify 'the classical school'; Radzinowicz, L., *A History of the English Criminal Law and its Administration, from 1750*, 5 vols., (London, Stevens, 1986); Radzinowicz, L., *Ideology and Crime*, (London, Stevens, 1966); Taylor, I., Walton, P., and Young, J., *The New Criminology*, (London, Routledge and Kegan Paul, 1973); most of these writers identify Beccaria as one of the earliest pioneers of 'classicism': Beccaria, C., *Of Crimes and Punishments*, (Indiana, Bobbs-Merill, 1963. First published in Italian as Dei Delitti e Delle Pene, 1764).

References

Balfour, M. (ed.), *Theatre and War, 1933-1945: Performance in Extremis*, (Oxford and New York, Berghahn Books, 2001).

Baim, C., Brookes, S., and Mountford, A. (eds.), *The Geese Theatre Handbook: Drama with offenders and people at risk*, (Winchester, Waterside Press, 2002).

Bandura, A., *Aggression: A Social Learning Analysis*, (Englewood Cliffs, N.J., Prentice Hall, 1973).

Bandura, A., *Social Learning Theory*, (Englewood Cliffs, N.J., Prentice-Hall, 1977).

Berghaus, G. (ed.), *Fascism and Theatre*, (Oxford and New York, Berghahn Books, 1996).

Berghaus, G., and Wolff, O. (eds.), *Theatre and Film in Exile*, (Oxford, Berg Books, 1989).

Berlo, J. C., 'Drawing and Being Drawn In: The Late Nineteenth Century Plains

Graphic Artist and the Intercultural Encounter' in *Plains Indians Drawings 1865-1935: Pages from a Visual History*, (New York, 1996).

Boyle, J., *A Sense of Freedom*, (London, Pan Books, 1977).

Collins, C., *Visions of a Fool*, (London, Penguin, 1945).

Dutlinger, A., *Art, Music and Education as Strategies for Survival 1941-45*, (New York, Herodias, 2001).

Dreyfus, H., and Rabinow, P., *Michel Foucault, Beyond Structuralism and Hermeneutics*, (Chicago, Harvester Wheatsheaf, 1982).

Eysenck, H. J., *Crime and Personality*, (St. Albans, Paladin, 1970).

Foucault, M., *Discipline and Punish*, (London, Penguin, 1979).

Foucault, Michel, *The Foucault Reader*, ed. Rabinow, P., (London, Penguin, 1984).

Fyvel, T. R., *The Insecure Offenders*, (London, Penguin, 1963).

Goldstein, A. P., *Psychological skill training*, (Elmsford, NY, Pergamon, 1981).

Goldstein, A. P., and Glick, B., *Aggression replacement training: A comprehensive intervention for aggressive youth*, (Champaign, IL, Research Press, 1987).

Goldstein, A. P., *The Prepare Curriculum*, (Champaign, Research Press, 1998).

Haag, E. van den, *Punishing Criminals*, (New York, Basic Books, 1975).

Jelavich, P., *Berlin Cabaret*, (Harvard University Press, 1993).

Johnson, B., 'Violent, man and boy', in *The Guardian*, (13/2/1996).

Kershaw, B., *The Politics of Performance*, (London, Routledge, 1992).

McGuire, J., and Priestly, P., *Offending Behaviour*, (London, B.T. Batsford, 1985).

Rowe, D. C., 'Inherited dispositions toward learning delinquent and criminal behaviour: New evidence', in L. Ellis and H. Hoffman (eds.) *Crime in Biological, Social and Moral Contexts*, (NY, Praeger, 1990).

Siegal, L. J., and Senna, J. J., *Introduction to Criminal Justice* (5th ed.), (St. Paul, MN, West Publishing, 1990).

Smith, P., *Cesare Lombroso, Crime Its Causes and Remedies*, (Montclair, N.J., 1968).

Solzhenitsyn, A., *The Gulag Archipelago*, (London, Collins and Harvill Press, 1975).

Stevens, R., 'Personal Identity', Block 5, D103, *Identities and Interaction*, (Milton Keynes, The Open University Press, 1991).

Texas Youth Commission, *Capital Offender Program* (Austin, TX, Texas Youth Commission, 1995).

Thompson, J., 'Making a break for it: Discourse and theatre in prisons', *Applied Theatre Researcher*, 2, (2001).

Thompson, J., *Drama Workshops for Anger Management and Offending Behaviour*, (London, Jessica Kingsley Publishers, 1999).

Thompson, J. B., 'The effects of the Present System of Prison Discipline on the Body and Mind', *Journal of Mental Science*, 12, (1867).

Young, J., 'Incessant chatter: recent paradigm's in criminology', in McGuire, M., Morgan, R., and Reimer, R., *Oxford Handbook of Criminology*, (New York, Clarendon Press, 1994).

A Study of Prisoners and Guards in a Simulated Prison

Craig Haney, Curtis Banks and Philip Zimbardo

The research reported in this chapter [originally published in 1973] was part of a larger project sponsored by the Office of Naval Research which was designed to develop a better understanding of the basic psychological mechanisms underlying human aggression. In this study, Dr. Zimbardo fabricated a simulation of the essential characteristics of a prison environment. From a highly selected group of college students, Dr. Zimbardo randomly assigned half as 'guards' (with all attendant powers) and half as 'prisoners' (under the complete subjugation of the 'guards'). Essentially then, a group of intelligent, 'normal' young men were put into a situation which demanded close contact over a period of several days. There was a well-defined authority/subordinate relationship between 'guards' and 'prisoners.' The 'prison' environment was further manipulated to promote anonymity, depersonalization, and dehumanization among the subjects. The study demonstrates how these variables combine to increase the incidence of aggressive behaviour on the part of the 'guards' and submissive and docile conformity on the part of the 'prisoners.'

Studies such as this one help to identify and isolate the various processes which motivate aggressive/submissive behaviour within a 'total institution' such as a prison. The Navy and Marine Corps have a direct interest in the conclusions drawn from this study in as much as parallels can be made between the forces which operated within Dr. Zimbardo's 'prison' and those which spawn disruptive interpersonal conflict in Naval prisons. More importantly, however, this study identifies some of the conditions which are likely to promote unrest when men are placed in situations which demand close contact for protracted periods of time. Such research increases the Navy's capability to develop effective training designs to eliminate conditions which elicit counter-productive conflict.

Introduction

After he had spent four years in a Siberian prison the great Russian novelist Dostoevsky commented surprisingly that his time in prison had created in him a deep optimism about the ultimate future of mankind because, as he put it, if man could survive the horrors of prison life he must surely be a 'creature who could withstand anything.' The cruel irony which Dostoevsky overlooked is that the reality of prison bears witness not only to the resiliency and adaptiveness of the men who tolerate life within its walls, but as well to the 'ingenuity' and tenacity of those who devised and still maintain our correctional and reformatory systems.

Nevertheless, in the century which has passed since Dostoevsky's imprisonment,

19

little has changed to render the main thrust of his statement less relevant. Although we have passed through periods of enlightened humanitarian reform, in which physical conditions within prisons have improved somewhat, and the rhetoric of rehabilitation has replaced the language of punitive incarceration, the social institution of prison has continued to fail. On purely pragmatic grounds, there is substantial evidence that prisons really neither 'rehabilitate' nor act as a deterrent to future crime in America, recidivism rates upwards of seventy-five per cent speak quite decisively to these criteria. And, to perpetuate what is also an economic failure, American taxpayers alone must provide an expenditure for 'corrections' of 1.6 billion dollars annually. On humanitarian grounds as well, prisons have failed: our mass media are increasingly filled with accounts of atrocities committed daily, man against man, in reaction to the penal system or in the name of it. The experience of prison creates undeniably, almost to the point of cliché, an intense hatred and disrespect in most inmates for the authority and the established order of society into which they will eventually return. And the toll it takes in the deterioration of human spirit for those who must administer it, as well as for those upon whom it is inflicted, is incalculable.

Attempts to provide an explanation of the deplorable condition of our penal system and its dehumanizing effects upon prisoners and guards, often focus upon what might be called the dispositional hypothesis. While this explanation is rarely expressed explicitly, it is central to a prevalent non-conscious ideology: that the state of the social institution of prison is due to the 'nature' of the people who administrate it, or the 'nature' of the people who populate it, or both. That is, a major contributing cause to despicable conditions, violence, brutality, dehumanization and degradation existing within any prison can be traced to some innate or acquired characteristic of the correctional and inmate population. Thus on the one hand, there is the contention that violence and brutality exist within prison because guards are sadistic, uneducated, and insensitive people! It is the 'guard mentality,' a unique syndrome of negative traits which they bring into the situation, that engenders the inhumane treatment of prisoners. On the other hand, there is the argument that prison violence and brutality are the logical and predictable results of the involuntary confinement of a collective of individuals whose life histories are, by definition, characterized by disregard for law, order and social convention and a concurrent propensity for impulsivity and aggression. In seeming logic, it follows that these individuals, having proven themselves incapable of functioning satisfactorily in the 'normal' structure of society, cannot do so either inside the structure provided by prisons. To control such men, the argument continues, whose basic orientation to any conflict situation is to react physical power or deception, force must be met with force, and a certain number of violent encounters must be expected and tolerated by the public.

The dispositional hypothesis has been embraced by the proponents of the prison status quo (blaming conditions on the evil in the prisoners), as well as by its critics (attributing the evil to guards and staff with their motives and deficient personality structures). The appealing simplicity of this proposition localizes the source of prison riots, recidivism and corruption in these 'bad seeds' and not in the conditions of the 'prison soil'. Such an analysis directs attention away from the complex matrix of social, economic and political forces that combine to make prisons what they are – and that would require complex, expensive, revolutionary actions to bring about any meaningful change. Instead, rioting prisoners are identified, punished, transferred to maximum security institutions or shot, outside agitators sought, and corrupt officials suspended – while the system itself goes on essentially unchanged, its basic structure unexamined and unchallenged.

However, the dispositional hypothesis cannot be critically evaluated directly through observation in existing prison settings, because such naturalistic observation necessarily confounds the acute effects of the environment with the chronic characteristics of the inmate and populations. To separate the effects of the prison environment *per se* from those attributable to *a priori* dispositions of its inhabitants requires a research strategy in which a 'new' prison is constructed, comparable in its fundamental social-psychological milieu to existing prison systems, but entirely populated by individuals who are undifferentiated in all essential dimensions from the rest of society.

Such was the approach taken in the present empirical study, namely, to create a prison-like situation in which the guards and inmates were initially comparable and characterized as being 'normal-average', and then to observe the patterns of behaviour which resulted, as well as the cognitive, emotional and attitudinal reactions which emerged. Thus, we began our experiment with a sample of individuals who were in the normal range of the general population on a variety of dimensions we were able to measure. Half were randomly assigned to the role of 'prisoner' the others to that of 'guard', neither group having any history crime, emotional disability, physical handicap or even intellectual or social disadvantage.

The environment created was that of a 'mock' prison which physically constrained the prisoners in barred cells and psychologically conveyed the sense of imprisonment to all participants. Our intention was not to create a *literal* simulation of an American prison, but rather a functional representation of one. For ethical, moral and pragmatic reasons we could not detain our subjects for extended or indefinite periods of time, we could not exercise the threat and promise of severe physical punishment, we could not allow homosexual or racist practices to flourish, nor could we duplicate certain other specific aspects of prison life. Nevertheless, we believed that we could create a situation of sufficient mundane realism to allow the role-playing participants to go beyond the superficial demands of their assignment into the deep structure of the characters they represented. To do so, we established functional equivalents for the activities and experiences of actual prison life which were expected to produce qualitatively similar psychological reactions in our subjects – feelings of power and powerlessness, of control and oppression, of satisfaction and frustration, of arbitrary rule resistance to authority, of status and anonymity, of machismo emasculation. In the conventional terminology of experimental psychology, we first identified a number of relevant conceptual variables through analysis of existing prison situations, then designed a setting in which these variables were operationalized. No specific hypothesis were advanced other than the general one that assignment to the treatment of 'guard', or 'prisoner' would result in significantly different reactions on behavioural measures of interaction, emotional measures of mood state and pathology, attitudes toward self, as well as indices of coping and adaptation to this novel situation. What follows is a discussion of how we created and peopled our prison, what we observed, what our subjects reported, and finally, what we can conclude about the nature of the prison environment and the psychology of imprisonment which can account for the failure of our prisons.

METHOD

Overview
The effects of playing the role of 'guard' or 'prisoner' were in the context of an experimental simulation of a prison environment. The research design was a relatively simple one, involving only a single treatment variable, the random assignment to either 'guard' or 'prisoner' condition. These roles were enacted over an extended period of time (nearly one week) within an environment that was physically constructed to resemble a prison. Central to methodology of creating and maintaining a psychological state of imprisonment was the functional simulation of significant properties of 'real prison life' (established through information from former inmates, correctional personnel and texts).

The 'guards' were free within certain limits to implement the procedures of induction into the prison setting and maintenance of custodial retention of the 'prisoners'. These inmates, having voluntarily submitted to the conditions of this total institution in which they now lived, coped in various ways with its stresses and its challenges. The behaviour of both groups of subjects was observed, recorded, and analyzed. The dependent measures were of two general types: 1) transactions between and within each group of subjects, recorded on video and audio tape as well as directly observed; 2) individual reactions on questionnaires, mood inventories, personality tests, daily guard shift reports, and post experimental interviews.

Subjects
The twenty-two subjects who participated in the experiment were selected from an initial pool of seventy-five respondents, who answered a newspaper advertisement asking male volunteers to participate in a psychological study of 'prison life' in return for payment of $15 per day. Each respondent completed extensive questionnaire concerning his family background, physical mental health history, prior experience and attitudinal propensities with respect to sources of psychopathology (including their involvements in crime). Each respondent also was interviewed by one of two experimenters. Finally, the twenty-four subjects who were judged to be most stable (physically and mentally), most mature, and least involved in anti-social behaviours were selected to participate in the study. On a random basis, half of the subjects were assigned the role of 'guard', half were assigned to the role of 'prisoner'.

The subjects were normal, healthy, male college students who were in the Stanford area during the summer. They were largely of middle-class socio-economic status and Caucasians (with the exception of one Oriental subject). Initially they were strangers to each other, a selection precaution taken to avoid the disruption of any pre-existing friendship patterns and to mitigate against any transfer into the experimental situation of previously established relationships or patterns of behaviour. This final sample of subjects was administered a battery of psychological tests on the day prior to the start of the simulation, but to avoid any selective bias on the part of the experimenter-observers, scores were not tabulated until the study was completed.

Two subjects who were assigned to be a 'stand-by' in case an additional 'prisoner' was needed were not called, and one assigned to be a 'stand-by' guard decided against participating just before the simulation phase began – thus, our data analysis is based upon ten prisoners and eleven guards in our experimental conditions.

PROCEDURE

Physical Aspects of the Prison

The prison was built in a thirty-five foot section of a basement corridor in the psychology building at Stanford University. It was partitioned by two fabricated walls; one was fitted with the only entrance door to the cell block and the other contained a small observation screen. Three small cells (6 x 9 ft.) were made from converted laboratory rooms by replacing the usual doors with steel barred, black painted ones and removing all furniture.

A cot (with mattress, sheet and pillow) for each prisoner was the only furniture in the cells. A small closet across from the cells served as a solitary confinement facility; its dimensions were extremely small (2 x 2 x 7 ft.), and it was unlighted.

In addition, several rooms in an adjacent wing of the building were used as guard's quarters (to change in and out of uniform or for rest and relaxation), a bedroom for the 'warden' and 'superintendent', and an interview-testing room. Behind the observation screen at one end of the 'yard' (small enclosed room representing the fenced grounds) was video recording equipment and sufficient space for several observers.

Operational Details

The 'prisoner' subjects remained in the mock-prison for twenty-four hours per day for the duration of the study. Three were arbitrarily assigned to each of the three cells; the others were on stand-by call at their homes. The 'guard' subjects worked on three-man, eight-hour shifts; remaining in the prison environment only during their work shift and going about their usual lives at other times.

Role Instructions

All subjects had been told that they would be assigned either the guard or the prisoner role on a completely random basis and all had voluntarily agreed to play either role for $15.00 per day for up to two weeks. They signed a contract guaranteeing a minimally adequate diet, clothing, housing and medical care as well as the financial remuneration in return for their stated 'intention' of serving in the assigned role for the duration of the study.

It was made explicit in the contract that those assigned to be prisoners should expect to be under surveillance (have little or no privacy) and to have some of their basic human rights suspended during their imprisonment, excluding physical abuse. They were given no other information about what to expect nor instructions about behaviour appropriate for a prisoner role. Those actually assigned to this treatment were informed by phone to be available at their place of residence on a given Sunday when we would start the experiment.

The subjects assigned to be guards attended an orientation meeting on the day prior to the induction of the prisoners. At this time they were introduced to the principal investigators, the 'Superintendent' of the prison (the author) and an undergraduate research assistant who assumed the administrative role of 'Warden'. They were told that we wanted to try to simulate a prison environment within the limits imposed by pragmatic and ethical considerations. Their assigned task was to 'maintain the reasonable degree of order within the prison necessary for its effective functioning', although the specifics of how this duty might be implemented were not explicitly detailed. They were made aware of the fact that, while many of the contingencies with which they might be confronted were essentially unpredictable (e.g., prisoner escape attempts), part of their task was to be prepared for such eventualities and to be able to deal appropriately with the variety of situations that might arise. The 'Warden' instructed the guards in the administrative details, including: the work-shifts, the mandatory daily completion of shift reports concerning the activity of guards and prisoners; the completion of 'critical incident' reports which detailed unusual occurrences, and the administration of meals, work and recreation programmes for the prisoners. In order to begin to involve these subjects in their roles even before the first prisoner was incarcerated, the guards assisted in the final phases of completing the prison complex – putting the cots in the cells, signs on the walls, setting up the guards' quarters, moving furniture, water coolers, refrigerators, etc.

The guards generally believed that we were primarily interested in the behaviour of the prisoners. Of course, we were as interested in the effects which enacting the role of guard in this environment would have on their behaviour and subjective states.

To optimize the extent to which their behaviour would reflect their genuine reactions to the experimental prison situation and not simply their ability to follow instructions, they were intentionally given only minimal guidelines for what it meant to be a guard. An explicit and categorical prohibition against the use of physical punishment or physical aggression was, however, emphasized by the experimenters. Thus, with this single notable exception, their roles were relatively unstructured initially, requiring each 'guard' to carry out activities necessary for interacting with a group of 'prisoners' as well as with other 'guards' and the 'correctional staff'.

Uniforms

In order to promote feelings of anonymity in the subjects each group was issued identical uniforms. For the guards, the uniform consisted of: plain khaki shirts and trousers; a whistle; a police night stick (wooden batons); and reflecting sunglasses which made eye contact impossible. The prisoners' uniform consisted of a loose fitting muslin smock with an identification number on front and back, no underclothes, a light chain and lock around one ankle, rubber sandals and a cap made from a nylon stocking. Each prisoner also was issued a toothbrush; soap; soap dish; towel and bed linen. No personal belongings were allowed in the cells.

The outfitting of both prisoners and guards in this manner served to enhance group identity and reduce individual uniqueness within the two groups. The khaki uniforms were intended to convey a military attitude, while the whistle and night-stick were carried as symbols of control and power. The prisoners' uniforms were designed not only to deindividuate the prisoners but to be humiliating and serve as symbols of their dependence and subservience. The ankle chain was a constant reminder (even during their sleep when it hit the other ankle) of the oppressiveness of the environment. The stocking cap removed any distinctiveness associated with hair length, color or style (as does shaving of heads in some 'real' prisons and the military). The ill-fitting uniforms made the prisoners feel awkward in their movements; since these 'dresses' were worn without undergarments, the uniforms forced them to assume unfamiliar postures, more like those of a woman than a man – another part of the emasculating process of becoming a prisoner.

Induction Procedure
With the cooperation of the Palo Alto City Police Department all of the subjects assigned to the prisoner treatment were unexpectedly 'arrested' at their residences. A police officer charged them with suspicion of burglary or armed robbery, advised them of their legal rights, handcuffed them, thoroughly searched them (often as curious neighbors looked on) and carried them off to the police station in the rear of the police car. At the station they went through the standard routines of being fingerprinted, having an identification file prepared and then being placed in a detention cell. Each prisoner was blindfolded and subsequently driven by one of the experimenters and a subject-guard to our mock prison. Throughout the entire arrest procedure, the police officers involved maintained a formal, serious attitude, avoiding answering any questions of clarification as to the relation of this 'arrest' to the mock prison study.

Upon arrival at our experimental prison, each prisoner was stripped, sprayed with a delousing preparation (a deodorant spray) and made to stand alone naked for a while in the cell yard. After being given the uniform described previously and having an I.D. picture taken ('mug shot') the prisoner was put in his cell and ordered to remain silent.

Administrative Routine
When all the cells were occupied, the warden greeted the prisoners and read them the rules of the institution (developed by the guards and the warden). They were to be memorized and to be followed. Prisoners were to be referred to only by the number on their uniforms, also in an effort to depersonalize them.

The prisoners were to be served three bland meals per day, were allowed three supervised toilet visits, and given two hours daily for the privilege of reading or letter-writing. Work assignments were issued for which the prisoners were to receive an hourly wage to constitute $15 daily payment. Two visiting periods per week were scheduled, as were movie nights and exercise periods. Three times a day all prisoners were lined up for a 'count' (one on each guard work-shift). The initial purpose of the 'count' was to ascertain that all prisoners were present, and to test them on their knowledge of the rules and their I.D. numbers. The first perfunctory counts lasted only about ten minutes, but on each successive day (or night) they were spontaneously increased in duration until some lasted several hours. Many of the pre-established features of administrative routine were modified or abandoned by the guards, and some privileges were forgotten by the staff over the course of study.

RESULTS

Overview

Although it is difficult to anticipate exactly what the influence of incarceration will be upon the individuals who are subjected to it and those charged with its maintenance, especially in a simulated reproduction, the results of the present experiment support many commonly held conceptions of prison life and validate anecdotal evidence supplied by articulate ex-convicts. The environment of arbitrary custody had great impact upon the affective states of both guards and prisoners as upon the interpersonal processes taking place between and within those role-groups.

In general, guards and prisoners showed a marked tendency toward increased negativity of affect, and their overall outlook became increasingly negative. As the experiment progressed, prisoners expressed intentions to do harm to others more frequently. For both prisoners and guards, self-evaluations were more deprecating as the experience of the prison environment became internalized.

Overt behaviour was generally consistent with the subjective self-reports and affective expressions of the subjects. Despite the fact that guards and prisoners were essentially free to engage in any form of interaction (positive or negative, supportive or affrontive, etc.), the characteristic nature of their encounters tended to be negative, hostile, affrontive and dehumanizing. Prisoners immediately adopted a generally passive response mode while guards assumed a very active initiative role in all interactions. Throughout the experiment, commands were the most frequent form of verbal behaviour and, generally, verbal exchanges were strikingly impersonal, with few references to individual identity. Although it was clear to all subjects that the experimenters would not permit physical violence to take place, varieties of less direct aggressive behaviour were observed frequently (especially on the part of the guards). In lieu of physical violence, verbal affronts were used as one of the most frequent forms of interpersonal contact between guards and prisoners.

The most dramatic evidence of the impact of this situation upon the participants was seen in the gross reactions of five prisoners who had to be released because of extreme emotional depression, crying, rage and acute anxiety. The pattern of symptoms was quite similar in four of the subjects and began as early as the second day of imprisonment. The fifth subject was released after being treated for a psychosomatic rash which covered portions of his body. Of the remaining prisoners, only two said they were not willing to forfeit the money they had earned in return for being 'paroled'. When the experiment was terminated prematurely after only six days, all the remaining prisoners were delighted by their unexpected good fortune. In contrast, most of the guards seemed to be distressed by the decision to stop the experiment and it appeared to us that they had become sufficiently involved in their roles that they now enjoyed the extreme control and power which they exercised and were reluctant to give it up. One guard did report being personally upset at the suffering of the prisoners, and claimed to have considered asking to change his role to become one of them – but never did so. None of the guards ever failed to come to work on time for their shift, and indeed, on several occasions guards remained on duty voluntarily and uncomplaining for extra hours – without additional pay.

The extremely pathological reactions which emerged in both groups of subjects testify to the power of the social forces operating, but still there were individual differences seen in styles of coping with this novel experience and in degrees of successful adaptation to it. Half the prisoners did endure the oppressive atmosphere, and not all the guards resorted to hostility. Some guards were tough but fair ('play rules'), some went far beyond their roles to engage in creative cruelty and harassment, while a few were passive and rarely instigated any coercive control over the prisoners.

Reality of the Simulation

At this point it seems necessary to confront the critical question of 'reality' in the simulated prison environment: were the behaviours observed more than the mere acting out assigned roles convincingly? To be sure, ethical, legal and practical considerations set limits upon the degree to which this situation could approach the conditions existing in actual prisons and penitentiaries. Necessarily absent were some of the most salient aspects of prison life reported by criminologists and documented in the writing of prisoners. There was no involuntary homosexuality, no racism, no physical beatings, no threat to life by prisoners against each other or the guards. Moreover, the maximum anticipated 'sentence' was only two weeks and, unlike some prison systems, could not be extended indefinitely for infractions of the internal operating rules of the prison.

In one sense, the profound psychological effects we observed under the relatively minimal prison-like conditions which existed in our mock prison made the results even more significant, and force us to wonder about the devastating impact of chronic incarceration in real prisons. Nevertheless, we must contend with the criticism that our conditions were too minimal to provide a meaningful analogue to existing prisons. It is necessary to demonstrate that the participants in this experiment transcended the conscious limits of their preconceived stereotyped roles and their awareness of the artificiality and limited duration of imprisonment. We feel there is abundant evidence that virtually all of the subjects at one time or another experienced reactions which went well beyond the surface demands of role-playing and penetrated the deep structure of the psychology of imprisonment.

Although instructions about how to behave in the roles of guard or prisoner were not explicitly defined, demand characteristics in the experiment obviously exerted some directing influence. Therefore, it is enlightening to look to circumstances where role demands were minimal, the subjects believed they were not being observed, or where they should not have been behaving under the constraints imposed by their roles (as in 'private' situations), in order to assess whether the role behaviours reflected anything more than public conformity or good acting.

When the private conversations of the prisoners were monitored, we learned that almost all (a full ninety per cent) of what they talked about was directly related to immediate prison conditions, that is, food, privileges, punishment, guard harassment, etc. Only one-tenth of the time did their conversations deal with their life outside the prison. Consequently, although they lived together under such intense conditions, the prisoners knew surprisingly little about each other's past history or future plans. This excessive concentration on the vicissitudes of their current situation helped to make the prison experience more oppressive for the prisoners because, instead of escaping from it when they had a chance to do so in the privacy of their cells, the prisoners continued to allow it to dominate their thoughts and social relations. The guards too, rarely exchanged personal information during their relaxation breaks. They either talked about 'problem prisoners', other prison topics, or did not talk at all. There were few instances of any personal communication across the two role groups. Moreover, when prisoners referred to other prisoners during interviews, they typically deprecated each other, seemingly adopting the guards' negative attitude.

From post experimental data, we discovered that when individual guards were alone with solitary prisoners and out of range of any recording equipment, as on the way to or in the toilet, harassment often was greater than it was on the 'Yard'. Similarly, video-taped analyses of total guard aggression showed a daily escalation even after most prisoners had ceased resisting and prisoner deterioration had become visibly obvious to them. Thus, guard aggression was no longer elicited as it was initially in response to perceived threats, but was emitted simply as a 'natural' consequence of being in the uniform of a 'guard' and asserting the power inherent in that role. In specific instances we noted cases of a guard (who did not know he was being observed) in the early morning hours pacing the Yard – as the prisoners slept – vigorously pounding his night stick into his hand while he 'kept watch' over his captives. Or another guard who detained an 'incorrigible' prisoner in solitary confinement beyond the duration set by the guards' own rules, and then he conspired to keep him in the hole all night while attempting to conceal this information from the experimenters who were thought to be too soft on the prisoners.

In passing we may note an additional point about the nature of role-playing and the extent to which actual behaviour is 'explained away' by reference to it. It will be recalled that many guards continued to intensify their harassment and aggressive behaviour even after the second day of the study, when prisoner deterioration became marked and visible and emotional breakdowns began to occur (in the presence of the guards). When questioned after the study about their persistent affrontive and harassing behaviour in the face of prisoner emotional trauma, most guards replied that they were 'just playing the role' of a tough guard, although none ever doubted the magnitude or validity of the prisoners' emotional response. The reader may wish to consider to what extremes an individual may go, how great must be the consequences of his behaviour for others, before he can no longer rightfully attribute his actions to 'playing a role' and thereby abdicate responsibility.

When introduced to a Catholic priest, many of the role-playing prisoners referred to themselves by their prison number rather than their Christian names. Some even asked him to get a lawyer to help them get out. When a public defender was summoned to interview those prisoners who had not yet been released, almost all of them strenuously demanded that he 'bail' them out immediately.

One of the most remarkable incidents of the study occurred during a parole board hearing when each of five prisoners eligible for parole was asked by the senior author whether he would be willing to forfeit all the money earned as a prisoner if he were to be paroled (released from the study). Three of the five prisoners said, 'yes', they would be willing to do this. Notice that the original incentive for participating in the study had been the promise of money, and they were, after only four days, prepared to give this up completely. And, more surprisingly, when told that this possibility would have to be discussed with the members of the staff before a decision could be made, each prisoner got up quietly and was escorted by a guard back to his cell. If they regarded themselves simply as 'subjects' participating in an experiment for money, there was no longer any incentive to remain in the study and they could have easily escaped this situation which had so clearly become aversive for them by quitting. Yet, so powerful was the control which the situation had over them, so much a reality had this simulated environment become, that they were unable to see that their original and singular motive for remaining no longer obtained, and they returned to their cells to await a 'parole' decision by their captors.

The reality of the prison was also attested to by our prison consultant who had spent over sixteen years in prison, as well as the priest who had been a prison chaplain and the public defender, all of whom were brought into direct contact with our simulated prison environment. Further, the depressed affect of the prisoners, the guards' willingness to work overtime for no additional pay, the spontaneous use of prison titles and I.D. numbers in non-related situations all point to a level of reality as real as any other in the lives of all those who shared this experience.

To understand how an illusion of imprisonment could have become so real, we need now to consider the uses of power by the guards as well as the effects of such power in shaping the prisoner mentality.

Pathology of Power

Being a guard carried with it social status within the prison, a group identity (when wearing the uniform), and above all, the freedom to exercise an unprecedented degree of control over the lives of other human beings. This control was invariably expressed in terms of sanctions, punishment, demands, and with the threat of manifest physical power. There was no need for the guards to rationally justify a request as they did in their ordinary life, and merely to make a demand was sufficient to have it carried out. Many of the guards showed in their behaviour and revealed in post-experimental statements that this sense of power was exhilarating.

The use of power was self-aggrandizing and self-perpetuating. The guard power, derived initially from an arbitrary and randomly assigned label, was intensified whenever there was any perceived threat by the prisoners and this new level subsequently became the baseline from which further hostility and harassment would begin. The most hostile guards on each shift moved spontaneously into the leadership roles of giving orders and deciding on punishments. They became the role model whose behaviour was emulated by other members of the shift. Despite minimal contact between the three separate guard shifts and nearly sixteen hours a day spent away from the prison, the absolute level of aggression as well as more subtle and 'creative' forms of aggression manifested, increased in a spiraling function. Not to be tough and arrogant was to be seen as a sign of weakness by the guards, and even those 'good' guards who did not get as drawn into the power syndrome as the others respected the implicit norm of *never* contradicting or even interfering with an action of a more hostile guard on their shift.

After the first day of the study, practically all prisoner rights (even such things as the time and conditions of sleeping and eating) came to be redefined by the guards as 'privileges' which were to be earned by obedient behaviour. Constructive activities such as watching movies or reading (previously planned and suggested by the experimenters) were arbitrarily cancelled until further notice by the guards – and were subsequently never allowed. 'Reward', then became granting approval for prisoners to eat, sleep, go to the toilet, talk, smoke a cigarette, wear eyeglasses, or the temporary dimunition of harassment. One wonders about the conceptual nature of 'positive' reinforcement when subjects are in such conditions of deprivation, and the extent to which even minimally acceptable conditions become rewarding when experienced in the context of such an impoverished environment.

We might also question whether there are meaningful non-violent alternatives as models for behaviour modification in real prisons. In a world where men are either powerful or powerless, everyone learns to despise the lack of power in others and in oneself. It seems to us, that prisoners learn to admire power for its own sake – power becoming the ultimate reward. Real prisoners soon learn the means to gain power whether through ingratiation, informing, sexual control of other prisoners or development of powerful cliques. When they are released from prison, it is likely they will never want to feel so powerless again and will take action to establish and assert a sense of power.

The Pathological Prisoner Syndrome

Various coping strategies were employed by our prisoners as they began to react to their perceived loss of personal identity and the arbitrary control of their lives. At first they exhibited disbelief at the total invasion of their privacy, constant surveillance, and atmosphere of oppression in which they were living. Their next response was rebellion, first by the use of direct force, and later with subtle divisive tactics designed to foster distrust among the prisoners. They then tried to work within the system by setting up an elected grievance committee. When that collective action failed to produce meaningful changes in their existence, individual self-interests emerged. The breakdown in prisoner cohesion was the start of social disintegration which gave rise not only to feelings of isolation, but deprecation of other prisoners as well. As noted before, half the prisoners coped with the prison situation by becoming 'sick' – extremely disturbed emotionally – as a passive way of demanding attention and help. Others became excessively obedient in trying to be 'good' prisoners. They sided with the guards against a solitary fellow prisoner who coped with his situation by refusing to eat. Instead of supporting this final and major act of rebellion, the prisoners treated him as a trouble-maker who deserved to be punished for his disobedience. It is likely that the negative self-regard among the prisoners noted by the end of the study was the product of their coming to believe that the continued hostility toward all of them was justified because they 'deserved it' (following Walster, 1966). As the days wore on, the model prisoner reaction was one of passivity, dependence, and flattened affect.

Let us briefly consider some of the relevant processes involved in bringing about these reactions.

Loss of Personal Identity

For most people identity is conferred by social recognition of one's uniqueness, and established through one's name, dress, appearance, behaviour style and history. Living among strangers who do not know your name or history (who refer to you only by number), dressed in a uniform exactly like all other prisoners, not wanting to call attention to one's self because of the unpredictable consequences it might provoke – all led to a weakening of self identity among the prisoners. As they began to lose initiative and emotional responsivity, while acting ever more compliantly, indeed, the prisoners became deindividuated not only to the guards and the observers, but also to themselves.

Arbitrary Control

On post-experimental questionnaires, the most frequently mentioned aversive aspect of the prison experience was that of being subjugated to the patently arbitrary, capricious decisions and rules of the guards. A question by a prisoner as often elicited derogation and aggression as it did a rational answer. Smiling at a joke could be punished in the same way that failing to smile might be. An individual acting in defiance of the rules could bring punishment to innocent cell partners (who became, in effect, 'mutually yoked controls'), to himself, or to all.

As the environment became more unpredictable, and previously learned assumptions about a just and orderly world were no longer functional, prisoners ceased to initiate any action. They moved about on orders and when in their cells rarely engaged in an activity. Their zombie-like reaction was the functional equivalent of the learned helplessness phenomenon reported by Seligman & Grove (1970). Since their behaviour did not seem to have any contingent relationship to environmental consequences, the prisoners essentially gave up and stopped behaving. Thus the subjective magnitude of aversiveness was manipulated by the guards not in terms of physical punishment but rather by controlling the psychological dimension of environmental predictability (Singer & Glass, 1972).

Dependency and Emasculation

The network of dependency relations established by the guards not only promoted helplessness in the prisoners but served to emasculate them as well. The arbitrary control by the guards put the prisoners at their mercy for even the daily, commonplace functions like going to the toilet. To do so, required publicly obtained permission (not always granted) and then a personal escort to the toilet while blindfolded and handcuffed. The same was true for many other activities ordinarily practiced spontaneously without thought, such as lighting a cigarette, reading a novel, writing a letter, drinking a glass of water, or brushing one's teeth. These were all privileged activities requiring permission and necessitating a prior show of good behaviour. These low level dependencies engendered a regressive orientation in the prisoners. Their dependency was defined in terms of the extent of the domain of control over all aspects of their lives which they allowed other individuals (the guards and prison staff) to exercise.

As in real prisons, the assertive, independent, aggressive nature of male prisoners posed a threat which was overcome by a variety of tactics. The prisoner uniforms resembled smocks or dresses, which made them look silly and enabled the guards to refer to them as 'sissies' or 'girls.' Wearing these uniforms without any underclothes forced the prisoners to move and sit in unfamiliar, feminine postures. Any sign of individual rebellion was labelled as indicative of 'incorrigibility' and resulted in loss of privileges, solitary confinement, humiliation or punishment of cell-mates. Physically smaller guards were able to induce stronger prisoners to act foolishly and obediently. Prisoners were encouraged to belittle each other publicly during the counts. These and other tactics all served to engender in the prisoners a lessened sense of their masculinity (as defined by their external culture). It followed then, that although the prisoners usually outnumbered the guards during line-ups and counts (nine vs. three) there never was an attempt to directly overpower them. (Interestingly, after the study was terminated, the prisoners expressed the belief that the basis for assignment to guard and prisoner groups was physical size. They perceived the guards were 'bigger,' when, in fact, there was no difference in average height or weight between these randomly determined groups.)

In conclusion, we believe this demonstration reveals new dimensions in the social psychology of imprisonment worth pursuing in future research. In addition, this research provides a paradigm and information base for studying alternatives to existing guard training, as well as for questioning the basic operating principles on which penal institutions rest. If our mock prison could generate the extent of pathology it did in such a short time, then the punishment of being imprisoned in a real prison does not 'fit the crime' for most prisoners – indeed, it far exceeds it! Moreover, since both prisoners and guards are locked into a dynamic, symbiotic relationship which is destructive to their human nature, guards are also society's prisoners.

References

Adomo, T. W., Frenkel-Brunswik, E., Levinson, D. J., and Sanford, R. N., *The Authoritarian Personality*, (New York: Harper, 1950).

Charriere, H., *Papillion*, (Robert Laffont, 1969).

Christie, R., and Geis, F. L., (eds.), *Studies in Machiavellianism*, (New York, Academic Press, 1970).

Comrey, A. L., *Comrey Personality Scales*, (San Diego: Educational and Industrial Testing Service, 1970).

Glass, D. C., and Singer, J. E., 'Behavioural after Effects of Unpredictable and Uncontrollable Aversive Events,' *American Scientist*, 6 (4), 457-465, (1972).

Jackson, G., *Soledad Brother: the Prison Letters of George Jackson*, (New York, Bantam Books, 1970).

Milgram, S., 'Some Conditions of Obedience and Disobedience to Authority,' *HumanRelations, 18* (1), 57-76, (1965).

Mischel, W., *Personality and Assessment*, (New York: Wiley, 1968).

Schein, E., *Coercive Persuasion*, (New York, Norton, 1961).

Seligman, M. E. and Groves, D. P., 'Nontransient Learned Helplessness,' *Psychonomic Science*, 19 (3), 191-192, (1970).

Walster, E., 'Assignment of Responsibility for an Accident,' *Journal of Personality and Social Psychology*, 3 (1), 73-79, (1966).

Pathologies of Hope in Drama and Theatre

Baz Kershaw

I'm still an atheist, thank God. (Luis Bunnel)

A Short Walk on the Wild Side

February, 1997. We're walking along the windy perimeter of a high concrete parade ground in one of Britain's newest remand centres for young offenders: it is called, with a gesture towards the rejuvenative, Lancaster Farms. The prison drama worker conducting us to our group in E-wing suddenly looks nervous as an unescorted suit approaches from the opposite direction. He greets her cheerily and enquires what we're up to with an affable smile, but true to type the eyes check us out with a cold efficiency that is horribly admirable: it is patently clear that this Governor knows all about the Panopticon, about systems of surveillance and control way more effective than anything dreamed up by Jeremy Bentham (Bozovic, 1995), George Orwell (1984), or Michael Foucault (1979). The quick deferential explanation from our minder seems to satisfy – 'College Drama Project, sir' – and he's on his way, him knowing that he doesn't really know what we're up to, us knowing that he won't want to know so long as it doesn't cause overt trouble on his patch, all of us knowing we could be playing with fire.

Creative 'Space'

Between the practised smile and the panoptic eye, between the politician and the policeman, between human rights and legalised oppression, in any system designed by some to control others, there will almost always be a space for resistance, a fissure in which to forge at least a little freedom. Such spaces and fissures are not best seen as openings into which drama can be inserted, like a scalpel that can be used to dissect the body of ideology. Rather, we should see them as crucially constituting the dramaturgies of freedom because they present an absence which creativity seeks to grasp, like the word on the tip of the tongue that you sense will become the *mot juste*, or that certain but vague vision of utopia hovering tantalisingly on the edges of nightmare spaces – or times – these absences are inherently dramatic, paradoxically because they cannot be perceived without the oppressive systems – the prison, the logos, the nightmare – which seek always to eliminate them. That is why creative work which produces and exploits them is customarily an unwelcome challenge to authority, an unpredictable disruption of norms, a kind of playing with fire.

Resistance and Transgression

All good histories of theatre demonstrate that drama can have this dangerous potential. Conversely, all good theories of drama or theatre as education also account for ways in which they can inculcate essential coping strategies: behavioural modes, thinking, or in the current jargon in Britain, transferable skills, that enhance the chances of an individual or group's survival in negotiating the demands of a rough and tumble world. But in this chapter I want to focus more on the proactive, interventionist, even disruptive possibilities opened up by the kinds of creative work found in Drama in Education, Theatre in Education, Drama Therapies, Community Theatre, Theatre of the Oppressed, Theatre for Development and for Liberation and others we haven't got names for yet. In choosing this focus I am not implying that drama projects which seek to develop coping strategies are second best. But I do think it is becoming increasingly important that drama and theatre practices continue to challenge and resist, and more importantly find ways to transcend, the new kinds of repression, oppression, exploitation, injustice and so on, which at this very moment are being invented in many parts of the world, even by people who think of themselves as friends of democracy.

The issues raised by resistant or transgressive practices in the arts, especially in a post-modern and globalised world, are of course complex. So to deal with them effectively in the short span of this chapter we need, in the best traditions of research, a relatively simple question. Here is mine: how do the practices of drama and theatre best engage with systems of formalised power to create a space of radical freedom. I frame the question in this way to indicate that I am just thinking about overtly politicised practices: 'formalised power' is about much more than the politics of the state, say. I also want to imply a particularly crucial ideological scope for the workings of drama and theatre. In referring to 'radical freedom' I am shadowing Raymond Williams's challenging definition of the radical as 'offer[ing] a way of avoiding dogmatic and factional associations while reasserting the need for vigorous and fundamental change' (1976, p. 210). In other words, the freedom my question invokes is not just freedom from oppression, repression, exploitation – what we could call the resistant sense of the radical – but also freedom to reach beyond existing systems of formalised power, freedom to create currently unimaginable forms of association and action – what I would call the transcendent sense of the radical.

I am choosing to approach the issue of potentially dangerous – fiery – practices in drama and theatre in this way partly because I want to interrogate those discourses of post-modernity which would place a limit on creative radicalism. Also because I wish to engage with questions of pluralism and relativism raised not just by post-modern and associated theory, but also by the spread of democracy in a globalised world. This entails a search for convincing accounts of the sources of the radical, both in the individual subject and in the collective action of groups involved in drama and theatre. Because, if we can convincingly identify the possibility of sources as such, then should we be so inclined, we can steer our drama and theatre work towards their creation.[1] Paradoxically, one of the best places to look for some sources of radicalism is where oppressions are at their most acute, at the heart of systems of formalised power, in the Panopticon itself.

Back to Prison

Five minutes into the Lancaster Farms session, a group of five 'lads' – as the warders called the inmates, who in return called the warders 'screws' – had joined up with three of our students, one of whom was called Matt. Now it was clear that the lads liked Matt's style. Where they might have one earring, Matt had a dozen, all in one ear, and where they were all pent-up high energy, he was languid and laid-back and appeared to be approaching the whole drama thing as an extended joke. His style seemed to give them access to creative space in which they invented a story about a king who throws a birthday party for his queen, who unfortunately flirts with one of the courtiers, so the king has their heads chopped off, thus triggering an orgy of official violence in which the rest of the court gets slaughtered, leaving only the king alive. Story sorted, the casting happens very quickly in a negotiation skilfully steered by Matt. The king is played by the only black man in the group with a cool intensity which seems to mimic but ironically inflect Matt's style, sitting up on a chair on the worktop of a study cubicle. The queen's throne is in the next cubicle, and she is played with fragile femininity by a young man who is clearly, in the real world of the prison, the butt of the group. The flirting courtier is done in habitual monosyllables by the physically strongest of the lads, the bully-boy who likes to throw his weight around, while the students do the other courtiers. The guards-cum-executioners are played by a couple of middle-rankers, two lads halfway up the pecking order of the whole workshop group of twelve inmates. In other words, the casting seemed to invert the usual pecking order of the lads.

The shifted power structure produced by the casting generates an impressive dynamic performance, with a concentration and intensity that belies the group's lack of drama experience. It is all very highly controlled, but still relaxed, so that even the stream of beheadings – done with the heads thrust through the gap in the back of a chair – achieves a jocular style, an ironic playfulness that distances yet seems fully to edge the horror of absolute power. The playfulness arises from the switchback of the dramaturgy: the queen is clearly devoted to the king, but flirts anyway; thinks she's safe when the flirting courtier is the first to be beheaded, but the king decides she's got to go too; having carried out the king's orders, first one guard then another think they're safe, but, having started, the king thinks he might as well go the whole hog and turns executioner himself; in his triumph at having got rid of the lot he suddenly realises he's all alone, and teeters on the edge of tears. I guess that the group's control of the material stems from their knowledge of popular gangster contemporary film noir, shades of Tarantino and maybe even David Lynch.

Now I think there was nothing particularly exceptional about this drama it has some similarities of approach to participatory projects undertaken in say, Zakes Mda (1993) in Lesotho or Penina Mlama (1991) in Tanzania; in Brazil by Augusto Boal (1979); in the Philippines by PETA (Philippines Educational Theatre Association) (1992); in India by MESCA (Media Exploration for Social and Cultural Education)

(1989); in Australia by FILEF (Federation of Italian Migrant Workers and their Families) (1987), and many others. I am discussing it, in fact, because of its relative ordinariness when seen in this global context, and because the fact that it is in some senses typical could help us to think through how ideologically resistant and transcendent impulses might be generated through a wide span of contemporary practices. So the issue is: what light might this simple prison play throw on our research question, about the ways in which theatre and drama can best engage with systems of formalised power to create a space of radical freedom?

If we approach it from the traditional perspective of political theatre – that is to say a Marxist, or socialist, or at least left-wing perspective – then I think it likely we would conclude that this was probably a reactionary spectacle, ultimately reinforcing hegemonic hierarchies of power despite its mildly satirical style. This was a fantasy inversion, like the Feast of Fools or carnival, which gave the lads a temporary illusion of power only to return them 'essentially' unchanged to the real servitude of the prison. However, post-modernity, of course, has rendered such a reading deeply problematic. The master-narratives devolving from the Enlightenment are now the subject of intense incredulity, with the result that – if for the moment we accept the full force of the post-modern paradigm – no discourse can confidently lay claim to the universal. It follows that no single interpretation of events can automatically predominate, so judgements based on notions of 'political theatre' which themselves derive from a totalising philosophy become especially suspect. The issue is made even more difficult by the impact of new critical theory on the analysis of art. Deconstructionist, poststructuralist, radical-feminist, post-colonialist, as well as post-modernist theories have promoted what I call the promiscuity of the political.

The Promiscuity of the Political

By 'promiscuity' I mean that in serious analysis of drama and theatre the idea of the political, in parallel with its usage in other disciplines, has been applied to a widening range of phenomena: thus, we have cultural politics, the politics of representation, the politics of the body, the politics of drama in education, and so on.[2] While, on the one hand, this trend may be seen as a welcome process of sensitisation to how power is embedded and circulates in all drama, theatre and performance, and therefore, in one sense, even as a 'democratisation' of the political, on the other hand, it has led to a continuing crisis about the ways in which drama and theatre might be considered to be 'political' or 'radical'. If all drama and theatre is political, then what might we mean by 'political'? The sources for this chronic uncertainty are not difficult to locate. So long as we allow that Barthes (1997) has finally done for the intentional fallacy by murdering the author; Foucault (1984) has incontrovertibly shown that power is everywhere; Derrida (1991) has uncoupled the signifier from the signified forever; Lyotard (1986) has raised incredulity about master-narratives to a new order of intensity; Butler (1990) has demonstrated that even gender is a cultural construct; and Baudrillard (1983) has possibly capped it all by banishing the real, we will be plagued by an acute, or maybe totally debilitating, insecurity. The anti-foundational theorists of post-structuralism and post-modernity, though offering all exhilarating release from oppressive systems of thought, may also threaten to plunge us into a miasma of ideological relativities which flows in the wake of the dematerialisation of the world.[3]

The implications of all this for the analysis and practice of theatre and drama are by no means all negative; from this critical angle the lads' prison drama takes on at least a more colourful complexion than we derived from the outworn notion of 'political theatre'. Viewed from the perspectives of identity politics, it was partly a liberalising affair – racism and homophobia countered by the elevation of the black man to king and the effeminate boy to queen – but it was also playing to oppressive stereotypes of sexist virile violence and limp-wristed gay weakness. From the perspectives of power politics, it was reinforcing ideas about the necessity of hierarchy, while critiquing the operations of institutionalised violence in the real figure of the bully and the imaginary figures of the guards. From the point of view of the politics of the criminal justice system, it mounted a parodic attack on the assumed rights of the powerful to punish as they please, at the same time as it gleefully submitted to a system of vengeance that made the real law seem entirely reasonable. And from the point of view of liberation politics, it provided a symbolic inversion of the rule of law as the real criminals took creative charge of an imaginary system of 'justice' that mocked the ideological foundations of the prison in which it was enacted, but ended up perhaps still too close to accepting the hierarchical values with which it had started, with the key change being that great energy had been expanded which might otherwise have been used to more subversive effect in the real world of the prison.

From this perspective – these perspectives – what matters in the ideological impact of the play-let is not its overall coherence, but the opportunity it gives for the expression of a multiplicity of voices which would normally be suppressed. From this perspective – these perspectives – what we were pursuing in Lancaster Farms overall was a liberating practice.

The Complexities of 'Freedom'

I am somewhat uncomfortable with this conclusion, though, and not simply because it entails a full-blooded embrace of contradiction. There are two more substantial aspects in this interpretation of the lads' drama that worry me. The first is that the admirable multivocality of the play did not seem to be matched by any positive unity of purpose in, say, a search for an explicitly agreed oppositional 'take' on its subject matter; whatever unity it created seemed to be based on an ironic rejection of existing structures of power which entailed that it always worked in their terms. This raises the second point, which is that while we might claim that it promoted the potential for a creative liberation from those structures, we would also need to note that it did not appear to explore to what ends such liberation might be put. To frame this more generally in relation to the equation embedded in the idea of 'radical freedom': for the lads the drama may have been mostly creating a 'freedom from' existing discipline, authority and so on, but hardly at all dealing with the 'freedom to' construct an alternative. In other words, their drama may have been working more in terms of resistant than transcendent radicalism.

Of course, this analysis raises other issues about the ways in which my 'take' on the drama may have prevented access to what was 'really' going on for the lads. This was the last session of five for them, and we did not record the short debrief which followed the performance, so I am unable to use what they said either to confirm or question my interpretation of what happened. This may be viewed as a fault in the design of the drama process as research (a point tellingly made by an Australian delegate when this argument was presented as a conference keynote), but also of course we probably need to be wary of the assumption that what people say about what they have learned from creative work is necessarily more accurate or closer to the 'truth' than the views of non-participants. In practice, such voicings may not give us particularly good access to the work's greatest value; in fact they may even risk the promotion of misinterpretation. There is not space here properly to explore this problem, but for me it underlines the importance of the analysis of the drama or theatre work itself as potentially the prime 'object' of study for this field of research. From this perspective, the aptitudes of the theatre critic – or the performance analyst – are highly relevant to research in drama in education: a Kenneth Tynan and an Elinor Fuchs should happily sit on our shelves beside Hornbrook and Heathcote![4]

Too quickly bypassing these research issues to return to the lads' drama: my analysis of their play-let raises the general question of how creative work might successfully achieve radical freedom, which in turn requires that we track back to my opening remarks about the sources of radicalism. The locations of such sources, I suggest, are likely to be found in areas with which post-modern theory customarily has difficulty dealing. Terry Eagleton (1996) identifies two principal ones in his mischievously entertaining book *The Illusions of Post-modernism*. He notes, for example, that the pluralism to which post-modernism is so securely wedded prevents it from constructing an effective notion of community, or of a common good other than a hybridised heterogeneity, a multiple choice of contrasting cultural positions, that makes the notion of 'common good' at best unintelligible, at worst redundant. This point is also admirably reinforced by the political theorist Anne Phillips, when she writes of contemporary democracy that:

> The new pluralism arises out of a radical tradition that sets its sight on future change. Because of this, it cannot rest content with a live and let live toleration that just enjoins each group to get on with its own private affairs. But, inspired as it is by a far-reaching egalitarianism that wants to empower currently disadvantaged groups, it is also more likely to '...validate all exclusive and fragmented politics of identity that blocks the development of wider solidarity' (Phillips, 1993).

Terry Eagleton also wittily outlines the second of the two key problems faced by post-modern theory; namely, the difficulty it has with the notion of human agency. He comments that post-modernists have 'little to say on the great liberal motives of justice, freedom, human rights and the like, since, these topics sit uncomfortably with its nervousness of the 'autonomous subject'' (p. 87). There are some post-modernists who have laboured hard, and from some points of view successfully, to refute such charges[5] – but of course the debate is far from settled. Hence, the epic tussle between the two great paradigms of modernity and post-modernity must still disturb one's lines of thought, particularly where questions of power and empowerment are at play. For our purposes now, one effect of this turmoil is plain, and that is: if we wish to see how contemporary drama and theatre might engage with the 'great liberal motives' underlying most conceptions of democracy, then we should be looking to resistant and transcendent practices which valorise the autonomous subject while reinforcing collective (or community) identities.

The rest of this chapter is a speculative exploration in search of some of the sources of radicalism in contemporary theatre and drama, focusing on a couple of ways in which it may create community and strengthen the autonomous subject. As there is not space to deal with the full complexity of the issues raised by such a project I will simply argue through a couple of highly selective and contrasting examples. The first is a massive participatory lantern procession called Glasgow All Lit Up! mounted in 1990 by the veteran British company, Welfare State International (see Coult and Kershaw, 1990). The second is a short play written by an inmate in another prison as a result of drama sessions with postgraduate students which I undertook in 1991. Despite their vast differences I would include both these projects under the general rubric of 'democratised performance'.

Glasgow All Lit Up!

Glasgow All Lit Up! was billed as 'The Biggest Lantern Procession in Europe'. This was the culmination of Glasgow's stint as European City of Culture, and, more importantly, of a long-term residency by Welfare State, which had some of the characteristics of Boal's Theatre of the Oppressed: it was participatory, it used a systematic creative methodology, it aimed to promote cultural democracy. So the company's work can be aligned with a worldwide range of theatre that uses vernacular forms and popular imagery to strengthen grass-roots activism, from the American Bread and Puppet Theatre to Teater Dynasti in Java, from the Negros Theatre League in the Philippines to Nixtayolero in Nicaragua, by some ngoma troupes in Tanzania, and by groups in many other countries.6

The chief creative activity of Glasgow All Lit Up! was lantern making. For a year and a half Welfare State artists trained local Scottish artists in techniques learned in Japan, and the local artists in turn worked with some two-hundred-and-fifty community organisations (including schools) throughout Strathclyde – the greater Glasgow area. In the early evening of 6 October 1990, following a day of torrential rain, these groups gathered at four locations to the north, south, east and west of the city centre. From there they converged on George Square to form a single procession of 10,000 people carrying, wheeling, and driving some 8000 lanterns.

Some of the lanterns were simple and tiny and could be carried by toddlers. Some were big and abstract and needed articulated trucks to carry them. Some truck-mounted ones were huge and politically satirical. The two mile-long procession snaked noisily down to Glasgow Green, a mile and a half from the city centre, where the big truck-lanterns drove in to form a semi-circular backdrop for a two-hundred strong community choir, while the smaller lanterns were hung onto collapsible towers that were gradually hauled up by cranes to form four glowing pyramids of light over forty-feet high at the corners of the Green. The end-piece to the gathering was a spectacle with musical accompaniment from the choir, staged by Welfare State artists, in which giant images from the Glasgow City crest – a tree, a bell, a fish and a bird-glowed and burned and flew through the air in a surreal animation that freed them from the rigour of their usual heraldic setting. A final big firework display ended the evening.

An analysis of this extraordinary event from a traditional 'political theatre' perspective would probably see it – surprise, surprise – as an incorporative carnival; as, in Terry Eagleton's (1981, p. 148) words, 'a licensed affair in every sense, a permissible rupture of hegemony' which ultimately reinforced the dominant values of its socio-political environment. Its willingness to dance to the tune of the dominant could be detected, for example, in its reliance on commercial sponsorship from British Gas, which, frisky for privatisation, insisted that the words 'Welfare State' should not appear on any advertising material. Also, it submitted to the complete control of the route by the authorities, and it was rumoured that the scale of the event gave the police and armed forces an opportunity surreptitiously to test out their disaster procedures. Also, its spectacular success no doubt reinforced the global competition between cities in their efforts to attract capital, which is embedded in the idea of the 'European City of Culture'. Moreover, the scale of the procession meant that it had to be organised through a military-like hierarchy, and the final orgasmic spectacle can be seen as simply legitimating existing structures of power by playing ineffectively with a bit of their symbolism. Hence, as an attempt at Cultural democracy, as an empowerment of local communities, Glasgow All Lit Up! was subverted by its own ambition, which caused it to engage with, and ultimately to succumb to, value systems that it had set out to oppose. For liberation, autonomy, self-determination, control over the construction of the subject – read containment, abnegation, manipulation by hidden forces, exploitation of the subject as object, and so on. From this perspective, just as with the lads' little play in Lancaster Farms, the event can be placed firmly in the realms of anti-democratic – or incorporated – art, because it did not sufficiently challenge or outwit the formalised power structures of its context.

This conclusion derives from a theoretical perspective that uses the notion of a dominant ideology to construct a binary either/or analysis: either Glasgow All Lit Up! successfully subverted the dominant or it was incorporated into it. But if we again adopt a more complex model by taking on board some of the pluralistic force of the post-modern paradigm, then we may be able to draw more hopeful conclusions about the event. What I am looking for is any ways in which Glasgow All Lit Up! may have enabled its participants to construct themselves collectively as 'autonomous democratic subjects' in order to achieve radical freedom. Once more it will be helpful to look in unlikely places, which in this case means among the thousands of children who took part in the event.

When the procession finally reached Glasgow Green the orderly ranks fractured into a confusion of mini-processions which split off to hang their lanterns on the rising lantern-pyramids. In the middle of the hubbub my attention was caught by a singular sight. This was a group of about thirty children aged from around six to nine years old, most of them carrying small, self-made lanterns shaped to form letters from the alphabet and spelling out the name of their school. They stood out from the surrounding confusion because for me there was a remarkable quality in their little procession: they were not processing like most of the other groups towards one of the lantern-pyramids, they were weaving their way around the sodden field, apparently with no particular direction in mind, but they were obviously not lost, nor directionless. They had a few adults in attendance, but the adults were following them, and they were processing in complete silence, with none of the usual chatter of excited children. They obviously were happy and self-possessed enough to be enjoying their procession for its own sake. Apparently they were processing for the enjoyment of the fact that it was their procession – not because they were part of some mega-celebration staged by Welfare State International, nor because this was a major civic happening that justified Glasgow as the European City of Culture. This was their event, they were staking a claim to their own creativity, and, I think, through making this their procession they may have been touching on a source of radical freedom.

So I want to suggest that this tiny procession represented, perhaps, a decentred and egalitarian collective, a celebration of localised unified difference. Maybe here was an image of communal autonomy and self-determination constructed through the processes of cultural democracy.

Theoretical Reflections

Now there are lines of argument in theatre anthropology and political theory that can be drawn on to reinforce this claim. For example, Victor Turner's (1982) study of ritual led him to develop the idea of 'communitas', by which he means a collective experience which is paradoxically both within and beyond the ideologies which shape society. Turner claims that:

> communitas does not represent the erasure of structural norms from the consciousness of those participating in it; rather its own style, in a given community, might be said to depend upon the way in which it symbolises the abrogation, negation, or inversion of the normative structure in which its participants are ... involved [in their everyday lives] (1982, p. 47).

Picking up these lines of thought, we may argue that the children's procession both presented an inversion of the anti-democratic aspects of its context and was also, in potential at least, an embodiment of certain crucial democratic rights; namely, those relating to the concept of collective autonomy. The political philosopher David Held (1987) argues that the concept indicates an underlying principle of both liberal and socialist democratic traditions, and states it in the following terms:

> individuals should be free and equal in the determination of the conditions of their own lives; that is, they should enjoy equal rights (and, accordingly, equal obligations) in the specification of the framework which generates the limits and opportunities available

to them, so long as they do not deploy this framework to negate the rights of others (1987, p. 271).

Held also stresses that the general principle means little if divorced from the specific, pragmatic 'conditions of its enactment'.

Now it is obvious that the 'enactment' of the children's procession was constructed through conditions which the children could not have determined in any critical way, and especially those conditions which pushed the whole event towards what I have called 'incorporative carnival'. However, it does not necessarily follow that, in the moment of making the mini-procession their own, the children would inevitably fail to achieve any sense of autonomy. At the very least we might justifiably claim that their action can be read in retrospect as a metaphor for 'the determination of the conditions of their own lives;' but also the nature of the performative, at least as conceived by performance theory and theatre anthropology, strongly suggests that the significance of the – metaphor may be, quite literally, embodied in the action. In other words, the children could well have had access to a basic process required for the construction of the collective democratic subject, and I would further argue that their action can be seen as not simply resisting the dominant ideologies of its context but also as transcending them. We can express this by saying that while it mimicked the main procession in being part of an incorporative carnival, it also, as it were, created a cultural space in which it could exercise a *modus operandi* of quite another order. It is a cornerstone of my argument that these kinds of liminal space – Turner calls them 'the seedbeds of cultural creativity' (1982, p. 28) – provide common sources of collective radical freedom to which drama, theatre and performance can give access.

I want to reinforce this point by expanding it to apply to the whole 10,000 strong procession, and this can best be done by seeing how the procession engaged with the law. In doing this I am taking the law as symbolic of the normative in the social, so that theoretically a creative transgression of the law may give access to liminality. I am aware that this is an ethical minefield, but that is the kind of territory which comes with any serious encounter with the fierily dangerous in drama and theatre, and Glasgow All Lit Up! ended up playing with a lot more fire, metaphorically speaking, than the actual flames that lit its thousands of lanterns.

This underlines the point that when we are dealing with liminality we will almost always end up encountering some kind of excess. And as Glasgow All Lit Up! wound its way through the city centre one of the most striking excesses in its narrative occurred in relation to ... traffic flow. Despite strenuous efforts of persuasion by Welfare State, the police had insisted that the roads of the route should remain open to vehicles, so that as the procession moved through the city the heavy Saturday evening traffic flowed in both directions alongside it. The plan agreed with the police was that after the four 'feed' processions formed into a single one on their approach to George Square, the roads crossing the route would be kept open through the maintenance of agreed 'gaps' in the procession and, if necessary, through stopping the procession while crossing traffic passed. Not surprisingly, most of the gaps disappeared once the full procession was formed; and probably the high energy of its flow made it impossible to interrupt without risk of a dangerous build-up of a potentially uncontrollable mass of bodies. The net result was that the city centre came to a standstill – for a time the narrative of the procession became the dominant discourse in the public domain of Glasgow city during that damp Saturday evening.

The procession did not so much break the law as force its suspension, and in the process it translated itself from a resistant discourse into a transgressive one. As a celebration of the creativity of the people of Glasgow it can be read as a resistant statement against, for example, the commodifications of consumerism or the usual exclusion of the majority from hands-on cultural production – it was making a claim for freedom from some of the limitations of post-industrial society. However, as a negotiation with authority it became a transgressive event, a claim for freedom to create a liminal space for its own unique types of empowering pleasure, a demand to make its own alternative forms of the social. It is in the nature of the liminal that its alternatives are hard to articulate: but we might say of the procession that it created a unity against the divisions that the law has to enforce in order to be the law, that it fostered a kind of civic energy which peacefully demonstrated how people may generate collective power. It is in this sense, at least, that both the children's mini-procession and the total procession that was Glasgow All Lit Up! might be taken to indicate some of the sources of radical freedom in drama and theatre.

The Freedoms of Oppression

I have been arguing that transgressive radical freedom may have been achieved collectively on the streets of Glasgow that night; but what might be possible in contexts that are much less accommodating? To address this issue I will finally turn to another of the blind spots that spasmodically plague post-modernism: the autonomous individual.

Post-modernism tends habitually to view the subject as detached from history and free-floating in a dematerialised (hyper-real) and indeterminate world, a fate which throws radical doubt on the subject's potential for autonomy. In contrast to this, I want to use my final example to explore how there is no necessary contradiction between the idea of the subject as embedded in histories and the possibility of free action by the individual. In doing this I will adopt a critical procedure that is potentially high risk in this context; namely, a very close analysis of a play-script. I take this risk in order to emphasise through this critical practice my point that it is the action (or its traces) of the work of drama/theatre itself which may give us best access to the reflections of participants on what they have achieved through such work. To highlight this argument we will return to prison, to see how even in the most constrained circumstances the creativity of the individual subject may make a claim on radical freedom.

In 1991 I undertook another prison project, this time with postgraduate students and in a category C, 'semi-open' establishment in which some internal gates are supposed to be kept open. We worked with a group of five men, and as usual tried to negotiate our way past the usual suspicions and mistrust through the usual group-building games. One of these ended in a joke-telling session which had the women students giving as good as they got in the way of sexist jokes. Their reward at the next workshop was to be presented with a screenplay that we might manage to make into a video or film, but then the chances that we would get permission to bring it out of the jail probably were exceedingly slim, given the nature of its contents. The screenplay was written by a young man whom I shall call Edgar Bond. He called it *The Rat Run*, though tellingly he would never write that on the script, which went officially by the title of *One Hour in the Semi-Open*.

The Rat Run dramatised the regime that the group claimed controlled individual journeys in the jail. Beside the regular mass movement of men from cell to showers, dining hall to workshops, and so on, the prisoners could be ordered on individual journeys, which often had a time limit set on them for getting from A to B. If the prisoner was late at B then his name would be recorded. Several such infringements could be counted against remission of sentence. And the prison, which occupies a historic castle, was a warren of corridors, stairways, alleyways, balconies leading to steel studded doors, barred gateways, huge-hinged portals. So there was always more than one way of getting from A to B – sometimes there were three or even four, and at almost every door you encountered a screw, who would be more or less inclined depending on what he knew of you or how he felt or whatever else might be in his head or heart right then – to promptly let you through or make you wait. This system is an example of what Foucault calls, in Discipline and Punish, the 'counter-law', the networks of semi-formalised, often unwritten, rules which are developed by institutions and organisations to cover areas that the law proper cannot reach.

The Rat Run represented one journey through this particular aspect of the prison's counter-laws, rooting out the drama buried deeply and discretely at the heart of its panoptic system. With amazing economy it explored the perverse disciplinarity of the idioms of incarceration, but it also suggested – both through its dramaturgy and through its position as a creative act in the whole penal discourse – entirely other possibilities, perspectives, and, I think, some sources of radical freedom. To begin to gain a clear perspective on these sources I shall focus on the paradox of what we might call the freedoms of oppression. The paradox stems from the idea that to be oppressed we must enter into oppression, but also that (to adopt Tom Stoppard's formulation) every entrance is an exit somewhere else (Hughes and Brecht, 1978). To approach the complexities of the freedoms of oppression I shall be exploring the following questions: how might radical freedom exist at the moment of greatest constraint; how can transgressive autonomy be nurtured in an exchange designed to destroy it?

The Rat Run

The screenplay tells the story of one con's typical journey from the prison gym to the education department. The high point of the play, its dramatic fulcrum, suggests the tortuous ontological routes that have to be forged in systems like the rat run for the incarcerated to create a bit of their own space. Up to this point the con has had to negotiate his way through five gates, in the process flogging unnecessarily up and down several flights of stairs and failing to get through three other gates, either because they were unmanned or because the attendant screw wouldn't let him through. Getting close to his destination, he eventually arrives at a gate where he's not supposed to be.

(*You arrive at the bottom gate, two screws in the office outside.*)

CON: Boss can you let us out please?
SCREW: Why?
CON: I'm trying to get to Ed.
SCREW: What wing are you off?
CON: 'A' wing.
SCREW: You're not allowed on this wing.
CON: I'm just trying to get to Ed.
SCREW: You're not allowed on this wing.

(*He still hasn't moved. all this is done shouting.*)

CON: I can't hear you.

(*The only way to get him to the gate.*)

SCREW: Why didn't you use the other gate?
CON: Because it's locked and there's no one there. I thought I could get through this way.
SCREW: You're not allowed on this wing.

(*Opens the gate.*)

CON: I'm only trying to get to Ed. If someone was on the other gate or if it was open as a semi-open should be, I wouldn't be here now.

Now, why does the screw let the con through a gate he's not supposed to use? The answer to this simple question, I think, has profound ramifications for the notion of radical freedom, and, by extension, for post-modernist's view of the subject as lacking autonomy through its detachment from history.

The screw has to come to the gate, and the con knows it, because the con's feigned deafness may lead to more shouting, which might draw attention to a lack of control in the system. More crucially, in such a tight system the screw must check why the con is pleading at a gate he's not allowed through, in case the con's insistence is the sign of some flaw in the operation of both the law and the counter-law – in concrete terms, that a locked gate that should have been open has forced him to be where he shouldn't be. The fact that this turns out to be the case is why the screw lets the con through the gate: in effect, the agent of the law is seduced into overturning it because it cannot conform to its own rules, its own perverse logic.

At this point the con is, as it were, creating a new law and hence making a space for his own autonomy, a partial empowerment. He can do this because he has fashioned a liminal space out of his encounter with the screw, a kind of virtual doorway or entry, a double threshold, through a technique that the script elsewhere calls 'blanking': to 'blank' someone is to refuse to negotiate an exchange on their terms. This refusal in the script, when the con pretends to be deaf, is what gets the screw to the gate and hence indicates the fissure in the system of the counter-law. At the moment of 'blanking' the con has achieved a radical freedom which allows him, so to speak, to rewrite the rules to his own advantage, hence producing a degree of autonomy and empowerment in this particular panoptic system.

So the mechanisms of discipline, which in fact generally hinge on an act of performance – in legal systems the law court is paradigmatic of this – can sometimes be turned back on themselves to produce resistant and transcendent empowerment, even within such a fine-tuned system as the rat run. And at another level of ideological negotiation, *The Rat Run* as a creative artefact demonstrated the self-reflexivity available to its author by signalling to us and then the prison authorities his awareness of the vulnerability of the law. In other words, the script itself demonstrated that Edgar Bond could see through the disciplinary mechanisms in such a way as to subvert, or perhaps even to negate them. All the prison authorities could do in response was to try to prevent its further dissemination through a weak form of censorship – they would not give us permission to take the audio recording we made with the group out of the prison, even though the group gave written approval for us to do so – but that, in its turn, only served further to expose their vulnerability. Also, although the authorities could exert control over that particular bit of the 'material capital' produced by the project, they had and have no final control over the 'symbolic capital' represented by the dramaturgy of the screenplay. There is no way at this stage that censorship, in this case, can repress the self-reflexive knowledge of the inevitable limits of the law produced by drama and theatre which encourages resistant and transcendent practices.

In calling on the paradox of the freedoms of oppression I am suggesting, too, that the source of such self-reflexive, performative knowledge can be found in the very disciplinary processes which aim to eliminate it. Even Foucault, in a relatively rare moment of (admittedly very guarded) optimism, seems to admit to this possibility when he writes:

> ...the prison with all the corrective technology at its disposal is to be resituated at the point where the codified power to punish turns into a disciplinary power to observe... [this is] the point where the redefinition of the juridical subject by the penalty becomes a useful training of the criminal ... (in Rabinow, 1984, p. 213).

From this perspective the old notion that prison is a training ground for criminals may take on a significant new inflection, perhaps, for the socio-cultural structures linking the criminal to the merely rebellious, and then to the dissident and the revolutionary, operate according to the same principles of attempted control and determined resistance. This is not, of course, to assert an identity between criminals and revolutionaries, nor to collapse moral judgement into political romanticism: the criminal can still be considered ethically wrong, or even wicked, even as he or she shares the same pedestal as the revolutionary hero. But I am arguing for a recognition that in panoptic systems the force of these varied forms of resistance and transgression – the revolutionary and the recidivist – may stem from linked sources, in the reflexivities of performance that can be fostered by drama and theatre. Such reflexivities are embedded crucially in the fact that drama and theatre do not exist without entrances and exits, and, of course, every entry is an exit somewhere else.

Conclusions

I have been arguing that drama and theatre can significantly contribute to the collective and individual creation of autonomous subjects, especially through an engagement with systems of formalised power in an effort to create radical freedom. Such freedom can be achieved through actions which combine resistant and transcendent ideological dynamics, which oppose dominant ideologies and also at least gesture to possibilities beyond them. Post-modernism is useful to this project because it's pluralism opens up a rich range of approaches to the creation of resistance. But it cannot give an adequate account of the possibility of transcendent action or thought because, paradoxically, despite some efforts in the contrary direction, it tends to make relativism an absolute and in the process undermines the possibilities of both community and the autonomous subject. However, I am suggesting, equally paradoxically, that when such ideological action is grounded in the contingencies of histories (through its engagement with formalised systems of power) then it may achieve a transcendent perspective in relation to those contingencies.

From this point of view, we can say that in my first example the lads in the prison may not have achieved a radical freedom precisely because they did not engage with the power structures of their immediate context directly and critically enough: the image of the king and his court did not sufficiently gesture beyond the hierarchies and contingent brutalities of the prison system, only reproduced them ironically; whereas, Glasgow All Lit Up! and *The Rat Run* had a greater chance of achieving this because they were so fully and directly engaging with the discourses of power in their particular settings. (I hope it is clear that I am not primarily talking about what was represented in the three examples, but rather how they were articulated to their context.) The paradoxical nature of this type of action can best be summarised, following Foucault, by saying that oppression produces at least the possibility, and possibly the necessity, of freedom.

The impact of the post-modern unfortunately demands that we develop quite complicated theoretical explanations for effective radicalism in drama and theatre. So I would like to finish with a very brief example which I think demonstrates that in practice the production of radicalism can be relatively straightforward, although never easy. The Chilian theatre director Hugo Medina has described how during Pinochet's reign of terror the people would show they knew the houses of torture by silently pointing at them as they walked past; everyone knew the significance of the pointed finger yet the dictatorship was powerless to prevent it because virtually everyone did it. Hence the everyday act of pointing was transformed into a collective gesture that was beyond the power of control of one of the most oppressive post-war regimes, because to eliminate it the regime would have had to destroy totally the people upon whom its power rested.[7]

In other words, there are forms of resistance which are decisively not articulated to the dominant structures of authority in ways that make them automatically recoupable by those structures, and those forms may produce a radical freedom that is not just negatively against a regime but also positively for some value or ideal that lies well beyond its ideological territory. Post-modernism usually has great difficulty in conceiving of this type of radical freedom, whereas drama and theatre which deliberately and critically engages in the power structures of its particular context has the potential, I think, actually to produce it. Even in the most obscure corners of the post-modern panopticon creative performance can insinuate pathologies of hope.

Notes

1. I am aware that my choice of the word 'source' can be interpreted as begging the question of the doctrine of first causes that post-modernism healthily challenges; I am using it in the sense of 'fountainhead' or 'a work supplying information or evidence' (Oxford English Dictionary), i.e. as a key point through which whole other systems of energy and knowledge can be sourced. It is a pity that its meaning in hawking is not much current, as it would add a further appropriate resonance to my search: 'The act of rising on the wing'.

2. See, for example: Holderness, Graham (ed.) *The Politics of Theatre and Drama* (London; Macmillan, 1992); Case, Sue Ellen & Janelle Reinelt (eds.) *The Performance of Power: theatrical discourse and politics* (Des Moines, University of Iowa Press, 1991); Diamond, Elm (ed.) *Performance and Cultural Politics* (London; Routledge, 1996); Campbell, Patrick (ed.), *Analysing Performance* (Manchester; Manchester University Press, 1996).

3. I realise this concluding generalisation oversimplifies the post-modern/post-structuralist scene, but I include it to indicate the extent of what is at stake in the paradigm shift from modernity to post-modernity.

4. A highly subjective selection of favourites; see: Tynan, Kenneth, *Tynan on Theatre* (Harmondsworth, Pelican, 1964); Fuchs, Elinor, *The Death of Character: perspectives on theatre after modernism* (Bloomington, Indiana University Press, 1996).

5. See, for example; Laclau, Ernesto & Chantal Mouffe, *Hegemony and Social Strategy: towards a radical democratic politics* (London; Verso, 1986); Trend, David (ed.) *Radical Democracy: identity, citizenship, and the state* (London, Routledge, 1996).

6. Useful recent texts include: Martin, Randy, *Socialist Ensembles: the theatre in Cuba and Nicaragua* (Minneapolis, University of Minnesota Press, 1994); Plastow, Jane, *African Theatre and Politics: the evolution of theatre in Ethiopia, Tanzania and Zimbabwe-a comparative study* (Amsterdam; Rodopi, 1996); Kerr, David, *African Popular Theatre* (Oxford; James Curry, 1995).

7. Hugo Medina at 'Performance, Politics and Ideology', University of Lancaster, April 1990; Prentki, Tim, 'Cop Out, cop in: carnival as political theatre', New Theatre Quarterly, Vol. VI, No. 24, November (1990), pp. 362-364. Consider also that the child

who beats her hands at the air in an ecstasy of frustration may be operating in the same matrix.

References

Barthes, Roland, *Image Music Text*, tr. Stephen Health (London, Fontana Press, 1977).

Baudrillard, Jean, *Simulations*, tr. Paul Foss, Paul Patton & Philip Beitchman (New York, Semiotext[e], 1983).

Bentham, Jeremy, *The Panopiticon Writings*, Miran, Bozovic (ed.) (London, Verso, 1995).

Boal, Augusto, *Theatre of the Oppressed*, Charles A. McBride & Maria-Odilia Leal McBride (London, Pluto Press, 1979).

Butler, Juddith, *Gender Trouble: feminism and the subversion of identity* (London, Routlcdge, 1990).

Coult, Tony & Baz Kershaw, *Engineers of the Imagination: the Welfare State Handbook*, revised edn. (London, Methuen, 1990).

Derrida, Jacques, *A Derrida Reader: between the blinds*, Peggy Kamuf (ed.) (Hemel Hempstead, Harvester Wheatsheaf, 1991).

Eagleton, Terry, *The Illusions of Post-modernism* (Oxford, Blackwell Publishers, 1996).

Eagleton, Terry, *Walter Benjamin: towards a revolutionary criticism* (London, Verso, 1981).

Epskamp, Kees P., *Theatre in Search of Social Change* (The Hague, CESO, 1989).

Erven, Eugene, *The Playful Revolution: theatre and liberation in Asia* (Bloomington and Indianapolis, Indiana University Press, 1992).

Foucault, M., *The Foucault Reader*, Paul Rabinow (ed.) (Harmondsworth, Penguin, 1984).

Foucault, Michel, *Discipline and Punish* (New York, Vintage Books, 1979).

Fotheringham, Richard (ed.), *Community Theatre in Australia* (Sydney, Currency Press, 1987).

Held, David, *Models of Democracy* (Oxford, Polity Press, 1987, p. 271).

Hughes, Patrick & George Brecht, *Vicious circles and Infinity: an anthology of paradoxes* (Harmondsworth, Penguin, 1978).

Lyotard, Jean-Francois, *The Postmodern Condition: a report on knowledge* (Manchester, Manchester University Press, 1986).

Mda, Zakes, *When People Play – People: development communications through theatre* (London, Zed Books, 1993).

Mlama, Penina, *Culture and Development: the popular theatre approach in Africa* (Uppsala, Nordiska Afrikaininstitutet, 1991).

Orwell, George, *1984* (Harmondsworth, Penguin Books, 1989).

Phillips, Anne, *Democracy and Difference* (Oxford, Polity Press, 1993, p. 17).

Turner, Victor, *From Ritual to Theatre: the human seriousness of play* (New York, PAJ Publications, 1982).

Williams, Raymond, *Key words: a vocabulary of culture and society* (London, Fontana, 1976, p. 210).

One Hour in the Semi Open

(aka The Rat Run)

(Con hanging around by a gate to 'A' wing.)

CON: Boss.

(Five minutes later.)

CON: Boss can you open the gate please?

(Five minutes more of hanging around, a screw turns up. You are let in. He goes off to somewhere else. You turn the corner.)

CON: Shit, typical.

(The doors locked, you bang on the floor. You're lucky, this time the door is opened nearly immediately.)

SCREW: Where have you been?

CON: Gym.

(You then go up two flights of stairs along the landing only to find...)

CON: Fuck it.

(Cell doors locked. You look around, no screw on the landing. But wait there's one walking about on the one's. The other two are reading papers in the office.)

CON: (Shouts.) Boss.

(Leaning over the railings.)

CON: Boss.
(Totally ignored. Just your luck, a deaf screw. Or is he blanking you? You then have to go down two flights of stairs.)

CON: Boss can you open my cell please?

SCREW: In a bit.

(You go back up and wait. Ten minutes pass, still no screw comes up. But during this time...)

SCREW: Thompson (Shouting from the one's for someone. Yet they can't hear you when you shout them. You go back down.)

CON: Boss can you open my door?

(Screw puts his paper down looking pissed off.)

SCREW: Alright.

(You then go up again and, shock he's behind you.)

CON: Ta.

(Screw walks off, no conversation. You get changed and go back down.)

CON: Boss can you let us out I've got to go to Ed.

(Screw reluctantly gets up and opens door he goes to lock it behind you.)

CON: Boss can you open the gate first?

(Knowing full well it will save you ten minutes of hanging around. You're free. Out onto the courtyard. No obstacles for a while. You get to the library gate, it's locked.)

CON: Boss.

(Rattling the gate. Five minutes.)

CON: Boss, Boss.

(No answer. You then walk to the other wing. The gates are locked, but there's a screw there.)

CON: Let us in Boss.
(He opens the gate. You walk up the first flight of stairs along the corridor, but the end gates are locked.)

CON: I don't believe this, it's bloody stupid.

(Up another flight of stairs again, the gate is locked.)

CON: Poxy, fucking stupid nick, moan, moan.

(You arrive at the bottom gate, two screws in the office outside.)

CON: Boss can you let us out please.

SCREW: Why?

CON: I'm trying to get to Ed.

SCREW: What wing are you off?

CON: 'A' wing.

SCREW: You're not allowed on this wing.

CON: I'm just trying to get to Ed.

SCREW: You're not allowed on this wing.

(He still hasn't moved. All this is done shouting.)

CON: I can't hear you.

(The only way to get him to the gate.)

SCREW: Why didn't you use the other gate?

CON: Because it's locked and there's no-one there. I thought I could get through this way.

SCREW: You're not allowed on this wing.

(Opens the gate.)

CON: I'm only trying to get to Ed. If someone was on the other gate or if it was open as a semi open should be, I wouldn't be here now.
(By this time you're really pissed off. You walk to the other gate again. But the screw stays put. You arrive at the other gate. It's still locked.)

CON: Boss, Boss, open up.

(Five minutes.)

CON: Let us in.

(The library screw comes out.)

SCREW: Where are you from?

CON: Ed Boss.

SCREW: Well you should come from the stairs, not from in there.

CON: I would come down the fucking stairs but I can't get up the fucking things in the first place.

(You then trudge up three flights of stairs. But it's not over yet, one more flight and the last door which of course is locked. Knock on the door and wait five minutes or so. The door opens.)

SCREW: Who are you?

CON: Robinson RTS.

SCREW: Where have you been?

(You look at him. Shake your head and start to move off.)

CON: Don't ask, you don't want to know.

(You arrive at the classroom but you're not exactly refreshed, relaxed and ready for a days work. A fag, a cup of tea and a punch bag are more the order.)

This is just one hour, one example of the freedom, rehabilitation, relaxed atmosphere of a semi open nick. Which does it's best to get you ready for the outside world. Let's hear it for the screws and the system, come on, one big cheer. No? Oh well, I understand.

THE END

From the Stocks to the Stage

Prison Theatre and the Theatre of Prison

James Thompson

This chapter is about the theatre *of* prison and how prison theatre needs to understand that wider performance in order to articulate its own rationale and values. The criminal justice system is, I contend, a space that has a complex relationship to performance, both historically and contemporarily. Prisons and punishment are performative. They construct special sites, appeal to certain audiences, involve ritualised acts and entertain or appal. Whether this be in the stylised practice of the trial, the role labelling of the person 'offender' or 'criminal' or in the close observation of a person's behaviour in the panopticon of the prison; in its many moments the criminal justice process is an arena full of heightened performative actions. Without expressly recognising the performative nature of the arena, theatre projects will struggle to locate themselves in that system. At worst there is a danger that the more brutal performances of punishment and the discursive justifications that are offered for them, can become a system of meaning that is operative in readings of prison theatre. An artist might assume that she or he is the child of a radical theatre heritage but by coming into prison, the work could be understood as a modern day version of the stocks. Because the performances of public shaming, deterrence and repentance are present and constantly reworked in modern prison systems, prison theatre could be read within the discursive constructions that these performances permit. Prisons and those within them have always been there as a display, a warning, a vision and a spectacle for the public gaze. This chapter asks does prison theatre belong to this history of performance or can it really lay claim to its own? Does it undermine the lurid spectacle of retribution or is it in danger of being a less explicit part of it?[1] This chapter is thus discussing the difficult relationship between prison theatre and prison as theatre: between performances in prison and the performance of prison.

The chapter will offer a brief analysis of the performance of punishment, concentrating in particular on the death penalty and contemporary discourses of retribution and toughness. Its primary focus will be how these are played out in the US system, arguing that in this context criminal justice processes have been particularly inflected with different forms of performance. I will argue these performances have changed over time, and are justified by different systems of explanation. The chapter will then examine in detail a contemporary practice that I believe makes a particular and deliberate use of the performative within a predominantly punitive system. This service explicitly uses performance techniques to display and shame but describes

57

them within the largely familiar discourse of prisoner rehabilitation. Their 'rehabilitation' programmes use exercises and approaches that will be familiar to theatre practitioners such as rehearsal, public presentations and role-play. By analysing a practice that uses many of the theoretical and discursive markers adopted by prison theatre (see for example Thompson, 1998a, 1999) while at the same time operating within a system that is strongly retributive, the fine line between theatre in prison and punishment as performance can be explored. The system to be examined will be the youth justice agency, the Texas Youth Commission, established through Governor George W. Bush's reforms that were implemented before he got embroiled in his more recent starring role.

Performing Punishment

The history of punishment is littered with examples of spectacle and performance. From the public hanging of thieves, humiliation in the stocks, to the guillotine and the burning of witches. These events sought in many different ways to impact on crime, criminal behaviour and the bodies of the offenders. They demonstrated the customs and fears of their time and aimed to have an affect on the audiences that witnessed them. They were both a public affirmation of a particular system of power and a public warning about transgression. In the same way that deterrence works in today's punishments, they aimed to go beyond the immediate incident of crime to impact on an audience. They were both actual and symbolic.

It is not my aim here to outline this history in detail, merely to argue that as crime is performed in the microcosms of interpersonal and inter-group behaviour, so the social and political response in the form of publicly sanctioned punishments has always had a performative element. It has always sought to move between a private attack on behaviour and a public demonstration of disapproval. The demand that an offender should be 'made an example of' is explicitly a call for his or her punishment to be performed. This activity has an impact on the society in which it occurs. In histories of penology, punishment is often analysed as evolving from particular social and ideological formations (Stern 1998, Garland 1990). The point to emphasise here is that this should also be understood as a 'two way process'. A particular approach to punishing wrongdoers is not only a product of a specific cultural and historical moment, it also acts on the society in which it exists. The penologist David Garland notes this explicitly when he says:

> In truth, the broad patterns of cultural meaning undoubtedly influence the forms of punishment. But it is also the case that punishments and penal institutions help shape the overarching culture and contribute to the generation and regeneration of its terms. (Garland, 1990, p. 249).

The relationship is thus interactive. The political, social and cultural histories of, for example, modern America shape its penal institutions, but also current penal practice impacts on the 'overarching culture'. The performances of 'toughness' in current public debates of crime policy (see below) are perhaps the externalised evidence of this 'two way' process. The debates both seek to affect penal policy and are a product of that policy. Again to quote Garland:

> The practices, institutions and discourses of penality all signify, and the meanings which are conveyed thereby tend to outrun the immediacies of crime and punishment and 'speak of' broader and more extended issues. Penality is thus a cultural text – or perhaps better, a cultural performance – which communicates with a variety of social audiences and conveys an extended range of meanings (Garland, 1990, pp. 252-3).

Penality is thus a performance both in the public discourse of crime and criminal justice policy and in the effects of the institutions of punishment on wider society. The whole process from arrest, through trial to imprisonment and the subsequent public discussion is a complex cultural 'text'.[2] Each element performs in a different way to various audiences, but vitally all are connected in a larger narrative. Often analysis seeks to isolate these moments and discuss them individually. What I believe is crucial is that the whole process of criminal justice is linked into a wide-ranging social performance. By way of example, in 1996 I visited a courtroom in Austin Texas and witnessed a judge loudly and bitterly admonishing a young offender. She however was not using vitriol and humiliation only within the performance conventions of the courtroom. She was also looking beyond her the narrow audience in that chamber, connecting implicitly with wider performances of toughness in public rhetoric. It is the position of prison theatre within this 'wide-ranging performance' that I am questioning in this chapter. 'Criminal justice' is an interconnected performance process with an 'extended range of meanings' creeping beyond each single moment. Shouting at a young man for the smile on his face, could be linked to a theatre project that aims to make young prisoners 'act' in different ways during an improvisation workshop. Both seek change in the performance of one, while demonstrating a particular performance of the system. One might operate within a discourse of toughness and the other of liberal concern, but does the emphasis on the performative in fact link two practices that on the surface we might assume are very different?

Although I have just argued that the criminal justice process needs to be understood as a whole, it is worth briefly discussing where the death penalty sits within this picture. I believe it is necessary to ask if there is a connection between the liveness of historical death penalty enactments, and the liveness of the prison theatre project that invites the public into prisons to witness prisoners in plays. The former although still in existence is now rare, but the latter is often an explicit desire of theatre projects in closed institutions. Is it stretching it too far to say that one could be the modern, sanitised version of the other? The discursive justifications are different (they arise from different cultural and historical moments) but are they both performances of punishment? In order to explore the connection I want to discuss in particular how the death penalty has changed and is changing currently in the US. Historically the death penalty and other forms of retribution were performed in public. Although there are differently scholarly analyses accounting for the demise of it as a public activity (see Garland, 1990, p. 141), Foucault notes that it was the ambiguity of these rituals that brought about their end (Foucault, 1977, p. 65). Their reception could not be controlled as crowds rather than being suitably warned by the vision of somebody being hanged started to use the occasions as times of both carnival and disorder. Garland explains:

> Instead of bearing respectful witness, the crowds came to mock the authorities and transform the condemned man into a popular hero (Garland, 1990, p. 141).

This battle for control of the reception of a performance led eventually to these events being taken inside prisons, from where the authorities could safely control the execution and limit the information that was let out. They clearly aimed to strictly control the script of the process. This script has become a new political battleground in the US. In one sense, the death penalty is now only played out on the level of discourse, but it is also, through extensive trials and appeals, a visual, mediatised process. The performance has been displaced from the clinical moment of death, to a series of very public and of course often televised occasions. These events, unlike the contested public executions of the past, although never offering a guarantee as to their reception, are far more easily controlled and edited.

Perhaps the most significant development however is not to be found simply in this public displacement, but in the transformation of the public execution into a private performance ritual. The presence at many executions of the victims' close relatives makes the death penalty in the US a very intimate performance between a small audience and a perpetrator.[3] The death is watched from behind a glass screen, with the convicted person on one side and the observers sat on a few rows of chairs on the other. The audience witnesses the administration of either the electricity or more commonly of the lethal injection. They watch a performance where they have an intimate connection with the actor and a pre-knowledge of the script. There is usually only one ending – unless there is a 'dramatic' last minute stay of execution. This event gives the appearance that the desire to impact on a social audience has been replaced with a simple ritual of the righteous enactment of vengeance for those immediately affected. However, this private moment is also relayed to and received by the outside world in a number of ways. It does become public property and part of the wider performance of punishment. Although it is framed as a legitimate act of private revenge, it still 'communicates with a variety of social audiences' and acts as a wider signifying cultural event. As part of the criminal justice process, it has an 'extended range of meanings'. The various film portrayals of this moment (see *Dead Man Walking*) and the detailed description of last meals and the moment of death in the media, links each death sentence to narratives and images in the popular imagination. Although the death penalty as an intimate ritual of the family watching a display behind a small glass screen is private, it still has a presence as a public performance.

This privatisation has also had the effect of making the public spaces surrounding death rows a place where reception of the execution is still contested. Without 'the body of the condemned', new rituals around the moment of death have emerged, reminding us of the 'carnival and disorder' of the executions of the past. Outside most US prisons on an evening of an execution, crowds will gather to either demonstrate for or against the death penalty. These crowds generate their own performances to celebrate or condemn the private ritual within the walls. In the past, the authorities brought the execution inside to prevent disorder. Public meetings now exist without the body present. The absence creates a vacuum into which rival groups emerge. In that space, they compete to offer meaning to the event. It is interesting to note that in Texas the authorities have also tried to prevent these public displays by changing the times of executions. By killing people during working hours, they have aimed to reduce the number assembling outside the gates of the Huntsville death row prison. This has had the effect of almost eliminating public demonstrations altogether. Similarly, Texas newspapers now very rarely comment on executions – there are more than one per month – and therefore execution has become a routine to the extent that public moments to contest the activity rarely occur. It is only when a disputed execution takes place that performance reappears. This happened notably when Karla Faye Tucker was executed. She was the first woman to die in Texas since the reintroduction of the death penalty. As a committed Christian her case caused much debate within the US, with coalitions calling for her to be saved and others urging on her execution. On the day she was finally killed, performance returned to Huntsville. Groups used the space outside the prison to articulate their position on her death. In the moment of a contested action, performative reactions arose again. *The Guardian* in the UK reported many examples;

> Several adults dressed as witches with tall black pointy hats (were) chanting 'have a nice day Karla Faye' [...]
> Melody Kirschke, a Christian musician, began singing Amazing Grace [...] On the grass outside the jail, it felt like a carnival [...] 'It's like going to the theatre,' grinned Hugger Bart, who had driven up from Houston to see the commotion (Joanna Coles, The Guardian 4/2/98).

The performative act of the death penalty in the absence of the body demanded a performative response. The 'witches' and the 'Christian musician' place their bodies centre stage.

I offer this brief analysis of the death penalty in order to question whether the popularity of certain forms of prison theatre could be understood as a response to the invisibility of the body of the prisoner in contemporary performances of punishment. The mediatised presentation of the justice process does not fulfil the public desire to see the live body of the offender. The performances outside the prison mentioned above are a displacement, but not a replacement of this desire. There is a visceral part of the criminal justice process, experienced in the throwing of fruit at the stocks or contemporary egg throwing at police vans holding particularly notorious prisoners, that has not been dissipated by the withdrawal of the body into the prison. Projects that have prisoners perform for public audiences – whether in prison or on the outside – cannot easily dismiss their link to this voyeuristic desire to see the body of the prisoner. Although these moments are of course not the extreme violence of the death penalty, the urge to see the live 'offender' cannot automatically be separated from the history of that spectacle. Of course, there will be different discourses explaining these phenomena, but because they are both performances, the old must be compared to the new. Although these projects might be announced as a public opportunity to counter the negative images of prisoners, they could easily be claimed by the discourse that hopes that punishment is the process of 'seeing that justice is done'. The death penalty was a direct way of 'seeing', and similarly young offenders on a stage during a conference can as easily be 'punishment in action' rather than a critical challenge to the dynamics of this process.[4]

Contemporary Audiences – New Displays

Most public discussions of crime are based on particularly mediated and constructed narratives. The stories of crime that enter the public imagination, that perform on the pages of newspapers and on the screens of televisions, are not arbitrary. They paint an explicitly partial picture of the nature and extent of criminal activity. A complex mixture of cultural and historical factors determines which crimes are most popularly presented and resonate most strongly with the public. The witch of yesteryear has been replaced by modern demons, but both say more about the society in which they were or are condemned than about the behaviour of the individuals concerned. The audience for these narratives has now become the audience for the policy makers who discuss crime in the public domain. Any person who works in this system, including prison theatre practitioners, enters these wider systems of performance. The stories of prison theatre projects therefore respond to and operate within these debates, and cannot hope that they exist in an unsullied space outside them. By 'doing prison theatre' (by writing this book) we are part of a contemporary performance of punishment and justice. Politicians, policy makers and now artist commentators sit between the performance of justice and the public audience as mediators and arbiters of meaning. They/we seek to control the reading of these moments. In particular politicians, journalists, pundits and social critics address and create a perception and vision of crime. Prison theatre makers need to question the narrative they create and if they do not actively state a 'vision of crime', they need to acknowledge that one that they do not control will be read 'by default' in their work. The dominant or most successful in this process develop a variety of performative devices to champion their perspective. Part of this process is done by what criminologist Jerome Miller calls 'rhetorical winks' 'whereby code phrases communicate a well-understood but implicit meaning' (Miller, 1996, p. 149).

> Violent crime is rising out of control
> Old people are not safe
> Our children are at risk of abduction.

These are all partial pictures of the crime situation but they appeal to deeply held sentiments and fears. Their constant reiteration helps create a climate in which an easy dichotomy between 'soft on crime/tough on crime' has become the central performance within the public debate. Appearing tough in policy towards offenders has become a benchmark for politicians wanting to appeal to public sensibilities. This performance importantly signals a personal quality with rich cultural and historical roots. The heroic performance of toughness has left audiences swooning for many years and its current manifestation within the field of crime policy, particularly in the US, has had staggering results.[5] Condemning your adversaries as 'soft' – as a friend of the criminal – has become the easiest form of political attack. The public policy response to the actions of offenders is now more than ever tied into the desires and fears of the viewing public rather than the intricate and complex activities of the offenders themselves. The vast majority of crimes are non-violent, petty and committed between people who know each other (Miller, 1996, pp. 1-9). But stating this is considered 'poor show'. The 'best' performances have conflict, tension, strangers and demons, and this is therefore what the politicians and commentators offer. They play to the gallery. Public policy debate in both the UK and the US is the state of 'being seen to be', not the state of 'being'. It is a constantly performed process. Within discussions of crime it is 'being seen to be' tough that is the vital characteristic.

This again becomes a problem for prison theatre practitioners in constructing their projects and publicising their work. In a time when the narrative of toughness dominates, prison theatre struggles not to become incorporated into this performance. For example, by taking pride in the fact that the most 'difficult and dangerous' prisoner has participated in a theatre project or hinting at the seriousness of our participant's crimes to different interested audiences, are we not operating within the same discourse? Prison theatre is 'hard'! Although at first it might appear that the work seeks to undermine the stigma attached to individuals in the system, the performance of toughness is not shifted so easily. It must be remembered that people admire the skill of the lion tamer, rather than the performance of the lion. By hearing about a theatre project in prison, the daring of the outside theatre practitioners is given the applause before the efforts of the prisoner participants. While the prison theatre project might hope that the prisoner is given credit and respect for their creative efforts, often the only credit given is to the system that has made them 'perform in this way'. Again, the question for this chapter is whether prison theatre can avoid becoming part of this performance: a performance that not only dehumanises the prisoner (see the lion metaphor) but one that has led to a huge rise in incarceration in both the UK and US.

In this climate new policies have been imagined and implemented. Public rhetoric and performances of toughness have led to electoral success and new programmes and systems being established. How 'toughness' is developed in practice is thus the concern of the next section and will be illustrated by examining one particular 'new' approach. As performances of public retribution in the past operated to display a certain configuration of power, the public toughness uttered by today's politicians has demanded fresh performances for the systems that are being constructed for these new times. Again, the question to ask is that if these new performances are emerging from this particular moment can prison theatre be understood as a practice permitted because it displays an era specific demand for certain performances of justice? For whom therefore does prison theatre perform?

The Texas Youth Commission

The Texas Youth Commission is the state agency responsible for the imprisonment of Texas' 'persistent juvenile offenders'.[6] With George W. Bush's election as Governor of Texas in 1994 and his campaign promise to 'do something' about juvenile crime (Donziger, 1996, p. 80), the Youth Commission became the focus for attention and legislative action. Not only was the size of the operation to be changed but also the content. The Deputy Superintendent from the new 'Orientation and Assessment' centre for the system explained that the pendulum had swung too far one way, and George Bush was instrumental in swinging it back.[7] His position was that young offenders were being treated too gently by the system and that now it needed to 'hold them accountable' more firmly. This did not mean to the Deputy a purely punitive system but an approach where 'accountability' and 'rehabilitation' were in balance. His pendulum was in the 'middle'.

The political context of Texas, and the strongly anti-rehabilitation climate, demands a very careful explanation of any state sponsored rehabilitation effort.[8] 'Accountability' in this context is a performative that both denies and permits different readings. I would contend that it is often what Harland calls 'an unhelpful code word for retribution' (Harland, 1996, p. 9). It is one of the 'rhetorical winks' mentioned above. The repeated desire to 'hold young people accountable' can be understood as a greater emphasis on punishing them, both by incarceration but also by making the rehabilitative process more austere and unpleasant. The question to ask is how much balance there really is in a system that proclaims the desire to hold 'accountable' the young people held within it. How did the performances of toughness and accountability impact on the realities of a system that imprisoned children aged between ten and eighteen? With 636 prisoners per 100,000 in the adult system, George Bush's mission to deal with the juvenile crime issue could have led an entirely punitive system based on increasing the volume of inmates. This section of the chapter thus asks did a rehabilitative intention survive and could it be effective or meaningful in this environment? If rehabilitation programmes are changed by a legislative mission for retribution, does this imply that any programmes in a prison system will be compromised by the performance conventions that surround them? In responding to this climate, the rehabilitation process in the TYC adopted what I will argue are practices that were performative and at times borrowed explicitly from theatre. Using theatrical methods within a framework of both 'accountability' and 'rehabilitation' thus becomes an important moment in the questions I am seeking to raise for the place of prison theatre. Performances in this context were used to show that the system was doing what it said it was: they operated as a display of 'holding young people accountable'.

'Rehabilitation' at TYC

The Texas Youth Commission has designed a system wide approach to working with young offenders called 'Resocialization'. This is a process in four stages that all detainees have to follow during what are predominantly indeterminate sentences. Young Offenders in Texas now receive sentences that have minimum time and an in built maximum of up to your twenty-first birthday. Even if they enter the system aged twelve on a six-month sentence (the minimum), they could stay until they are twenty-one if they do not comply or demonstrate successful completion of each of the stages. If they do not 'perform' appropriately. The majority of any sentence will be spent in a 'State Home' – a secure regime – with only the latter part being spent in a 'half way house' where they are able to work, with restrictions, in the local community. There are determinant sentences within the system officially only for the very serious offences, but under pressure the TYC system is finding more and more judges wanting to give longer determinant sentences. Under such a sentence a young person must return to the judge aged eighteen and will get one of three options. Either transferral to adult prison to finish her or his time, immediate release or return to the TYC system until she or he is twenty-one. The reality is that the debate is over adult prison or TYC and thus compliance with the Resocialization programme becomes an important criteria.

TYC has introduced a four pronged philosophy – correctional therapy, education, discipline and vocational study. All aspects of these four continue from the moment a person arrives at the 'Orientation and Assessment Center' (Marlin, central Texas) until they leave a half way house (such as Turman House in Austin). It is the particular relationship between the 'correctional therapy' and the 'discipline' that will be the focus here. Whether one bleeds into the other and how the performance of tough discipline is transferred into performative elements of the 'therapy' are vital parts of the argument that I am making in this chapter.

Correctional Therapy

The most popular rehabilitation intervention strategies both in the UK and the US for adolescents and young offenders are in some form cognitive behavioural. It is not the place here to outline in detail the analytical assumptions behind such popularity. However, it is enough to say that programmes that contain a cognitive behavioural approach are believed to demonstrate substantial decreases in re-offending rates and a reduction in 'delinquent attitudes' amongst offender groups (Andrews and Bonta, 1994, Gendreau, 1996). These programmes broadly seek to discover the cycles of behaviour in offenders and how those cycles are maintained by the thinking patterns of the young person. They intervene on an individual level seeking to develop consequential thinking, decision making, perspective taking and victim empathy (see Balfour, 2000, Thompson, 1999 and 2003). The TYC broadly accepts the logic of these programmes and has built much of their curriculum around these theories.

Although much of this curriculum would be familiar to UK practitioners therefore, it is framed very differently. The TYC curriculum was written as part of a process that also saw the Texas legislature changing juvenile justice law. It was to be the blueprint for the new system and therefore had to be mediated through the demands of a strongly conservative House and Senate. The 'Resocialization Curriculum' of the TYC (TYC 1995) is now the core programme across all institutions. To illustrate the impact of wider performances of retribution, it is important to search for the signs or 'markers' that become incorporated into the documents describing practice as well as analysing the actual practice. The first point to note is that the document goes to great lengths to stress personal responsibility and accountability. As I have already mentioned 'accountability' is an intensely problematic word – 'an unhelpful code word' (Harland, 1996, p. 9). It is a device that can be read by various audiences in ways to suit their own perspectives. Here there is a political expediency in its use as it clearly performs a reassurance to a legislative audience whose members had gained their places through their advocacy of a strongly 'tough on crime' agenda.

'Accountability' and 'responsibility' are political, contested constructs here incorporated in to an apparently 'clinical' rehabilitation programme as though they were 'scientifically' fixed and concrete. There is a mixing of these markers within a programme that is otherwise constructed around 'psychological' terms and justifications. While it may be appropriate to criticise this, it can be understood as a politically necessary combination in a very conservative context. What is interesting is whether this should be read as a punitive sweetener ensuring the survival of the rehabilitative agenda or an illustration that the actual rehabilitative process was itself retributive. Does the balance explained by the Deputy Superintendent really exist?

I will start to answer this by elaborating on a number of other 'sweetening' rhetorical flourishes and by demonstrating how they led to more confusions with the 'scientific' or 'psychological' approach. One of the strongest of these is the programme's direct appeal to the fundamental basis for its practice being in the notion of the social contract.

> The resocialization programme 'is based, at a minimum, on the notion of social contract – i.e., that members of a society agree to uphold certain rules of behaviour for the good of all its members, that individuals must be accountable for their own actions.' [Emphasis original] (TYC Core Curriculum in Resocialization, 1995, p. 1.8).

The TYC gives a rehabilitation programme an intensely political framework. Rehabilitation and future behaviour is tied into notions of a particular political ideology. Many political theorists and sociologists would argue that social contract theory is an inappropriate analysis of modern western societies, and whether you agree with it or not, its inclusion here means that rehabilitation becomes linked to notions of correct political thought. Again, my main argument is that this is a device calculated to perform to the belief system of the legislature and other policy makers. You emphasise (embolden) what you want your audience to hear most strongly. The political overtone is important because the new TYC programme has to perform at a political level as much as it had to appear sound at the level of rehabilitation theory. Of course, the question to ask is what is the effect of the sweetening rhetoric on the practice? Does that practice continue to display itself to the wider public audience, or once passed by the politicians does it only focus on the 'private world' of prison?

Using a theory of social contract created through consensus sits very awkwardly with the other main theoretical base for the Resocialization programme. The behaviour of young people and young offenders is explained as part of 'Biopsychosocial

Interaction' (TYC, 1995, p. 1.5). The programme here argues that while most adolescents tend to be self-centred, they do have their needs met by their parents or other carers. Young Offenders however either have their needs unmet or over met, leading to a greater self-centred orientation to others and society. 'Biopsychosocial Interaction' recognises biological influences, social learning (including socio-economic situation, ethnic background and subcultural influences), cognitive behavioural, emotional and personality issues. Although this is a rich interaction of many crime causation theories, it seems to sit firmly in a positivist tradition with a heavily mediated concept of human will. I am not saying this interactive approach denies human agency but it does place it in a context of many relating, heavily determining factors. This seems to fit uncomfortably with the notion of accountability and a freely entered social contract. I do not believe this contradiction is resolved and therefore it is important to examine how this tension is played out in treatment practice itself. There is a discrepancy if you are attempting to 'resocialize' young offenders in a manner that is 'respectful of cultural differences [and] validates the reality of their developmental experiences' but at the same time 'is based at a minimum, on the notion of social contract' (TYC, 1995, p. 1.8). If you believe in the reality of their developmental experiences, can you also believe that they are freely accountable for their actions – that they had unfettered choice in committing the acts they did? Another public display for the legislature or does the emphasis on 'at a minimum' indicate that the performance of 'accountability' is the heart of the practice?

The Rehabilitative Process

In order to discuss some of the points I raise above I am going to look in more detail at a number of moments in the TYC's rehabilitation or 'resocialization' process. I want to illustrate how wider performances in the public arena do become translated into the minutiae of criminal justice programmes. The argument thus seeks to link the activities inside TYC establishments to performances in the wider public arena, opening the possibility that a similar connection can be proposed between performances in prison and the performance of prison. This section in particular asks whether the retributive undertone of the programme's documentation contributes to a 'balance' or does it turn a process of rehabilitation into a system of punitive display? What does this say for performances in the UK system? Do theatre projects turn the objective of rehabilitation into a performance of justice being done, or do they 'contribute' to the process of rehabilitation?

In 'Marlin Orientation and Assessment Center', where all new juvenile prisoners in the state of Texas are sent, the young people are given a sharp reminder that they have lost their right to make decisions when they were sentenced. They now have to do as they are told and not question. All have their heads shaved, crew cut army style. All are given bright orange smock tops and loose fitting orange trousers. They will have to march in single file everywhere they go, with their hands held in the small of their backs (this was supposedly so that they 'couldn't wave gang signs') and their chins touching their chests. They are allocated dorms with other 'peers', eat their meals in seven minutes without talking or moving their heads to the side, and must participate actively in 'the programme'. If they ever want to talk to a member of staff or visitor, they must stick out two fingers in a pointing motion in front of their chests. The routine is intensive. Seven full days a week of group therapy (on their institutional behaviour and on their offending) and education. At other state homes to which they will eventually graduate, the hairstyle remains but a less garish uniform (more likely to be prison issue jeans and T-shirts) is adopted. At the same time that they are being 'orientated' in Marlin, they will also undertake a series of very detailed assessments determining where they will be sent to finish their sentence. These are to determine the health – physical and mental – intelligence level and any special needs a young person might have. There are state homes for general offenders and then specialised regimes for drug users, sex offenders, capital offenders and mentally disordered offenders. Not all that need specialised treatment receive it due to financial restrictions on these services.

This institutional culture is both part of the Resocialization programme and the context in which it operates. It is supported by the staff as the means to provide the necessary control to undertake the intervention work, and more importantly it was approved of by the state legislature who are ultimately funding the system. Marlin as the first place of entry is vital in this process of developing a system wide culture and exists as a showcase for developing political and social support. I believe the TYC has created Marlin as a place that appeals to the audience that demanded tough responses to juvenile crime. It is a spectacle – perhaps appalling to some and heart warming to others. I cannot deny that as a witness to this performance, I read 'gulag' rather than a democratic country's institution of reform.[9] However, I must understand that I was not the primary audience for whom it was created. My reading of the sight of young men with heads lowered to their chests, marching in bright orange smocks, was that this was a sight of humiliation and shame. It was a striking and disturbing image. More disturbing considering the fact that the language used to describe the regime in my interview with the Deputy Superintendent minutes before my 'tour' had not prepared me for it. I had not translated the code, his 'rhetorical winks', to create this vision. Clearly the regime creates an impressive exhibition for those who want toughness and a linguistic comfort zone interpreting what they see is a logical, humane and necessary approach to dealing with young offenders. Behind the 'linguistic markers' was a performance of brutal, numbing control. While the rhetoric was coded, mixing terms such as 'accountability' with expressions demanding uncompromising behavioural therapy, the practice also marked itself with signals – cut hair, lowered heads, orange smocks – which could be read as the retribution for which the legislature were searching. Dressing the inmates and teaching them particular routines demonstrates and performs a policy with an audience in mind. The legislative demand had determined a show and what they got was marching lines of young men and boys, heads lowered, shuffling in silence in garish, demeaning costumes. Significantly, many of the legislators had visited Marlin. It was the first place that visitors (such as myself) went to be impressed with the result of George W's crack down on juvenile crime. They held open days for local dignitaries and the press – the *live* performance of shame was apparently loudly applauded.

Marlin was not the only moment that used performative devices to show 'justice being done'. I want to continue by analysing two further moments that used explicitly performative techniques as part of the 'resocialization' programme. The first of these is called the Basic Layout – a memorised, personally tailored revelation device. The second is the psychodrama used as part of the 'Capital Offender Treatment Programme' in one of the specialist centres that the young people can graduate to once they have passed through Marlin. The former is intensely theatrical, the latter familiar to theatre practitioners as a drama workshop: both are problematically linked to the wider performances of punishment that I am discussing here.

The Basic Layout

The Basic Layout is a personal and public declaration of a TYC resident's name, offence, and length of sentence, with other elements added at different stages of his or her sentence. The young people are expected in the 'Orientation and Assessment' phase to learn by rote the first version, which contains the basic information plus the name of their victim and how this victim suffered from the crime committed against them. The 'off-by-heart' nature and often monotonic relaying of these statements is seen as unproblematic at this stage as only later in their sentence will they be expected to internalise the true meaning of what they are saying. In a pattern familiar to various performance processes, the system believes that learning by rote eventually is incorporated in the body of the 'offender'. The Basic Layout increases in length and complexity as the individual moves through the resocialization stages. By the time a person is ready to leave TYC, it might be two minutes long and will include the way they intervene in their own thinking and behaviour as well as a 'success plan' for the future.

It is not only the content of the layout that is deemed important but also the presentation. A TYC resident should stand straight up, hands behind their back and look you directly in the eye when they speak it.[10] They must demonstrate in their demeanour, their belief in the seriousness of what they are saying. No shuffling of feet, aimless smiling or shifting of heads.[11] The explanation of this procedure is that by naming the offence and particularly their victim, they will stop the process of denial and minimisation. In addition, it is assumed that through the Basic Layout they will be forced to accept the consequences of their own actions and eventually articulate how they are to move forward. There is a belief that frequent repetition will lead to an internalising of its components and conclusions. It will move from a performed monotone to a 'real' personal statement of change.

The belief that this declaration when performed with fluency becomes 'real' is of course problematic. It might be 'heart-felt' but there is no automatic connection between a fluently performed statement and the performer's adherence to the values inherent in the script they are uttering. Many Shakespearean actors would have been arrested and imprisoned over the years if the performance and the person become conflated so easily. While this critique of the process is obvious, there is another important question for the layout that must be considered. It is also not about the behaviour of the offender. The Basic Layout is central to the process of holding a young

69

person 'accountable'. In all my visits during 1996-7 to TYC establishments, I had many young people stand in front of me, look me in the eyes and make their statement. This was a public proclamation. It was a performance for visitors, and thus specifically for public consumption. It was both a form of apology and but also a moment of unease and shame for the young person. It demonstrated that they were no longer in control and that they now performed what the programme wanted to hear. The layouts I heard from much longer-term TYC residents were always more fluent and 'polished'[12] but the layouts of the new arrivals always had a sense of desperation and occasionally fear. The description of their crime, how they now felt sorry for it and the grim detail of the effect upon their victim, said to the anonymous visitor/s and in front of other inmates, made this an excruciating moment of self-inflicted shame. A public act of blaming where the presented body of the offender is flagellated by their own words. Prison theatre?

Many rehabilitation programmes seek to create a contract with participants, a kind of personal commitment to change (see Mountford and Farrall, 1998 for example from a theatre-based programme). This they argue is an important treatment mechanism and is an attempt to shift some power and control of the process to the group. However we must question how these can make you a watched object of a programme and the wider audience for that particular approach, rather than build a personal commitment to change. The young offenders who performed on a stage during the conference in Wolverhampton mentioned above, were, according to their director, 'making amends' for their crimes through this performance. Performing to 'make amends' is situated, I believe, in the same value arena as the Basic Layout described here, and the more brutal public acts of justice from elsewhere and yesteryear. The link in these cases between the stocks and the stage appears quite strong, as the demand for accountability is realised through public display.

The Capital Offender Programme

As they move through the TYC system, some of the young people with particular needs can progress to one of the specialised programmes for 'capital offenders', 'sex offenders' or 'addicted offenders'. I am going to concentrate here on the 'Capital Offender Programme' for young people convicted of murder as this programme is situated at a crucial point in criminal justice debates in Texas.[13] Since adults (over eighteen) would be liable for the death penalty for similar offences, this programme operates in a climate where many believe that the young person's age has allowed them to 'escape justice': they are the lucky ones. Again, this programme needs to be examined to discover whether it is constructed to appease that clamour or whether it is only a reaction to the needs of the very troubled young people for whom it is designed. Created in this tense interface, this programme uses the most explicitly theatrical methodology of all TYC programmes. It uses a form of psychodrama to examine moments in the past of the participants. During the intensive programme the young men role-play the moment of their crime in detail, they replay the incident in the role of their dead victim and recreate many of the most troubling events of their pasts.

> The group module is experientially based in order to facilitate access to emotions typically buried by cognitive defences. Rather than allow the juvenile offender to edit, distort and desensitize their offences by relying on verbal reports, they are required to role-play many aspects of their life stories (TYC Capital Offender Programme, 1995, p. 1).

Although the 'requirement' to complete the role-plays implies a lack of voluntary consent, this is not my major concern here. Accessing emotions buried by cognitive defences is a highly explosive therapeutic endeavour. Framed as it is above, it is also a strongly confrontational one – it aims to dig up/perform the 'real' that has become 'buried' by distorting words. Paradoxically performance is presented as a truth to counter the fabrication of discourse – those verbal reports. I believe that a programme needs be clear how the painful 'truth' that might be uncovered could be eased and perhaps more appropriate defences offered. I am anxious that the desire to break open young people is articulated without the same attention being given to how they are to be reconstructed. Verbal reports may distort and desensitise, but we all use and need them to construct meaning for our lives.

I have witnessed one 'live' version of this process from behind a screen, and seen one on a video during a conference. During the 'live' event, the young men knew I was there as I was introduced to the group before the session started. However, the experience echoed the privatised rituals of the death penalty I discussed above. Seated in a narrow gallery behind one-way glass, I was that private witness to the performance of acutely painful acts. For reasons of confidentiality, I am not permitted to discuss what I saw. It was video taped 'for the record', but this live performance was for my and the psychologist's eyes only.[14] I have discussed elsewhere the vision of young people going through these Psychodrama sessions (Thompson, 1998b, pp. 197-210), and how alarming they were. The emotionally distraught young people I witnessed might have been offered support to reintegrate the knowledge of the origins of their damaged lives into their current life but my observation of the programme hinted at a punishing agenda. Watching young people writhe in emotional pain as they 'relived' past trauma might be contained within the logic of a clinical discourse, but I felt I was witnessing a spectacle of punishment. These young men were in agony and since some of them would have been executed had they been one year older when they committed their offences, it almost seemed that this programme was a psychological/simulated version of the ultimate punishment.

The video I witnessed was presented to an Office of Juvenile Justice and Delinquency Prevention (OJJDP) Conference audience in Baltimore in December 1996. The fact that the director of this treatment programme was an invited speaker at a national conference illustrates that the private becomes public performance in a direct way. This event was a vital part of the public affirmation of this 'therapeutic intervention'. I have described the video in detail in an article written soon after this event and it is produced here in full because it is not covered by the confidentiality of the other 'live' version. The 'live' session was considerably more chilling than this:

Giddings State Home Texas Youth Commission, Texas. A session of the 'Capital

71

Offender Programme' is taking place. About seven young men all under eighteen, all convicted of a homicide or a similar offence, are in the middle of recreating the crime of Carlos [not his real name]. The majority of the men are Hispanic or African-American. All have shaved heads. All wear the plain T-shirt and jeans uniforms. They have graduated from wearing the bright orange smocks that they sported when they first arrived in the Texas Youth Commission. Four of them are sat in chairs in a mock up car – they mime driving, talking and smiling. A member of staff plays a young man they start talking to from the window of their car. They argue. Carlos pulls a large – mimed – gun from his jeans – and points. A caseworker's voice shouts, 'shoot him Carlos'. Carlos mimes a single shot. 'You shot him seven times Carlos, seven times'. Carlos mimes another shot. 'That's twice, shoot him again.' The person being shot is on the floor pleading for his life. 'Three. Shoot him Carlos.' Carlos is standing over him, pointing the gun at the body, his arm recoils as he shoots him again. 'That's four – seven times Carlos.' Tears stream down Carlos' face – he sobs that he can't do it. 'Shoot him Carlos.' And then the group chant the numbers – five, six, seven. Carlos stands there, still miming the gun dangling in his hand. The dead body is asking him why he did it. Another staff member is standing next to Carlos – 'Why did you kill my son?' She's pleading with him. Carlos slumps down in the imaginary car seat and cries. The woman playing the mother continues – 'why did you kill your friend?' (Ibid, pp. 197-8).

I do not want to dismiss these sessions entirely. Stripping away distortions held about the affect of your actions and helping young people understand the painful origins of their current behaviour could be an important part of a rehabilitative programme. The problem is witnessing the anguish of the young people going through this experience in a political context that demands retribution. This pain performed well at the OJJDP conference and was of course sanctioned by the Texas legislative system. The session described above was relentless. When the young man started crying, his pain was doubled by the urging of the caseworkers and the repeated 'why did you kill your friend?' At the moment of vulnerability, in both the sessions that I saw, the young person was targeted for the most pressure. This was difficult to watch. Maybe I am squeamish, and have not understood that holding people 'accountable', 'rehabilitating them' must be a painful process. But in the same way that a public hanging would churn my stomach, these acts made me avert my eyes in disgust. Clinically effective or not, these spectacles were an extremely distressing and disturbing show. I freely admit that this is a product of my cultural values that are contingent to the particularities of my history. However, I would assert that values must be articulated when a system pretends to be executing a programme that is 'clinical', 'necessary' and not bound by ideology. If the programme proclaims itself 'value-free', I have few worries about reading it through the value system that I bring.

Conclusion

This chapter might be accused of being unnecessarily bleak. In a book on prison theatre, am I arguing the work is no better than other more gruesome performances of punishment? If the retributive climate of Texas has led to a youth justice system that chooses explicitly theatrical methods in its programmes, am I arguing that the rise of prison theatre in other systems is part of other similarly punishing agenda? Yes and no. What I am arguing is that prison theatre is permitted and then understood within the wider performances of punishment. A closer interrogation of how a particular society's punishment system is organised and performed will reveal how prison theatre *may be* viewed. The conference performance, touched upon twice already, was a theatre piece by young offenders organised by the community outreach wing of a regional theatre in the UK that displayed them 'making amends', 'performing apology' through an improvised show on a conference stage. This spectacle adopted the rhetoric of a criminal justice agenda in the UK and made the theatre process part of an execution of that particular 'justice' rather than a critique or alternative to it. The theatre was bound down and defined by that policy context and it therefore became an instrumental part of a particular belief system. Prison theatre in working in a range of moments in the criminal justice system, might hope to be critical of many of its values, but it can too easily become the exhibitor of them. The assumption by the people involved in this type of project that their work belongs to a critical tradition is defied by the performance of their work in the moment.

I do have a positive note for this conclusion however and it is linked to my final words on the TYC 'capital offender programme' discussed above. Prison theatre will be in danger of belonging to the discourse of the stocks as long as it avoids proudly articulating the values of its practice. Because it can too easily be comprehended as an opportunity for 'seeing justice being done', practitioners must either loudly proclaim its purpose in their own eyes, or what 'justice' is to them. The values need to be operative in both the discursive justifications and the actual moments of the practice. This might mean that a public performance is not done, because the practitioners doubt that the reception will be anything other than a satisfaction of an audience's voyeuristic desire. It might mean refusing other audiences to the work, because the performance will then fulfil the particular agenda of one part of the system. It might mean avoiding words which echo the rhetoric of 'toughness' that infect discussions of prison work. The work is not 'rigorous', 'challenging', 'disciplined' or 'no easy option'. By using these terms, we not only invite comparisons with those punishments that clearly are these things, but also we explain the theatre process as a punitive one. Punishment is theatrical, but if theatre is punishment, I want nothing to do with it. Programmes that therefore attach themselves to an explicit value system, however contingent those values are understood to be, can at least carve a space that competes with other systems of explanation. Perhaps one of the best examples of this at the moment are the 'Staging Human Rights' projects being run by People's Palace Projects[15] and the Centre of the Theatre of the Oppressed in Brazil. With the workshops, the rehearsals, the performances and the public discussions of the work so tightly bound into an overt human rights agenda, these projects potentially counter other performances of punishment, rather than being read as an example of them.

Theatre is an escape. Theatre is deep reflection. It can be rewarding, joyous, serious, entertaining or beautiful. If it is 'holding people to account', 'making them see the error of their ways', 'making amends', 'showing justice being done', 'confronting them with the consequences of their behaviour', 'forcing them to understand the affects of their actions on others' – it has a noble tradition, yes, but one strewn with rotten fruit and gibbets. Prison theatre can play with the performance traditions in the spaces that it meets rather than becoming another version of them. It can perform new stories of crime and punishment that do not rely on the narratives of retribution or the self-aggrandising rhetoric of toughness. This takes great will, a statement of clear intent and a careful preparation of the activity. Although we must understand the specificity of the values that theatre practitioners bring to these places of punishment, we must not be afraid of articulating what those values are. Theatre can redirect gazes, shift perceptions and change the display. It can debate the serious pain in the system, without itself being part of the infliction of pain that is the system. It should not seek to deny the suffering caused by those labelled 'offender', but operate to challenge the easy performances that claim they are they answer to these difficult issues. Performances of the death penalty, private and public, declaratory Basic Layouts, orange robes and role-played drive-by shootings all deserve to be met with a vigorous practice that champions different accounts, new stagings and alternative visions of justice.

Notes

1. My belief that spectacles of retribution are damaging to individuals and communities and make little contribution to lessening the real pain that is caused by crime, is of course a particular and contested one. I make no apologies that it is taken as a starting point in this chapter, but I do acknowledge that others might have a very different view.
2. See Schechner (2002, pp. 192-3) for a discussion of the problems of 'text' as a metaphor in analysis performance.
3. It must be noted that in the case of Timothy McVeigh, the Oklahoma bomber, there were over three hundred family members who watched his execution relayed on video screens (Schechner, 2002, p. 179).
4. See the review of a performance by young offenders during a theatre conference in Wolverhampton in 2000 *Theatre and Punish / discipline and display*. This performance was as much an exercise in shaming as it was about promoting the skills and capabilities of these young people (Thompson, 2000).
5. For example the US has proportionally five times the number of prisoners as does the UK and the UK has the second highest proportionally in Europe (Donziger, 1996, p. 38).
6. All my comments on this system are related to visits I made to TYC establishments in 1996/7 and interviews with staff undertaken at the same time. Although I understand therefore that some of the procedures may have changed, my analysis of them I believe is still relevant for the argument I am making here.
7. Interview with Deputy Superintendent Melvin Haisler, 9 October 1996, Marlin Orientation and Assessment Center, Marlin, Texas.
8. See Austin American Statesman 'Long-term prisoners due less rehab under state

proposal' p. 1, 6 September 1997. Also see *The Guardian*, 3 February 1997, p. 1 and p. 12 on the execution of Karla Faye Tucker.

9. The word gulag is chosen specifically because the American system has been compared to a 'gulag' in the excellent analysis by Nils Christie *Crime Control as Industry: towards gulags 'western style'*, (1993).

10. It must be added that the practice of looking you directly in the eyes is a very Texan custom. A normal greeting with a stranger would include a handshake and strong eye contact. TYC trainers stressed the importance of the eye contact without the recognition that it is a very culturally loaded concept. It was uncomfortable for my English sensibilities and it was brought to my attention that Hispanic Texans (Tejanos/as) would also view it differently.

11. This was all relayed to me during a TYC training course at Corsicana State Home, 3 and 4 March 1997.

12. A term used by trainer during a TYC training course at Corsicana State Home, 3 and 4 March 1997. From personal notes.

13. Of the young people I met in the example given below all had murder convictions except one who had an attempted murder conviction.

14. As I discuss in the death penalty analysis, I have no doubt that this private 'confidential' moment becomes exhibited for public consumption in a host of different ways beyond the exact moment. The presentation of the video of one session 'with permission of the participants' is one way that this punishment meets its audience.

15. See www.peoplespalace.org

References

Andrews, D. A., and Bonta, J., *The Psychology of Criminal Conduct* (Cincinnati, Anderson, 1994).

Balfour, M., 'Drama, Masculinity and Violence', *Research In Drama Education*, Vol. 5, 1 pp. 9-21 (2000).

Cloud, D. L., *Control and Consolation in American Culture and Politics: rhetoric of therapy* (London, Sage, 1998).

Christie, N., *Crime Control as Industry: towards gulags 'western style'* (London, Routledge, 1993).

Donziger, S. R., *The Real War on Crime: the report of the National Criminal Justice Commission* (New York, Harper Perennial, 1996).

Foucault, M., *Discipline and Punish: the birth of the prison* (New York, Pantheon, 1977).

Garland, D., *Punishment and Modern Society: a study in social theory* (Oxford, Clarendon, 1990).

Gendreau, P., The Principles of Effective Intervention with Offenders, in: A.T. Harland (ed.) *Choosing Correctional Options that Work* (London, Sage, 1996).

Goffman, E., The Presentation of Self in Everyday Life (New York, Doubleday, 1959).

Goldfried, M. R., and Davison, G. C., Clinical Behavior Therapy (New York, Holt Reinhart and Winston, 1976).

The Guardian, 4 February 1998, 'The Ghoulish and Good Gather for Last Hours.' Joanna Coles. p. 12.

Harland, A. T., (ed.) Choosing Correctional Options that Work (London, Sage, 1996).

Hollin, C., Cognitive-Behavioral Interventions with Young Offenders (New York, Pergamon Press, 1990).

McGuire, J., and Priestley, P., Offending behaviour: skills and stratagems for going straight (London, Batsford, 1985).

Miller, J., Search and Destroy: African-American males in the criminal justice system (Cambridge, Cambridge University Press, 1996).

Mountford, A., and Farrall, M., The House of Four Rooms: Theatre, Violence and the Cycle of Change, in: J. Thompson (ed.) Prison Theatre: perspectives and practices (London, Jessica Kingsley Publishers, 1998).

Schechner, R., The Future of Ritual: writings on culture and performance (London, Routledge, 1993).

- Performance Studies: an introduction (London, Routledge, 2002).

Stern, V., A Sin Against the Future: imprisonment in the world (London, Penguin Books, 1998).

Texas Youth Commission, Core Curriculum in Resocialization (Austin, TX, Texas Youth Commission, 1995).

- Capital Offender Program (Austin, TX, Texas Youth Commission, 1995).

Thompson, J., (ed.) Prison Theatre: perspective and practices (London, Jessica Kingsley Publishers, 1998a).

- 'Theatre and Offender Rehabilitation: observations from the US'. Research in Drama Education, Vol. 3, 2, pp. 197-210 (1998b).

- Drama Workshops for Anger Management and Offending Behaviour (London, Jessica Kingsley Publishers, 1999).

- 'Theatre and Punish / discipline and display'. Research in Drama Education. Vol. 5, 2, pp. 272-275 (2000).

- Applied Theatre: bewilderment and beyond (London, Peter Lang, 2003).

The Prosocial Gang

Arnold P. Goldstein, Barry Glick, Wilma Carthan,

Douglas A. Blancero

Rock Brigade
Harlem Ranger Cadet Corps
Black Crusaders
Brothers Gaining Equality through Excellence
Nighthawks
Puerto Rican Young Lords
East Harlem Youth Action Programme
Brown Berets
Homeboy Tortillas

The phrase *prosocial gang* appears on its face to be an obvious contradiction. Gangs, we all know, are antisocial, not prosocial. The world of criminal justice asserts this, the media proclaim it daily, and, a great deal of sociological, psychological, and other data clearly affirm and describe such antisocialness. Juvenile gangs, the consensus has it, are bad; they regularly commit an array of aggressive and criminal acts, and ought to be discouraged, disbanded, and dispersed. America, responding to this anti-gang consensus, is increasingly mobilized to reduce gang membership and gang activities. Unlike the 1950s and 1960s, when social workers were the country's primary gang-relevant professionals, and detached (from the agency or office) street work was the primary intervention activity, the police are today's gang specialists, and intelligence-gathering, deterrence, arrest, and incarceration are their gang-relevant pursuits. The change grew from several sources, but most especially from the heightened and often lethal gang-initiated violence that has so frequently characterized America's drug market-places and streets.

Also contributing to this shift, however, was the purported failure of detached worker programming. The central goal of such street work intervention was value transformation. Working with the gang as a unit whenever possible or with substantial cliques thereof, detached workers employed an array of counselling, vocational, and recreational techniques and activities in order to enhance gang youths' problem-solving skills, autonomy, self-esteem, cooperativeness, and competence *vis-à-vis* 'conventional' behaviours. Stated most generally, value transformation was the hoped-for route to the prosocial gang.

It was a notion with great inherent appeal, and by the early 1960s, many dozens of

American cities had ongoing, detached worker programmes. Several evaluations of their effectiveness then followed and, to the surprise of many workers – given the then popularity of the approach – most such evaluations were negative. Results seemed to be consistently indicating that gang youth values and delinquent behaviour were not favourably impacted by detached worker programming. Worse, some claimed that by working with the gang as a unit, workers were providing it with added recognition and legitimacy and thereby increasing its cohesiveness and durability. As a result of such findings and interpretations, detached worker youth gang interventions rapidly faded away, to be replaced by more individualized approaches designed for, among other purposes, weaning youth away from gang membership.

We wish to assert here that it is our belief that detached worker programming was not a failure and that, in fact, its efficacy remains unknown. As Klein (1968b) courageously describes *vis-à-vis* his own detached worker programme, and as we strongly suspect was true for the large majority of such efforts, the actual worker youth programming very frequently never took place. Klein's 'detached' workers, for example, spent twenty-five per cent to fifty per cent of their time attached, in the agency, not the streets; twenty-five per cent of their time travelling to and from their assigned neighbourhood or waiting around, alone on the street; and only approximately twenty-five per cent of the time engaged in actual activities with gang youths. Given caseload size, this translated to approximately five minutes per youth per week. Far from proving the ineffectiveness of detached worker programming, and its value transformation rationale, such failure of programme implementation more parsimoniously suggests an indeterminacy of effectiveness. Even if carefully planned and evaluated, as many such programmes were, if only carried forth minimally, its effectiveness is yet to be determined.

Add to this (non)finding and (non)refutation of the value transformation strategy two apparent facts: First, current criminal justice, 'weed and seed' efforts to arrest gang leadership, in the hope that the gang as a then leaderless organization will dissolve, have rarely succeeded. Instead, youths rapidly coalesce around new leadership, or old leadership continues undeterred by incarceration. Second, boys need other boys. The need for a like-minded, compatible peer group exists, and further is a healthy, normal quality of adolescence in particular. These several factors, namely, the general failure of criminal justice 'gang-busting' efforts, the legitimacy and even desirability of adolescent peer groups, and the apparent indeterminacy of effectiveness for earlier, gang youth value transformation efforts combine to serve as the strategic underpinning for the project we describe in this chapter. It is, as will be seen, an effort to work with a series of intact gangs, as gangs, in order to move their members in more constructive directions and begin creating a series of prosocial gangs.

Thus, for us, the phrase *prosocial gang* clearly is not a contradiction. This chapter opens with a list of such youth groups, and others exist. Some were prosocial in intent and action from their beginning. Others formed first into a juvenile gang, engaged for an often extended period of time in illegal behaviours, and then, through various combinations of their own and agency/community worker efforts, shifted in both their overt behaviours and underlying attitudes toward distinctly prosocial standards. Such movement has happened in the past, and can be facilitated in the future. This chapter is a journey into one such facilitative attempt.

Aggression Replacement Training – Background and Procedures

Until the early 1970s there existed primarily three major clusters of psychological interventions designed to alter the behaviour of aggressive, unhappy, ineffective, or disturbed individuals – psychodynamic/psychoanalytic, humanistic/nondirective, and behaviour modification. Each of these diverse orientations found concrete expression in procedures targeted to the group of persons of central concern to the present programme, aggressive adolescents – the psychodynamic in psychoanalytically oriented individual psychotherapy (Guttman, 1970), activity group therapy (Slavson, 1964), and the varied array of treatment procedures developed by Redl and Wineman (1957); the humanistic/client centered in the applications to juvenile delinquents (e.g., Truax, Wargo, & Silber, 1966) of the client-centered psychotherapy of Carl Rogers (1957), the alternative educational programmes offered by Gold (1978), and the approach to school discipline put forth by Dreikurs, Grunwald, and Pepper (1971); and the behaviour modification in a wide variety of the interventions reflecting the systematic use of contingency management, contracting and the training of teachers and parents as behaviour change managers (O'Leary, O'Leary, & Becker, 1967; Patterson, Cobb, & Ray, 1973; Walker, 1979). Though each of these intervention philosophies differs from the others in several major respects, one of their significant commonalities is the shared assumption that the targeted client had somewhere within himself, as yet unexpressed, the effective, satisfying, non-aggressive, or healthy behaviours whose expression was among the goals of the intervention. Such latent potentials, in all three approaches, would be realized by the client if the intervener were sufficiently skilled in reducing or removing obstacles to such realization. The psychoanalyst sought to do so by calling forth and interpreting unconscious material blocking progress-relevant awareness. The client-centered therapist, who in particular believed that the potential for change resides within the client, sought to free this potential by providing a warm, empathic, maximally accepting intervention environment. And the behaviour modifier, by means of one or more contingency management procedures, attempted to see to it that when the latent desirable behaviours or approximations thereto did occur, the client received contingent reinforcement, thus increasing the probability that these behaviours would recur. Therefore, whether sought by means of interpretation, provision of a positive intervention climate, or by dint of offering contingent reward, all three approaches assumed that somewhere within the individual's repertoire resided the desired, effective goal behaviours.

In the early 1970s an important new intervention approach began to emerge – psychological skill training, an approach resting upon rather different assumptions. Viewing the helpee more in educational, pedagogic terms rather than as a client in need of therapy, the psychological skills trainer assumed he was dealing with an individual lacking, deficient, or at best weak in the skills necessary for effective and satisfying interpersonal and intrapersonal functioning. The task of the skills trainer became, therefore, not interpretation, reflection, or reinforcement, but the active and deliberate teaching of desirable behaviours. Rather than an intervention called psychotherapy, between a patient and psychotherapist, what emerged was training, between a trainee and a psychological skills trainer.

The roots of the psychological skills training movement lie within both education and psychology. The notion of literally seeking to teach desirable behaviours has often, if sporadically, been a significant goal of the American educational establishment. The Character Education Movement of the 1920s and more contemporary Moral Education and Values Clarification programmes are but a few of several possible examples. Add to this institutionalized educational interest in skills training, the hundreds of interpersonal and planning skills courses taught in America's more than two thousand community colleges, and the hundreds of self-help books oriented toward similar skill-enhancement goals that are available to the American public, and it becomes clear that the formal and informal educational establishment in America provided fertile soil and explicit stimulation within which the psychological skills training movement could grow.

Much the same can be said for American psychology, as it too laid the groundwork in its prevailing philosophy and concrete interests for the development of this new movement. The learning process has above all else been the central theoretical and investigative concern of American psychology since the late nineteenth-century. This focal interest also assumed major therapeutic form in the 1950s, as psychotherapy practitioners and researchers alike came to view psychotherapeutic treatment more and more in learning terms. The very healthy and still expanding field of behaviour modification grew from this joint learning-clinical focus, and may be appropriately viewed as the immediately preceding context in which psychological skills training came to be developed. In companion with the growth of behaviour modification, psychological thinking increasingly shifted from a strict emphasis on remediation to one that was almost equally concerned with prevention, and the bases for this shift included movement away from a medical model concept toward what may most aptly be called a psycho-educational theoretical stance. Both of these thrusts – heightened concern with prevention and a psycho-educational perspective – gave strong added impetus to the viability of the psychological skills training movement.

Perhaps psychology's most direct contribution to psychological skills training came from social learning theory and in particular from the work conducted by and stimulated by Albert Bandura:

> The method that has yielded the most impressive results with diverse problems contains three major components. First, alternative modes of response are repeatedly modelled, preferably by several people who demonstrate how the new style of behaviour can be used in dealing with a variety of ... situations. Second, learners are provided with guidance and ample opportunities to practice the modelled behaviour under favourable conditions until they perform it skillfully and spontaneously. The latter procedures are ideally suited for developing new social skills, but they are unlikely to be adopted unless

they produce rewarding consequences. Arrangement of success experiences, particularly for initial efforts at behaving differently, constitute the third component in this powerful composite method... Given adequate demonstration, guided practice, and success experiences, this method is almost certain to produce favourable results (1973, p. 253).

Other events of the 1970s provided still further stimulation for the growth of the skills training movement. The inadequacy of prompting, shaping, and related operant procedures for adding new behaviours to individuals' behavioural repertoires was increasingly apparent. The widespread reliance upon deinstitutionalization, which lay at the heart of the community mental health movement, resulted in the discharge from America's public mental health hospitals of approximately 400,000 persons, the majority of whom were substantially deficient in important daily functioning skills. And it had grown particularly clear that what the American mental health movement had available to offer lower social class clients was grossly inadequate in meeting their psychotherapeutic needs. These factors, that is, relevant supportive research, the incompleteness of operant approaches, large populations of grossly skill deficient individuals, and the paucity of useful interventions for a large segment of American society – all in the context of historically supportive roots in both education and psychology – came together in our thinking and that of others as demanding a new intervention, something prescriptively responsive to these several needs. Psychological skill training was the answer, and a movement was launched.

Skillstreaming

Our involvement in this movement, a psychological skills-training approach termed Skillstreaming, began in the early 1970s. At that time, and for several years thereafter, our studies were conducted in public mental health hospitals with long-term, highly skill-deficient, chronic patients. As the research programme progressed, and demonstrated with regularity successful skill enhancement effects (Goldstein, 1981), focus shifted from teaching a broad array of interpersonal and daily living skills to adult psychiatric inpatients to a more explicit concern with skill training for aggressive individuals. Trainee groups included spouses engaged in family disputes violent enough to warrant Police intervention (Goldstein, Monti, Sardino, and Green, 1979), child-abusing parents (Solomon, 1978; Sturm, 1979), and most especially, overtly aggressive adolescents (Goldstein, Sprafkin, Gershaw, and Klein, 1980).

  With regard to adolescent trainees, Skillstreaming has been successful in enhancing such prosocial skills as empathy, negotiation, assertiveness, following instructions, self-control, and perspective taking. Beyond these initial demonstrations that Skillstreaming enhances skill acquisition for such youngsters, these beginning studies also highlighted other aspects of the teaching of prosocial behaviours. Fleming (1976), in an effort to capitalize upon adolescent responsiveness to peer influence, demonstrated that gains in negotiating skill are as great when the Skillstreaming group leader is a respected peer as when the leader is an adult. Litwack (1976), more concerned with the skill-enhancing effect of an adolescent anticipating that he will later serve as a peer leader, showed that such helper role expectation increases that degree of skill acquired. Apparently, when the adolescent expects to teach others a skill, his own level of skill acquisition benefits, a finding clearly relevant to Reissman's helper therapy principle (1965). Trief (1976) demonstrated that successful use of Skillstreaming to increase perspective-taking skill (i.e., seeing matters from other people's viewpoints) also leads to consequent increases in cooperative behaviour. The significant transfer effects both in this study and in the Golden (1975), Litwack (1976), and Raleigh (1977) investigations have been important signposts in planning further research on transfer enhancement in Skillstreaming.

As in earlier efforts with adult trainees, the value of teaching certain skill combinations to adolescents was also examined. Aggression-prone adolescents often get into difficulty when they respond with overt aggression to authority figures with whom they disagree. Golden (1975), responding to this type of event, successfully used Skillstreaming to teach such youngsters resistance-reducing behaviour, defined as a combination of reflection of feeling (the authority figure's) and assertiveness (forthright but non-aggressive statement of one's own position). Jennings (1975) was able to use Skillstreaming successfully to train adolescents in several of the verbal skills necessary for satisfactory participation in more traditional, insight-oriented psychotherapy. And Guzzetta (1974) was successful in providing means to help close the gap between adolescents and their parents by using Skillstreaming to teach empathic skills to parents.

The overall conclusions that may justifiably be drawn from these several early empirical evaluations of our work with aggressive adolescent, as well as other trainees, are twofold.

1. Skill acquisition: Across diverse trainee populations (including aggressive adolescents in urban secondary schools and juvenile detention centers) and target skills, skill acquisition is a reliable training outcome, occurring in better than ninety per cent of Skillstreaming trainees. It is acknowledged that gains demonstrable in the training context are, relatively speaking, rather easily accomplished, given the potency, support, encouragement, and low threat value of trainers and procedures in that context. The more consequential outcome question by far pertains to trainee skill performance in real-world contexts (i.e., skill transfer).

2. Skill transfer: Across diverse trainee populations, target skills, and applied (real-world) settings, skill transfer occurs with approximately forty-five to fifty per cent of Skillstreaming trainees. Goldstein and Kanfer (1979), as well as Karoly and Steffen (1980), have indicated that across several dozen types of psychotherapy involving many different types of psychopathology, the average transfer rate on follow-up is between fifteen and twenty per cent of patients seen. The forty-five to fifty per cent rate consequent to Skillstreaming is a significant improvement upon this collective base rate, though it must immediately be underscored that this cumulative average transfer also means that the gains shown by half of the trainees were limited to in-session acquisition. Of special consequence, however, is the consistently clear manner in which

skill transfer was a function of the explicit implementation of the laboratory-derived transfer-enhancing techniques discussed later in this chapter.

> Interpersonal, aggression-management, cognitive, and related psychological skill deficiencies among delinquent gang youths have multiple origins, instigators, and maintainers. Such deficiencies, as well as proficiency in alternative, antisocial behaviours, grow first from the powerful and often almost unremitting presence of antisocial models in the three arenas of life in which the youngster spends almost all of his time – family, peers, and mass media. In each of these domains, that is, at home, in school or on the street, and in front of the television set, the youngster is repeatedly exposed to vivid, frequent, expert, and rewarded displays of aggression, egocentricity, impulsiveness, and other behaviours in the full spectrum of antisocial living (Bandura, 1973; Comstock, 1983).

As the youngster himself begins to engage in such antisocial behaviours, he is often much more likely to be frequently, immediately, regularly, and richly rewarded for his (antisocial) efforts than punished for them. Regretfully, aggression pays. Thus, punitive and at times abusive parents, encouragement and examples from peers, and a flood of expert portrayals in the mass media help initiate a process or lifestyle that finds considerable real world reward – in tangible, social, and self-esteem-enhancing expressions.

The persistence of such behaviours is, at minimum, a joint function of the potency of its roots, the pervasiveness of its reward, and the heretofore relative impotency of intervention efforts. Skillstreaming appears to have been a fine beginning in creating an effective, prosocial-enhancing intervention, but only a beginning. Delinquent youngsters do reliably learn a full curriculum of prosocial behaviours by means of this method, but skill acquisition is not enough. For skill transfer to occur at equally high levels, more must be added to the intervention effort. The roots and maintainers of aggression and related behaviours are diverse and multi-channel. So too must remediation be. The youngster must learn not only what to do (a behavioural matter) but also *why to do it* (a cognitive and motivational matter) and *how to control* alternative impulsive and antisocial behaviours (an affective matter). Thus we built upon Skillstreaming, and constituted an intervention we termed Aggression Replacement Training (ART), an intervention that seeks to impact upon youngsters simultaneously along three different but complimentary channels: cognitive (via Moral Education), affective (via Anger Control), and *behavioural* (via Skillstreaming). Therefore, we held, to aid in maximizing transfer and maintenance of gain, two additional interventions need to be implemented when dealing with aggressive, delinquent adolescents: Anger Control Training and Moral Education.

Anger Control Training

Individuals may fail to utilize appropriate interpersonal skills because their knowledge of them is weak or lacking, and hence should be offered the kind of performance-enhancement training that Skillstreaming provides. But poor skill performance may also be in part a result of inhibitors to skilled performance in individuals who do possess the skill, at least to some degree. In the case of chronically aggressive gang youths, the target trainees for the present training and evaluation programme, prosocially skilled behaviour may be rare not only, or because, they are weak in prosocial alternatives to aggression, but also because they have great difficulty in inhibiting or controlling the aggression itself. In addition to performance-enhancement training (Skillstreaming) therefore, such youngsters might simultaneously benefit from training designed to reduce performance inhibitors. Such an anger control training intervention, consisting largely of training in relaxation, self-disputation of instigating self-statements and interpretations, use of calming techniques, and other self-control procedures, has been developed by Feindler and Fremouw, 1983; Moon and Eisler, 1983; and Novaco, 1975.

Moral Education

Kohlberg's (1976) especially well-calculated approach to enhancing prosocial values is essentially a non-indoctrinative procedure for developing higher levels of moral reasoning. Youngsters are not told in this method what to believe, but instead are exposed to a series of experiences designed to enhance the likelihood that their moral reasoning will progress toward higher, more constructive (just, fair, less egocentric) levels. These experiences, in synopsis, involve first of all the constituting of groups of adolescents currently functioning at two or three different stages or levels of moral reasoning. A series of group discussions then ensues. In these meetings, the adult leader serves as discussion facilitator, not value arbiter of good or bad, right or wrong. The leader's responsibility is to pose moral dilemmas and have them fully examined. These are descriptions of real-life problem situations whose diverse solutions reflect conflicting moral values. Kohlberg and others have repeatedly shown that such moral reasoning discussions, when engaged in by persons at differing levels of moral reasoning, will arouse in many of the discussants substantial levels of cognitive conflict (about their present values), which functions to move them upward, as it were, to new and higher levels of moral reasoning. While this moral reasoning enhancement effect has been a frequent finding by Kohlberg and others, a causal relationship between such prosocial valuing and overt prosocial behaviour has been a much less frequent research result. Prosocial values by themselves are often not a sufficient foundation for the emergence of prosocial behaviour. It is in part for this reason that Aggression Replacement Training, the intervention central to the present project, also provides the concrete techniques of overt prosocial behaviour training and antisocial behaviour inhibition.

We have described the rationale underlying our decision to constitute ART with three complementary interventions. In the material that follows we wish to detail the specific procedures that operationalise Skillstreaming, Anger Control Training, and Moral Education. We will follow this operational discussion with a presentation of the actual curricular materials employed when implementing ART.

Skillstreaming Procedures

In Skillstreaming, small groups of chronically aggressive adolescents with shared psychological skill deficiencies are:

1. Shown several examples of expert use of the behaviours constituting the skills in which they are weak or lacking (e.g., *modelling*);

2. Given several guided opportunities to practice and rehearse these competent interpersonal behaviours (e.g., *role-playing*);

3. Provided with praise, reinstruction, and related feedback on how well their role-playing of the skill matched the expert model's portrayal of it (e.g., *performance feedback*); and

4. Encouraged to engage in a series of activities designed to increase the chances that skills learned in the training setting will endure and be available for use when needed in the school, home, community, institution, or other real-world setting (*transfer training*).

Modelling

Skillstreaming requires that trainees first be exposed to expert examples of the behaviours we want them to learn. The five or six trainees constituting the Skillstreaming group are selected according to their shared skill deficiencies. Each skill to be taught is broken down into four to six different behavioural steps, each set of steps constituting the operational definition of the given skill. Using either live acting by the group's trainers or audiovisual modelling displays, actors portray the steps of the skill being used expertly in a variety of settings relevant to the trainee's daily life. Trainees are told to watch and listen closely to the way the actors in each vignette follow the skill's behavioural steps.

Role-Playing

A brief spontaneous discussion almost invariably follows the presentation of a modelling display. Trainees comment on the steps, the actors, and very often, on how the situation or skill problem portrayed occurs in their own lives. Since our primary goal in role-playing is to encourage realistic behavioural rehearsal, a trainee's statements about his or her difficulties using the skill being taught can often develop into material for his or her role-play of it. To enhance the realism of the portrayal, the main actor is asked to choose a second trainee (co-actor) to play the role of the significant other person in his or her life who is relevant to the skill problem. It is of crucial importance in the role-play that the main actor seek to enact the steps he or she has just seen and heard modelled.

The main actor is asked to briefly describe the real skill problem situation and the real persons involved in it with whom he or she could try these behavioural steps in real life. The co-actor is called by the name of the main actor's significant other during the role-play. The trainer then instructs the role-player to begin. It is the trainer's main responsibility to be sure that the main actor keeps role-playing and attempts to follow the behavioural steps while doing so.

The role-playing is continued until all trainees in the group have had an opportunity to participate, even if all the same steps must be carried over to a second or third session. It should be noted that while the behavioural steps of each role-play in the series remain the same, the actual content can and should change from role-play to role-play. The skill deficiency problem as it actually occurs, or could occur, in each trainee's real-life environment should be the content of a given role-play. When the role-play is completed, each trainee should be better armed to act appropriately in the given reality situation.

Performance Feedback

Upon completion of each role-play, feedback is briefly given. The goals of this activity are to let the main actor know how well he or she followed the skill's steps or in what ways he or she departed from them, to explore the Psychological impact of the enactment on the co-actor, and to provide the main actor with encouragement to try out the role-play behaviours in real life. In these critiques, the behavioural focus of Skillstreaming is maintained. Comments must not take the form of general evaluative comments or broad generalities, but must focus on the presence or absence of specific, concrete behaviours.

Transfer of Training

Several aspects of the Skillstreaming sessions just described have as their primary purpose augmentation of the likelihood that learning in the training setting will transfer to the trainee's real-life environment.

1. *Provision of general principles*. Transfer of training has been demonstrated to be facilitated by providing trainees with general mediating principles governing successful or competent performance in training and in real world settings. The provision of general principles to Skillstreaming trainees is operationalised in our training by the presentation in verbal, pictorial, and written form of appropriate information governing skill instigation, selection, and implementation principles.

2. *Overlearning*. Overlearning is a procedure whereby learning is extended over more trials than are necessary to produce initial changes in the trainee's behaviour. The overlearning, or repetition of successful skill enactment, in the typical Skillstreaming sessions is substantial, with the given skill taught and its behavioural steps (1) modeled several times, (2) role-played one or more times correctly by the trainee, (3) observed live by the trainees as every other group member role-plays it, (4) read by the trainee from a chalkboard and on the Skill Card, (5) written by the trainee in his or her Trainee's Notebook, (6) practiced *in vivo* one or more times by the trainee in response to skill-relevant events in, or introduced into, his or her real life environment.

3. *Identical elements*. In perhaps the earliest experimental concern with transfer enhancement, it was found that when there was a facilitative effect of one habit on another, it was both to the extent that and because they shared identical elements. The

greater the similarity of physical and interpersonal stimuli in the Skillstreaming setting and the home, school, or other setting in which the skill is to be applied, the greater the likelihood of transfer. The 'real-lifeness' of Skillstreaming is operationalised in several ways. These operational expressions of identical elements include (1) the representative, relevant, and realistic content and portrayal of the models, protagonists, and situations in the live modelling or modelling tapes, all designed to be highly similar to what trainees are likely to face in their daily lives; (2) the physical props used in, and the arrangement of, the role-playing setting to be similar to real-life settings; (3) the choice, coaching, and enactment of the co-actors to be as similar as possible to the real-life figures they represent; (4) the manner in which the role-plays themselves are conducted to be as responsive as possible to the real-life interpersonal stimuli to which the trainee will actually have to respond with the given skill; (5) the *in vivo* homework assignments; and (6) the training of natural peer groups whenever possible.

4. *Stimulus variability*. Several studies have demonstrated that positive transfer is greater when a variety of relevant training stimuli are employed. Stimulus variability is implemented in our Skillstreaming studies by use of (1) rotating group leaders across groups; (2) rotating trainees across groups; (3) having trainees re-role-play a given skill across relevant settings; and/or (5) using multiple homework assignments for each skill.

5. *Real-life reinforcement*. Agras (1967), Gruber (1971), Tharp and Wetzel (1969), and dozens of other investigators have shown that stable and enduring performance in application settings of newly learned skills is very much at the mercy of real-life reinforcement contingencies. We have found it useful to implement supplemental programmes outside the Skillstreaming setting to help ensure that trainees obtain the reinforcements they need and thereby maintain their new behaviours. These programmes include provision for both external social reward (provided by people in the trainee's real-life environment) and self-reward (provided by the trainee).

Anger Control Training Procedures

As noted earlier, in contrast to Skillstreaming's goal of facilitating prosocial behaviour, Anger Control Training teaches youngsters how to control their level of anger arousal. Anger Control Training sessions utilize modelling, youth role-playing, and group performance feedback procedures similar to those employed in Skillstreaming. As the homework effort does in Skillstreaming, Hassle Logs are used in Anger Control Training to help tie the training to real-world events – in this instance, actual provocations the youth has experienced. See Figure 1 for an example of a Hassle Log.

In a series of sessions, usually once weekly, participating youths learn a series of links in a chain of anger-control responsiveness. The first link, Triggers, is an effort to help participants identify the external events and internal self-statements that elicit anger. What provokes the youths? Having begun to master this initial concern, the youths then turn their attention to identifying the particular physiological/kinesthetic cues that let them know that it is anger, and not fear, anxiety, or any other affect, that they are experiencing. Cues of anger – tensed biceps, flushing cheeks, hair on neck standing erect, sinking stomach sensation – tend to be idiosyncratic.

Having identified the stimulus involved (Triggers) and that it is anger one is experiencing (Cues), youths are taught a series of effective anger-reducing techniques. In our Anger Control Training programme, these include deep breathing, counting backward, imagining a peaceful scene, contemplating the long-term consequences of alternative behavioural sequelae to the anger being experienced, and the use of Reminders. Reminders are, in a sense, the opposite of internal triggers. The latter are self-statements (explanations, instructions) that instigate heightened levels of anger. Reminders (also explanations, instructions, and the like) are designed to lower anger arousal. Some Reminders are generic and can be used widely (e.g., 'chill out,' 'calm down,' 'cool off'). Some are situation specific (e.g., 'Jane didn't trip me on purpose, she always sits at her desk in that sloppy way').

If the links described thus far are used properly, the trainee may reward himself or herself, a procedure taught as the next link. Finally, since Aggression Replacement Training typically involves youths attending both Skillstreaming and Anger Control classes every week, by the sixth or seventh week of the programme, the youth is armed with a sufficient number of Skillstreaming skills that he or she can complete the role-playing of an anger-lowering response to a provocation by showing the group the correct behaviours to use instead of aggressing, namely a Skillstreaming skill. By means of these components, chronically angry and aggressive youths are taught to respond to provocation (others' and their own) less impulsively, more reflectively, and with less likelihood of acting-out behaviour. In short, Anger Control Training teaches youngsters what not to do in anger-instigating situations.

Moral Education Procedures

Armed with both the ability to respond to the real world prosocially and the skills necessary to stifle or at least diminish anger, will the youngster who chronically acts out choose the prosocial alternative? To enhance the likelihood that he or she will, one must enter into the realm of moral values.

When faced with the choice of behaving aggressively (usually a richly and reliably rewarded response) or prosocially (often a behaviour ignored by others), the latter will be the more frequent choice the greater the youth's sense of fairness, justice, and concern for the rights of others. As noted earlier, in a long and pioneering series of investigations, Kohlberg (1969, 1973) demonstrated that exposing youngsters to a series of moral dilemmas, in a discussion group context that includes youngsters reasoning at differing levels of moral thinking, arouses cognitive conflict whose resolution frequently advances a youngster's moral reasoning to that of the higher-level peers in the group. The dilemmas employed ideally are interesting; relevant to the world of adolescents; and involved with issues of fairness, justice, or the needs or rights of others. Examples of such dilemmas (Gibbs, 1986) are as follows:

Figure 1. Hassle Log

Name   Date
Morning   Afternoon   Evening

Where were you?
Classroom   Friend's House   Youth Center
Store   Movie   Car
Home   Park   On a Job
Street   Outside   Other

What happened?
Somebody insulted me.   Somebody took something of mine.
Somebody told me to do something. Somebody was doing something
I didn't like.   I did something wrong.
Somebody started fighting with me.
Other:

Who was that somebody:
A friend   Parent   Teacher/Principal   Coach
A stranger Brother/Sister Girlfriend/Boyfriend   Other

What did you do?
Hit back   Told peer   Ran away
Ignored it   Yelled   Used Anger
Control   Cried   Broke
something
Cursed   Used Skillstreaming skill   Told someone
Walked away calmly   Talked it out

How did you handle yourself?
1   2   3   4   5
Poorly   Not so Well   Okay   Good   Great

How angry were you?
Burning   Really angry   Moderately angry
Mildly angry, but still okay   Not angry at all

Sam's Dilemma

Sam and his best friend, Dave, are shopping in a record store. Dave picks up a record he really likes and slips it into his backpack. Dave then walks out of the store. Moments later, the security officer and the store owner come up to Sam. The store owner says to the officer, 'That's one of the boys who were stealing records.' The security officer checks Sam's backpack but doesn't find the record. 'Okay, you're off the hook, but what's the name of the guy who was with you?' the officer asks Sam. 'I'm almost broke because of shoplifting,' the owner says. 'I can't let him get away with it.' What should Sam say or do? Why? What would be the consequences?

Regina's Dilemma

'Your father called to say he had to work late,' Regina's mother told her one night as they sat eating dinner. But Regina knew better. She had passed her father's car on the way home from school. It was parked outside the Midtown Bar and Grill. Regina's mother and father had argued many times about her father's stopping off at the bar on his way home from work. After their last argument, her father had promised he would never do it again. 'Do you think I should believe your father?' Regina's mother asks her. What should Regina say or do? What would be the consequences?

The arousal of cognitive conflict and perspective-taking necessary for the enhancement of moral reasoning is most likely to occur when a range of reasoning levels is present in the dilemma discussion group. For that reason, Aggression Replacement Training Moral Education groups typically consist of twelve members, in contrast to six each in Anger Control Training and Skillstreaming. Trainers distribute the dilemma, read it aloud as the youths follow along, elicit a dilemma solution and its underlying reasons from each youth, rate each such response for the moral reasoning stage it reflects, and then conduct a twenty to thirty minute series of debates regarding alternative dilemma solutions among youths at adjacent moral reasoning stages until all have participated.

While moral reasoning stage advancements in youths participating in moral education is a frequent finding, efforts to utilize it by itself as a means of enhancing actual overt moral behaviour have yielded mixed success (Arbuthnot & Gordon, 1993; Zimmerman, 1983). Perhaps this is because such youngsters did not have in their behaviour repertoires the actual skill behaviours either for acting prosocially or for successfully inhibiting the antisocial. We thus reason that Kohlbergian Moral Education has great potential for providing constructive direction toward the prosocial and away from the antisocial in youngsters armed with the tools of both Skillstreaming and Anger Control Training.

The Aggression Replacement Training Curriculum

Table 1.1 is a listing, respectively, of the Skillstreaming skills, Moral Reasoning dilemmas, and Anger Control Training steps employed by us in our initial ART evaluation research, presented in detail in the chapter that follows. Utilizing this curriculum, our first two studies operationalised ART via a ten week programme; and the specific skills, dilemmas, and steps employed were selected following extensive consultations with a broad sample of delinquency facility staff. Our third evaluation, a longer ART programme, expanded upon these contents, and the current programme – our fourth efficacy evaluation – is yet a further expansion in length and contents. In this present programme, reflecting not only the greater programme intensity just noted but also enhanced programme prescriptiveness, we have varied skill, dilemma, and step contents from participating gang to participating gang in order to be fully responsive to their skills training preferences as the youths themselves defined them. Here is what we consider (Table 1.1) our 'core' curriculum – used in its entirety in our initial research and in large part filtered into the present programme.

TABLE 1.1 Aggression Replacement Training Curriculum

Skillstreaming	Moral Reasoning	Anger Control
I. *Expressing a Complaint* 1. Define what the problem is, and who's responsible for it. 2. Decide how the problem might be solved. 3. Tell that person what the problem is and how it might be solved. 4. Ask for a response. 5. Show that you understand his or her feelings. 6. Come to agreement on the steps to be taken by each of you.	1. The Used Car. 2. Dope Pusher. 3. Riots in Public Places.	*Introduction* 1. Rationale: Presentation and discussion. 2. Rules: Presentation and discussion. 3. Training procedures: Presentation and discussion. 4. Contracting for ACT participation. 5. Initial history taking regarding Antecedent provocations – Behavioural response – Consequences.

		(A-B-C)
11. *Responding to the Feelings of Others (Empathy)* 1. Observe the other person's words and actions. 2. Decide what the other person might be feeling and how strong the feelings are. 3. Decide whether it would be helpful to let the other person know you understand his or her feelings. 4. Tell the other person, in a warm and sincere manner, how you think he or she is feeling.	1. The Passenger Ship. 2. The Case of Charles Manson. 3. LSD.	*Assessment* 1. Hassle Log: Purposes and mechanics. 2. Anger self-assessment: Physiological Cues. 3. Anger Reducers: Deep breathing training Refocusing: Backward counting Peaceful imagery.
111. *Preparing for a Stressful Conversation* 1. Imagine yourself in the stressful situation. 2. Think about how you will feel and why you will feel that way. 3. Imagine that other person in the stressful situation. Think about how that person will feel and why. 4. Imagine yourself telling the other person what you want to say. 5. Imagine what he or she will say. 6. Repeat the above steps, using as many approaches as you can think of. 7. Choose the best approach.	1. Shoplifting. 2. Booby Trap. 3. Plagiarism.	*Triggers* 1. Identification of provoking stimuli a) Direct triggers (from others) b) Indirect triggers (from self) 2. Role-play: Triggers + Cues + Anger Reducer 3. Review of Hassle Logs
IV. *Responding to Anger* 1. Listen openly to what the other person has to say. 2. Show that you understand what the other person is feeling. 3. Ask the other person to explain anything you don't understand.	1. Toy Revolver. 2. Robin Hood Case. 3. Drugs.	*Reminders (Anger Reducer #4)* 1. Introduction to self-instruction training. 2. Modelling use of Reminders under pressure. 3. Role-play: Triggers +

4. Show that you understand why the other person feels angry. 5. If it is appropriate, express your thoughts and feelings about the situation.		Cues + Reminders + Anger Reducer. 4. Homework assignments and review of Hassle Log.
V. *Keeping Out of Fights* 1. Stop and think about why you want to fight. 2. Decide what you want to happen in the long run. 3. Think about other ways to handle the situation besides fighting. 4. Decide on the best way to handle the situation, and do it.	1. Private Country. 2. New York vs. Gerald Young. 3. Saving a Life.	*Self-Evaluation* 1.Review of Reminder homework assignments. 2. Self-evaluation of post-conflict Reminders. (a) Self-reinforcement techniques. (b) Self-coaching techniques. 3. Review of Hassle Log post-conflict Reminders 4. Role-play: Triggers + Cues + Reminders + Anger Reducer + Self-evaluation.
VI. *Helping Others* 1. Decide if the other person might need and want your help. 2. Think of ways you could be helpful. 3. Ask the other person if he/she needs and wants your help. 4. Help the other person.	1. The Kidney Transplant . 2. Bomb Shelter. 3. Misrepresentation.	*Thinking Ahead (Anger Reducer #5)* 1. Estimating future negative consequences for current acting out. 2. Short-term versus long-consequences. 3. Worst to least consequences. 4. Role-play: 'If … then …' thinking ahead. 5. Role-play: Triggers + Cues + Reminders + Anger Reducers + Self = evaluation + Skillstreaming skill.
VII. *Dealing With an Accusation* 1. Think about what the other person has accused you of. 2. Think about why the person	1. Lt. Berg. 2. Perjury. 3. Doctor's Responsibility.	*The Angry Behaviour Cycle* 1. Review of Hassle Logs. 2. Identification of own anger provoking behaviour. 3. Modification of own

might have accused you. 3. Think about ways to answer the person's accusations. 4. Choose the best way, and do it.		anger-provoking behaviour. 4. Role-play: Triggers + Cues + Reminders + Anger Reducers + Self-evaluation + Skillstreaming skill.
VIII. *Dealing With Group Pressure* 1. Think about what the other people want you to do and why. 2. Decide what you want to do. 3. Decide how to tell the other people what you want to do. 4. Tell the group what you have decided.	1. Noisy Child. 2. The Stolen Car. 3. Discrimination.	*Full Sequence Rehearsal* 1. Review of Hassle Logs. 2. Role-play: Triggers + Cues + Reminders + Anger Reducers + Self-evaluation + Skillstreaming skill.
IX. *Expressing Affection* 1. Decide if you have good feelings about the other person. 2. Decide whether the other person would like to know about your feelings. 3. Decide how you might best express your feelings. 4. Choose the right time and place to express your feelings. 5. Express affection in a warm and caring manner.	1. Defense of Other Persons. 2. Lying in Order to Help Someone. 3. Rockefeller's Suggestion.	*Full Sequence Rehearsal* 1. Review of Hassle Logs. 2. Role-play: Triggers + Cues. + Reminders + Anger Reducers + Self-evaluation + Skillstreaming skill.
X. *Responding to Failure* 1. Decide if you have failed. 2. Think about both the personal reasons and the circumstances that have caused you to fail. 3. Decide how you might do things differently if you tried again. 4. Decide if you want to try again. 5. If it is appropriate, try again,	1. The Desert. 2. The Treat. 3. Drunken Driving.	*Full Sequence Rehearsal* 1. Review of Hassle Logs. 2. Role-play: Triggers + Cues. + Reminders + Anger Reducers. + Self-evaluation + Skillstreaming skill.
using your revised approach.		

Notes

1. An extended presentation of Anger Control Training procedure appears in Feindier and Ecton (1986) and Goldstein and Glick (1987).
2. An extended presentation of the procedures of moral education appears in Goldstein and Glick (1987) and Zimmerman (1983).

References

Agras, W. S., 'Transfer during systematic desensitization therapy', *Behavior Research and Therapy, 5*, (1967) 193-199.

Arbuthnot, J., & Gordon, D. A., Personality. In H.C. Quay (ed.), *Handbook of juvenile delinquency*, (New York, John Wiley,1983).

Bandura, A., *Aggression: A social learning analysis*, (Englewood Cliffs, NJ, Prentice Hall, 1973).

Comstock, G., Media influences on aggression. In A. P. Goldstein (ed.), *Prevention and control of aggression*, (Elmsford, NY, Pergamon, 1983).

Dreikurs, R., Grunwald, B. B., & Pepper, F. C., *Maintaining sanity in the classroom*, (New York, Harper & Row, 1971).

Feindler, E. L., & Ecton, R., *Anger control training*, (Elmsford, NY, Pergamon, 1986).

Feindier, E. L., & Fremouw, W. J., 'Stress inoculation training for adolescent anger problems', in D. Meichenbaum & M. E. Jaremko (eds.), *Stress reduction and prevention*, (New York: Plenum,1983).

Fleming, D., *Teaching negotiation skills to pre-adolescents*, (unpublished doctoral dissertation, Syracuse University, 1976).

Gibbs, J. C., *Small group sociomoral treatment programs: Dilemmas for use with conduct-disordered or antisocial adolescents or preadolescents*, (unpublished manuscript, Ohio State University, 1986).

Gold, M., 'Scholastic experiences, self-esteem, and delinquent behavior: A theory for alternative schools', *Crime & Delinquency, 17*, 290-309 (1978).

Golden, R., *Teaching resistance-reducing behavior to high school students*. (unpublished doctoral dissertation, Syracuse University, 1975).

Goldstein, A. P, *Psychological skill training*, (Elmsford, NY, Pergamon, 1981).

Goldstein, A. P. & Glick, B., *Aggression replacement training: A comprehensive intervention for aggressive youth*, (Champaign, IL, Research Press, 1987).

Goldstein, A. P., Glick, B., Irwin, M. J., Pask-McCartney, C., & Rubama, L., *Reducing delinquency: Intervention in the community*, (Elmsford, NY, Pergamon, 1989).

Goldstein, A. R., & Kanfer, R. H., *Maximizing treatment gains: Transfer enhancement in psychotherapy*. (New York, Academic Press, 1979).

Goldstein, A. R., Monti, P. J., Sardino, T. J., & Green, D. J., *Police crisis intervention*, (Elmsford, NY, Pergamon, 1979).

Goldstein, A. P., Sprafkin, R. P., Gershaw, N. J., & Klein, P., *Skillstreaming the adolescent: A structured learning approach to teaching prosocial skills*, (Champaign, IL., Research Press,1980).

Gruber, R. P., 'Behavior therapy: Problems in generalization', *Behavior Therapy, 2,* (1971) pp. 361-368.

Guttman, E. S., 'Effects of short-term psychiatric treatment for boys in two California youth authority institutions', in D. C. Gibbons (ed.), *Delinquent Behavior,* (Englewood Cliffs, NJ: Prentice Hall, 1970).

Guzzetta, R. A., *Acquisition and transfer of empathy by parents of early adolescents through structured learning training,* (unpublished doctoral dissertation, Syracuse University 1974).

Jennings, R. L., *The use of structured teaming techniques to teach attraction enhancing skills to residentially hospitalized lower socioeconomic emotionally disturbed children and adolescents: A psychotherapy analogue investigation.* (unpublished doctoral dissertation, University of Iowa 1975).

Karoly, P., & Steffen, J. J. (eds.), *Improving the long-term effects of Psychotherapy,* (New York, Gardner,1980).

Klein, M. W., Impressions of juvenile gang members. *Adolescence, 3,* (1968a) pp. 53-78.

Klein, M. W., *The Ladino Hills project* (Final report), (Washington, DC, Office of Juvenile Delinquency and Youth Development, 1968b).

Klein, M. W., *Street gangs and street workers.* (Englewood Cliffs, NJ, Prentice Hall, 1971).

Klein, M. W., & Crawford, L. Y., 'Groups, gangs and cohesiveness', in J. F. Short (ed.), *Gang delinquency and delinquent subcultures,* (New York, Harper & Row, 1968).

Kohlberg, L.,'Stage and sequence: The cognitive-developmental approach to socialization', in D. A. Goslin (ed.), *Handbook of socialization theory and research,* (Chicago, Rand McNally, 1969).

Kohlberg, L., *Collected papers on moral development and moral education.* (Cambridge, MA., Harvard University, Center for Moral Education, 1973).

Kohlberg, L., 'Moral stages and moralization: The cognitive-developmental approach', in T. Lickona (ed.), *Moral development and behavior: Theory, research, and social issues,* (New York: Holt, Rinehart, & Winston, 1976).

Litwack, S. E., *'The use of the helper therapy principle to increase therapeutic effectiveness and reduce therapeutic resistance: Structured teaming therapy with resistant adolescents,'* (unpublished doctoral dissertation, Syracuse University, 1976).

Moon, J. R., & Eisler, R. M., 'Anger control: An experimental comparison of three behavioral treatments', *Behavior Therapy, 14,* (1983), pp. 493-505.

Novaco, R. W., *Anger control: The development and evaluation of an experimental treatment,* (Lexington, MA., D. C. Heath, 1975).

O'Leary, K. D., O'Leary, S., & Becker, W. C., 'Modification of a deviant sibling interaction pattern in the home', *Behavior Research and Therapy, 5,* (1967), pp. 113-120.

Patterson, G. R., Cobb, J. A., & Ray, R. S., 'A social engineering technology for retraining the families of aggressive boys', in H. E. Adams & I. P. Unikel (eds.), *Issues and trends in behavior therapy,* (Springfield, IL., Charles C. Thomas, 1973).

Raleigh, R., *Individual versus group structured learning therapy for assertiveness training with senior and junior high school students,* (unpublished doctoral dissertation, Syracuse University, 1979).

Redl, F., & Wineman, D., *The aggressive child,* (New York, Free Press, 1957).

Reissman, F., 'The helper therapy principle', *Social Work, 10*, (1965), pp. 27-32.

Rogers, C. R., *Client-centered therapy: Its practice, implications, and theory*, (Boston, Houghton Mifflin, 1951).

Rogers, C. R., 'The necessary and sufficient conditions of therapeutic personality change,' *Journal of Consulting Psychology, 21*, (1957), pp. 95-103.

Slavson, S. R., A *textbook in analytic group psychotherapy*, (New York, International Universities Press, 1964).

Solomon, E., *Structural learning therapy with abusive parents*, (unpublished doctoral dissertation, Syracuse University, 1978).

Sturm, D., *Therapist aggression tolerance and dependent tolerance under standardized conditions of hostility and dependency*, (unpublished doctoral dissertation, Syracuse University, 1979).

Tharp, R. G., & Wetzel, R. J., *Behavior modification in the natural environment*, (New York, Academic Press, 1969).

Trief, P., *The reduction of egocentrism in acting-out adolescents by structured learning therapy*, (unpublished doctoral dissertation, Syracuse University, 1976).

Truax, C. B., Wargo, D. G., & Silber, L. D., 'Effects of group psychotherapy with high accurate empathy and nonresponsive warmth upon female institutionalized delinquents,' *Journal of Abnormal Psychology, 71*, (1966) pp. 267-274.

Walker, H. M., *The acting-out child: Coping with classroom disruption*, (Boston, Allyn & Bacon, 1979).

Zimmerman, D., 'Moral education', in Center for Research on Aggression (ed.), *Prevention and control of aggression*, (Elmsford, NY., Pergamon, 1983).

Prison Poem

By 'Ali'

This stinking fucking shithole
full of stinking fucking hags,
who love to pinch your undies
and blagg your fucking fags.
Big black facey yardys
with big black attitude,
watch you down their noses
and moan about the food.
Lazy, sweaty scagheads
go sliding down the walls,
pestering for units
to make their desperate calls.
Don't look at Noncing Nancy
the scum the whole wing hates,
don't let her smoke your roaches
or you'll soon be branded mates.
Stinking filthy toilets
with tampons free for all,
where dykes do their recruiting
and smudge bogies down the wall.
Clinging to the brickwork
lies silent, festering mould,
fed by steamy showers
and the freezing fucking cold.
You can hear the jingle jangle
of keys in corridors,
locking up the bitches
cunts and slags and whores.
The night brings junkies screaming
contorted by their cramps,
The morning brings them begging
for DF's, burn and stamps.
This stinking fucking shit hole
this cage of social scum,
too sad and dumb to realise
or care what they've become.
This stinking fucking shit hole
this HMP, this HELL.

Somebody's Daughter Theatre

Celebrating Difference with Women in Prison

Maud Clark

I no longer believe in the necessity of prisons, I see the model of 'prison' as archaic and totally ineffective, the system itself simply reinforcing and compounding issues that have brought women to prison.

My understandings come from working directly and intensively with prisoners and ex-prisoners in Melbourne in theatre for twenty years. In this work I have witnessed the power of theatre to activate questioning about current structures and policies that directly impact on women and to posit other possibilities other than prison.

When I first went into prison as a drama student over twenty years ago I only knew what I had been trained to believe about prisons and prisoners. It took me some time to understand what prison actually does to women and how important it is to our society for people like me to believe in the myth of the necessity of prison and the necessity of keeping 'prisoners' separate. These myths about prison and prisoners are the only way such abuse of fellow human beings can be tolerated.

But most importantly, I had no idea that I believed the myth that prisoners were *different* to me, that somehow they were *different* from 'normal' women and that this belief defined me as not being one of 'those' women. Not being one of 'those' women gave me power and protection. Believing prisoners were different meant I was safe and that what happened in the prison world was OK.

It is actually a body memory for me when I realised that I held this prejudice. I was standing in a circle of women prisoners in a workshop and knew that the women standing around me were not different, that in fact I could be one of them. It was a frightening and a defining moment and I recognized that the bottom line was that I had not seen these woman as equals. This realisation made me feel suddenly unsafe.

Over the years I have come to understand just how unsafe being one of those women can be. Back then, I didn't even know that there was such a thing as a strip search or being urined, naked; I had no comprehension of the devastation of separation from those you love – and, if I'd been told, I wouldn't have recognised it because it was happening to them and they were different, they somehow wouldn't feel it in the same way as I would. When I realised I was no different it meant I or anyone I knew

101

could be a prisoner, it forced me to confront the brutality and inhumanity that is the life of a woman prisoner.

This memory is important because in the main the people who control women; the decision makers that determine the laws and conditions that keep our prisons in operation and audiences who do not question the necessity of prisons believe as I used to. There are beliefs and expectations that go with the label prisoner – crim, junkie, murderer – that separate these people from being woman, lover, mother, sister that keep us from seeing the person and keep us comfortable with the fact of prisons. There is a belief that somehow women choose to be prisoners and that in the same way they have made choices to arrive at the prison, that these women will have choices when they are released.

Also the women in the prison expect those that work with them will carry this belief of difference/separation, they do not expect to be met equally – and in most cases they are right. I have come to understand that for most women in the prison system this 'separation' has started many years before they came to prison, and that this 'separation' in the main affects the poorest and most vulnerable in our society. We punish our most powerless.

For transnational prisoners the separation, prejudice and isolation that they suffer in effect places these women in a prison within a prison. They are isolated because of race, language and culture – the stereotyping and separation that happens to these transnational prisoners based on 'difference', in fact happens to all women prisoners.

Of course the separation for women from other countries is much harsher and more clearly underlined. I think of a Japanese woman who was in prison months before a dictionary was procured. From the moment she had been picked up at the airport, throughout police questioning, court proceedings, to sentencing and imprisonment not only was there no one that she knew, there was no one that she could talk to; it was many months before she was able to communicate.

There have been a number of Lebanese women imprisoned, two have been released recently, one imprisoned for nine years; she had five children, five children she did not see for nine years. The other was imprisoned for seven years, in that time her father died, her mother died and her daughter grew to be a young woman. When her mother died she lost any connection with her daughter through phone or letters as the father's family shunned her. At the end of their sentences these women were driven to the airport and deported.

In Melbourne, Vietnamese women are placed together because they look the same and come from the same general geographical area, it is presumed they will understand each other, will want to be together, that it will be better for them to be together. In fact it is simply easier for the system for them to be clumped together and in doing so it isolates this community more from the mainstream of the prison hence strengthening already strong prejudice. This presumption that these women want to be together is wrong – often there is great conflict – e.g. with women from North and South Vietnam huge tensions exist.

It is the same set of presumptions operating when we clump women together in prison – there is the presumption of sameness. In the same way that prejudice against the Vietnamese women grows in the prison community because of this isolation, in the wider community outside of the prison our perceptions of prisoners similarly become more distorted because women in prison are so isolated.

The understandings that in fact unite women in prison come from their shared experiences of separation, of disempowerment, of the continual physical abuse they face daily in the prison environment.

Prison management is able to discriminate against women from other countries because they have less power in the prison community and therefore they are usually more compliant. A Vietnamese woman has her day leaves reduced from eight to two hours, the next week the day leave is cancelled altogether. This would not happen to more vocal members of the prison population. Again it is exactly why our prisons still operate – prisoners have no voice in our current structures.

The decisions made that control these women's lives are based on the world views and experiences of individuals who have no comprehension of the experiences and lives of the women concerned.

What real understanding do we have of the woman who is a courier when that is the only way she can feed her child, or the woman who has killed the violent partner that has abused her for years. What understanding of the woman who steals or prostitutes for the money to pay for her drugs, who has been abused since she was a child and finds it impossible to function without deadening the pain. When she is placed within the prison she is medicated so highly from the medical centre in the prison that when she is taken to court the judge refuses to hear the case. Women are imprisoned for drug use and are released addicted to psych medication officially administered to them.

A very spirited twenty-five year old woman, who has been in and out of institutions and prisons since she was nine, was at her work place in the prison when she jumped onto a table and started singing along with the radio, 'Never gonna give you up, never gonna let you down' – other women sang with her, the officer in charge was beside himself and sent her out. Within minutes she heard herself called to the medical centre – her medication was increased considerably, immediately. Yet she was imprisoned for her drug use.

So where does theatre fit in and particularly for women from other countries?

To begin, working truly creatively you can't work with inequality. There can be no 'us' and 'them' – working creatively means an equal meeting place. It means really 'seeing' and really 'hearing' someone. This might sound pretty basic and that this is what happens in all human interaction – unfortunately it does not and it is less likely to happen in situations where there is a strong imbalance of power. You have to really 'see' someone to catch the source of their creative spark – to feed it, to nurture it. This is a great privilege because you are actually working with the heart of someone – you are working with soul.

In really 'seeing' and 'hearing' there can be no room for stereotypes, you can play with stereotypes, play with masks but that is all they are; the faces we use to survive. Working with women from other countries this is even more potent because we carry so many conceptions about who someone is based on race; which is exactly the same stereotyping that occurs in belief about prisoners.

Ironically it is through the meeting as unique individuals that true connectedness takes place. When we did the play *The Malways* a number of Vietnamese women performed, they told the story of their journey as 'boat people' to Australia – after the performance the attitude of the prison population had changed from one of prejudice to inclusion.

Theatre is about voice – this is very important in a prison situation where women don't have one. Having your own voice, not someone speaking for you, about you and defining who you are, be it – lawyers, judges, psychologists, policy makers – but speaking your own truth and being heard. As one woman says 'people are talking about me, my life, but getting it wrong, not saying the truth. It's not me. But I'm not allowed to talk' (Call My Name, Somebody's Daughter Theatre, 1994).

A lot of time is spent on breathing, finding your own breath, finding your centre. To breathe deeply puts us in contact with what we're really feeling, for many women this has never been safe – to stay with what they are really feeling.

Much of the work is body work – being in your body, allowing the body to be massaged, allowing the body to run, roll on the floor. Many women have been abused – eighty per cent of the women have been sexually abused and if we look at physical abuse that figure is in the high nineties. How often women echo the words, 'fly away, numb myself … I must leave myself. Never enter my body'. The first time incest was mentioned was in 1988 at Fairlea in Melbourne. It was thought that it would be best if a woman who had not been abused perform the particular scene. Again I was totally ignorant of the extremity of this abuse. Out of eight performers seven were incest victims. After the performance many women in the prison started talking about their own abuse for the first time. The psychologist was inundated. The code of silence had been lifted.

Theatre work is about being totally inside the body – reclaiming your own body – feeling your cells come alive. Trusting your body, trusting someone to massage your body. This work is extremely potent in an environment where your body is not your own – where it can be invaded with strip searches, handcuffed, observed though cameras.

Theatre is about creating a world woven with women's own stories – that's the bridge, that's the meeting point. Not moving away from who they are, where they have come from but claiming it – not having their experiences dissected for meaning but finding their own knowings.

Many want to dismiss our work in art, music, theatre as 'therapy', therefore it is not real art – not to be taken seriously. In dismissing the work as 'therapy' it thereby diminishes the worth, the creativity of prisoners, again separating these women from ourselves. I am not here diminishing the work of therapists but this is not what we are, there is no pretence of wanting to dissect experiences for therapy but for creation. This is extremely important for the women as there is no judgement, no reporting. It is therapy only in so far as art, music, theatre has been therapy for our communities for centuries and some of the most talented, artists, performers, writers are in our prisons.

I cannot tell you how many times people have said – but these people have to be professional actors they can't be prisoners. Why can't they?

Finally and very importantly if theatre is working, audiences will be taken on a journey, they will feel what the character feels, their heart will be engaged their imagination awakened, they will understand the experience not only from their head but the very cells in their body. This is where theatre can activate change and to posit possibilities for structures other than prison. The myths that we hold about prisons and prisoners can be broken down. And if this journey is made with actors who happen to be prisoners or ex-prisoners it is breaking down some very strong world views held by audiences.

I will not only hear but feel what it is for a seventeen or a seventy year old woman to stand naked while an officer inspects her body, feel the officers eyes inspect her scars, flinch as she lifts her breasts, separates her legs further. Feel how much harder it is for her if she is bleeding when she has to wee into a jar, naked with her hands in the air. Feel the violation as a fifty-seven year old woman, who was in a domestic violence situation for years, is made to bend over and part her cheeks, repeatedly and then stand as officers stare at the scars on her body, particularly interested in the one that looks like a ships anchor.

In making that journey with her, I am no longer separate and observing, I feel it.

I feel the violation, the rape. As an audience I am likely to find this abuse intolerable and then start to look more closely and discover that eighty per cent of women in prison have been sexually abused. Discover that this abuse is usually extremely violent and usually started in childhood. I might begin to understand that women don't choose prison and gain understandings of the pathways that have led them there. In making a journey with a woman I will feel the devastation of being separated from her children and might come to question why this happens, understand that the children are being punished as well as the mother. I might begin to see that we can accept all of this only if we see these women as different and that they deserve punishment. If I then come to question 'punishment' I might begin to understand that our structures need to be changed. That prison is not an answer.

Theatre does have this power, to illuminate what we could not see before because it is about finding connectedness as human beings. The very connectedness that women in prison have been denied.

A female teacher worked closely with a woman who had had her child with her in the prison for the first three years of her daughter's life. It was time for her daughter to leave the prison and her mother still had four years of imprisonment. It was only when this teacher came to a performance some eight years later and made the journey through the performance that she said she understood the excruciating pain of that separation. Last year we performed in Canberra, the DPP came to the performance and immediately went home and faxed every judge and magistrate in the state to say – 'you must see this!' A Federal MP went away from the performance to try to arrange a performance at Government House. They understood that the individuals making decisions about womens lives needed to have some real understandings of their lives. We see it as imperative to work with schools, not only because it might help teenagers who are heading down the same paths as the women themselves, but also because these are the decision makers of the future, the men and women who are going to be making decisions that will determine the conditions and possibilities of prisoners lives.

Prison does not work, it is a brutalising, archaic system whose violence perpetuates itself. Working in small communities does work – where individuals can be actually seen. In the end it doesn't matter whether a woman is fired by music or economics, what matters is that she has real choices, finally what matters is that we are brave enough to try other ways.

An officer came to see the play, *Call My Name* a play exploring women's experiences in prison, the officer came stumbling from the theatre saying, 'If this is what I've been doing – it's wrong.'

The Role of the Camshaft in Offender Rehabilitation

Chris Johnston

'I'm gonna fuck it off'. He leaned back in his chair in that way I've only seen prisoners do, leaning back so far that a slight nudge on the two chair legs taking the weight, would send him flying. Risk, edge, on the edge of control, on the edge of collapse. 'Don't do that.' 'What?' 'Don't fuck it off.' Trying to be positive, I'm reminded how pathetic it often sounds, 'being positive'. We both looked again at the piece of kinetic sculpture on the table. 'It's whack', he went on, amplifying the point by putting his legs up on the table, allowing the chair to tilt even further back, but now getting some counterbalance from the table. 'I mean if you walked into a ...fuckin...' – he tries to remember where it is we're going to exhibit the sculptures – ... 'place... art... gallery... whatever – and saw THAT – you'd go 'That's shit! Wouldn't you? Well, wouldn't you?' Trying to frame a reply, the thing that worried me more than anything else, was that the truthful answer was probably 'Yes'.

Artists and creatives who rage against the system, turn instinctively to others who rage. For there's a reluctance in us to channel personal creativity into products that simply oil the sophisticated clockworks of consumerism; instead we seek out alternative patterns of production and collaboration in the hope that some measure of autonomy is achievable. Perhaps it may even be possible, we conjecture, to build a sub-culture within the host culture that simply cannot be infiltrated and commodified. If we establish a ring of wagons secure enough, we might just maintain our alternative value-set for sufficiently long to keep at bay the baying, bloody enthusiasms of the crazed meritocrats who swoop around us.

The great community arts movement of the seventies, which struggled and sprawled messily on into subsequent decades, was a reflection of this aspiration. When Ed Berman first started up and rolled out his Fun Bus at Inter-Action's headquarters in Camden Town, he helped to shift decisively the focal point of creative arts work from 'the place to which others must come' to 'the place where people already are' (my parenthesis). Ed was the inspiration for many, and despite his flirtation in later life with the government of Margaret Thatcher, his determination not to wait for the working class to recognise the validity of community arts practice but to deliver it wholesale and free to schools and centres and streets, created a model that still perseveres. Other pioneers were making similar journeys. It was not long since Charles Parker had walked out from the BBC with a portable tape recorder under his arm to record workers in their workplaces, later to present their stories, naked of any critical or social contextualising, on the BBC in his seminal, documentary radio ballads. He went on to found Banner Theatre with the express purpose of making a direct conduit between the voices of workers and the ears of audiences. Partnerships of this kind, between Ed Berman's Professor Doggge's Troupe and estate residents in Camden Town on one hand, and between Parker's fellow actors and industrial workers on the other, have been made, broken and remade in a thousand combinations since. And in the centre of each is often found this shared empathy between creatives who have felt themselves to be disenfranchised – and workers and others who very clearly were.

Rideout was formed in 1998 by myself and Saul Hewish to run arts programmes in prisons. We had earlier each headed up companies with a national remit – Saul had been director of Geese Theatre (UK) and I had been director of Insight Arts Trust – and now we wanted some freedom to run projects without the responsibilities of maintaining companies and fulfilling annual contracts with statutory bodies. We wanted the opportunity to establish new, experimental partnerships with that often confused, difficult but creative constituency of serving prisoners. We were fortunate enough to be offered a contract with a Young Offenders Institution in the West Midlands and became involved in developing a module to complement their Cognitive Skills Programme. This became ubiquitously known as an 'Experiential Testing Programme.' (I don't know why but it's always comforting to boast you're running something with a title no one can understand). What it in fact means is that we test a group of some eight to ten young prisoners on their ability to put their 'newly-acquired' cognitive skills into practice, through a series of individual and group challenges. After their main course is finished, our task is to assess the learning. We still run this programme and the Prison Services Offending Behaviour Programme Unit centrally has taken an interest in our work, although our suspicion is that we're a little too maverick to become 'built-in' to their accredited programme. And besides, we don't use the orthodox language, those key phrases and definitions which have been carried over from the originators of the programmes in Canada, Robert Ross and Liz Fabiano. The Cognitive Skills Programme itself, to which our ETP is a coda, normally happens over several weeks and takes the prisoners through a variety of challenges which are intended to kick-start a more comprehensive, intellectual reflexivity than they are likely to be familiar with.[1]

But we quickly became aware of how limited was the range of experiences which could be generated within a programme of this kind. It is limited primarily by the conceptual parameters of cognitive skills orthodoxies which promote the importance of thinking skills above all else. Empathic and affective skills are less valued here, and there is, in our opinion, insufficient attention paid to the social and psychological profile of the individual offender at the time of this new learning. We would argue that thinking skills are useful of course, essential even, but their usefulness is relative to the point of development which the offender is at. Sharpening thinking skills in an offender who has made no significant decision to change their lifestyle or life choices may leave the teachers open to the charge of merely improving the offender's ability to commit crime successfully. And a cognitive skills course will very likely not even seriously raise the key question of a change in personal culture. Or if it does, the rigidity of the programme means there is little scope for the teacher to interrogate or challenge a pupil outside the centrally determined series of questions and tasks. (All sessions within such programmes are video recorded and sent to the Prison Service for scrutiny. Comments and criticisms are sent back if it is felt that the teacher is straying too far from the orthodoxy.) There is clearly a debate to be had here, not just about the issue of the central control of such programmes, but also about why there is so little effective collaboration between creatives, educationalists and others in the development of new programmes which are appropriate for our own prisoners.

So we've been constantly looking for opportunities to develop other programmes that allowed a wider remit of research and development. In particular, such programmes would probe more deeply into the personal mythology of the offender and the unique circumstances of their offending. They would also very likely incorporate a conscious search for the location of the dreaming self. For within cognitive skills work there is no place for engagement with, or understanding of, the role which fantasy plays in the psyche of the offender. In fact much of the purpose of that project is the very elimination of fantasy, the scraping out of illogical, fantastical thought from the head. For if a thought or an assumption cannot survive the rigours of reductionist, positivist argument then, it will be argued, it has no place in the strategic patterns of the learning individual in this context. And that's fair enough, to a degree. For if John, on his second day at work, tells the boss he John should be doing the boss' job and getting the boss' money, and if when asked why, cannot offer a better argument than he has a fantastic girlfriend who needs to be taken out, then he very likely is thinking fantastically. He is not thinking realistically. And if, on receiving a rejection to this proposal, John goes on to 'lamp' the boss in his own office for his cheekiness, then it's clear that his thinking around the issue of employment needs some very serious overhaul. It's possible that John is in fact locked into a kind of fantasy idea about what he is capable of doing and what he deserves. So a Cognitive Skills course, which strips down his thinking and examines its patterns, as one might strip down a car and lay it out in a garage, is a pretty good idea. And if it helps John go into his next job with his thinking head better screwed on, and a more realistic understanding of conventional boss-employee relationships, that can't be a bad thing.

Nevertheless this instinct for fantasy is human. In the above imaginary story, it's been channelled into the wrong area. But once displaced from there, where does it go? Perhaps it's not just a question of eliminating the fantasy thinking, but understanding the relationship between different kinds of thinking. And then helping the offender to relocate the fantasy thinking into a different area altogether. Because it won't necessarily just 'disappear'. The individual won't suddenly just stop thinking fantastically because he's told that his thinking is dysfunctional. It'll simply be projected on to a different screen. After all, the instinct to fantasise and creatively re-imagine 'reality' away from its moorings is as old as cave paintings.

'What's the point of fucking it off when you just spent three days making it?' Ok, three days was a bit of an exaggeration, he didn't actually work on it for three days, but he was in the room for three days. And he must have done some work on it otherwise we'd never have got to this point. 'Dunno. It's shit.' 'It's not shit, it's good.'

'It doesn't even work.' 'That's because you haven't tightened the elastic bands like we said was necessary. If you did that, then it would work.' 'I'm tired.' This is always the moment when I have to stop myself screaming with pain and laughter. When a nineteen year old, doing time, nothing to do all day, with all his meals provided and with more opportunity to sleep than a dormouse in winter, complains about being tired. But I check the impulse and try a different tack. 'I suppose you were up all night wanking.' 'Maybe.' Now before you reach for your indignation, Dear Reader, I should point out that I'm not the first to raise this subject. The prisoner in question has already shared with us that he thrashes the monkey three or four times a day. I think it came into a discussion about his future career. Did I mention what that was going to be? He wants to be a porn star. When he announced this, there was considerable unanimity in our project team that we should do our damnest to dissuade him. Not that this was really necessary, since the idea was clearly a prison-inspired fantasy cooked up by too much time away from girls, tuning in to Channel Five and staring down at his own cock. But we did it anyway, pointing out how the porn industry was run by sleazebags and hyenas and how everyone got treated like meat. We desisted from presenting the argument that he wouldn't be able to keep it up for long enough at critical moments, because that would have only earned us another withering stare of derision and contempt. So we simply made our puritan points and left it open for further discussion. 'You need to tighten your elastic band, do the sandpapering and then you can paint it – after that, the sculpture's finished.' We both looked back at the sculpture, me in hope, him in despair.

Given the focus within cognitive skills work on thinking and logical analysis, we've been concerned that the 'core' or 'interior part' of the individual psyche is remaining unengaged. That the imaginative/feeling part of the self stays for the most part untouched by all the talk of 'Causes and Consequences', 'Stop and Think', 'Consider all Factors' and 'Other Peoples Views'. (CAC, SAT, CAF & OPV.) The fact that the individual dreams of being a porn star may actually be a key factor in any dialogue with him about constructing a different life. It doesn't mean we support the ambition, certainly not, but it might reasonably be argued that 'starting where the individual actually is', looking at the imaginative and mythological viewpoint through which he or she now looks at the world, may lead us to a better understanding of the impulses, aspirations and self-understandings which currently make up the functioning person within the personality. And if we don't understand this internal dreaming, and simply try and 'graft on' an apparently more wholesome set of lifestyle goals, they may just fall off again within a matter of months. And judging by re-offending rates, that is pretty much what happens. (Although it's still true that those who take any kind of course inside do better than those who take none.) Besides, we know that for many young offenders, their experience of crime is based on a kind of easy dreaming in which fantastic solutions to problems are preferred over mundane, difficult ones. The individual, faced with a problem, fantasises a solution in desperation, then goes out to execute this, often making a hash of the whole thing and then regretting it. (Although not always – let's not kid ourselves that crime never pays – the number of young offenders inside who are proud of their success rate is significant.). But supposing on this occasion, the individual offender does meet inglorious failure, then never mind, for through both conscious and – probably – unconscious reassessment of the incident, it can be redefined subsequently as a glorious, heroic failure (which was only failure at all due to the most appalling bad luck on the day). So this dreaming is both anticipatory and reflective. It's part of the preparation and the evaluation. It's pursued ahead of time, building up in the mind a sequence of predictive images (what will happen during 'the job') – and this helps to avoid grappling with the issue of possible injury to others ('I'm only going to show him the knife') – and it's employed retrospectively to exonerate the self from blame. Should the evaluation take place in prison, then others are there to help with that, comforting the offender with assurances that all this was more bad luck than bad judgement. The incident can be painted in the colours of heroic, glorious failure in an honest struggle against the odds. This is not the dreaming self of Arnold Mindell of which the individual psyche is unaware, whose affects are only realised through dreams and involuntary gestures, but the active, conscious recreation of reality in order to achieve a kind of privileged status within society, that of the honourable trickster who has been ruthlessly compelled by society to live outside the law. In Rideout's work in the Midlands we work almost exclusively with young offenders, and here the dreaming is to be seen both at its most vivid and its most transparent. The act of dreaming is a kind of self-hypnosis in which unsustainable aspirations are buckled on like the armour of ancient warriors. Those who argue intellectual rigour against it, are either fought or discounted because they have not the same privileged access to the experiences of these warriors. These young men have seen the promised land, and it belongs to them. It will be theirs. But – of course – unfortunately – they have wrought it almost entirely within their imaginations. And the imagination, let it be said, is a well-fortified castle which the teachers of cognitive skills can only throw straws at. This castle needs to be approached a different way.

There's always a danger in beginning to generalise about any group of people, that you betray those individuals who do not fit the generalisation. So it needs to be made plain that we're not identifying here those who because of stress or bad judgement or sudden wild anger commit a crime which is notable for the fact that no other crimes are listed under it on the offender's sentencing report. We're talking instead about another group who are sometimes identified as 'career criminals' (which always suggests to me a rather unlikely image of a suit, a tie and briefcase) or those who are simply too lazy or who have been betrayed so frequently by carers and parents and authority figures, that they have never learnt for long any different way of life other than stealing, selling drugs or doing fraud to survive. For these individuals, the dreaming becomes compensatory, to comfort the self and to placate any rising sense of empathic morality which might spring from thinking about how others' might be hurt by the crimes. And too, the dreaming also provides an escape from the prospect of having to sink into the dull, shameful, degrading series of tasks which make up gainful employment.

It's only by recognising how central a role imagination plays in the definition – and redefinition – of self, that we can begin to construct programmes which do more than vaguely tinker with ideas of rehabilitation. But in saying this, it's also important to define 'imagination' quite broadly – so it encompasses firstly, memory (and how we perceive or re-make/re-member past events), secondly, how we see ourselves in the present (our perception of our self in relation to others as well as our abilities) and thirdly, our sense of what the future might be (which is a largely speculative and subjective exercise, although the parameters of speculation are always defined for us). Taking all these images, regrets, grievances and anticipations together as a kind of world view, adding in our learned fears and acquired hopes, we can begin to define the shape of a personal mythology. Of course no personal mythology consists entirely of unique, individual elements, for much of it has been burnt into us by our shared cultures. Besides, we have deliberately borrowed much of it from others who we feel are fellow travellers on the same road. Criminal code is an interesting example of how such attitudes are borrowed, for while it is easy to have this articulated by prisoners, it is also possible to identify differences of interpretation, and too, a split sometimes between an expressed opinion ('You should never grass') and a personal practice ('If the other is not a 'right' person, he doesn't deserve that defence'). And this raises the question of to what extent any personal mythology is actually conscious. What is often recognisable in groups of prisoners is a quality of an absence of self-knowledge – young offenders often simply don't 'know themselves' (in the sense in which they understand why they act the way they do.) Yet they will only occasionally admit to such lack of self-knowledge, preferring to resort to criminal code or cliché to answer questions about the motivation for particular behaviours. But this absence of self-knowledge does not necessarily mean the absence of a personal mythology, as long as one admits that part of this mythology is itself unconscious. And indeed chroniclers of myth from Jung onwards, in particular Joseph Campbell, have asserted the intimate connectedness between the role of myth and the need for social groups to carry through life, a set of unconscious collective sentiments.

Of course this is not mythology in the strict sense of the word because it is has no mythological shape. It is not understood or 'carried' as story, although key 'mythologised' incidents might be cited by a prisoner as central to the way they look at the world. Incidents which happened to them, their brother, their friend, their co-defendant, etc. But the point is that this interiorised amalgam of sentiments, desires and experiences could be articulated as mythology because it has all the essential elements which myth or story requires. Rehabilitation work may therefore usefully set itself the task of doing precisely this; creating a narrative out of these raw elements almost as an archaeologist would drain a seabed to reveal the contours of a civilisation that once lived on that land, before the seas came. In this way the personal mythology is given shape, definition and imagery. Once this is achieved, then (and not before) the components of that myth can be interrogated, challenged and possibly rewritten. It is with this nod to Narrative Therapy therefore that we established templates for the pilot programme which anticipated Repeating Stories, our six-week sculpture project. Here we worked hard in the limited time available, to identify and give shape to these personal mythologies. For one prisoner, we found that drawing on pirate stories drew us closest to a realisation of his set of beliefs. Once dramatised in scenarios, the value system of the offender became far more transparent – it came alive in a way which simply wasn't possible while it was a series of short cryptic sentences describing his view of society. Despite the rather obvious (and artificially wrought) device being employed, we were able to conjure a scenario which put flesh and blood on his changing opinions. And, crucially, we were able to conjure for him a scenario that enabled him to act out – within this mythological universe – 'the leaving of the pirates'. For he had articulated an intent to leave behind his criminal life of old once he left prison. So, within the fiction, he first tried to persuade his bloodthirsty cohorts to abandon piracy as he planned to. In this he failed. So, there was nothing left for it then but to accept the punishment which pirates traditionally mete out to mutineers. He was forced to walk the plank at sword-point (so to speak) and jump into the sea (OK, off the chairs on to the chapel floor).

We were looking at a rectangular box about three foot wide, two foot across and six inches deep, on top of which sat most prominently, an abstract wooden sculpture of a man, a kind of ogre with nails coming out of his head. This wooden sculpture did also look rather like an angry phallus, although it was debatable whether, at this precise moment, this should be pointed out. Two smaller abstracts of wood also sat on the box. Each of these three figures sat on a 'track' cut into the box, allowing them to be moved by pulleys within. Inside the box was a series of crisscrossing pieces of string and elastic which facilitated the movements. So the spectator pulled a cord on the side of the box, and the figures moved. According to the sculptor, the larger figure represented a bully who was threatening the smaller figure. If you pulled a lever, the 'bully' started to move towards the 'victim', but as this happened, the third figure, the 'rescuer', moved to intervene. It was this third figure which represented the young man who had made the sculpture. Well, that's what he said. It was a neat enough idea, and it pretty much fulfilled the brief we'd set, even though there was no specific reference to offending within the piece. We had been cheered by the notion that this particular prisoner had cast himself in the role of the rescuer as his behaviour on the project to date had suggested that rescuer wasn't conventionally his natural role. It was clear that the image could also be read in different ways. He wanted to be seen as the rescuer, and we wanted to encourage that sense of identity, but to what extent had he been the bully? Or the victim? What we could be sure of, is that this three-way relationship was important to him, despite his reluctance to complete the sculpture. At times it was also very clear that he wanted to destroy it. But why? Because he preferred to be seen as incapable of achieving anything? Because he preferred to be seen as a victim himself of his own rages? Or perhaps because to complete would be to hand us some kind of victory. And that's not even beginning to ask questions about the moving phallus.

Sometimes it's a good idea to raise the issue of the alternative perception – what a more psychotherapeutic pair of eyes might see in a piece of work – but also, sometimes, it isn't. Sometimes to do this may be seen as taking the piss, or as a kind of damning judgement on the creator's work – especially since it accesses terms of reference unfamiliar to the creator. So it was a matter of taking each situation separately on this project, and often we kept quiet. Another sculptor built a model of a prison cell in the middle of a busy road. In the cell he put a photograph of himself, reading a magazine. It was beautifully made, with a door on a hinge, and a bed which folded into the wall. The sculpture perfectly conjured his narcissistic disinterest in the real world. But would it have helped to articulate this perception? He had earlier refused to continue an exercise at the very point we pointed out to him that he possibly found it difficult to ask others for help. He'd presented his body map to us (a large two-dimensional map of his key experiences located on parts of his drawn body) and talked about his experiences of stealing cars. He'd needed money, he'd said. That's why he'd stolen the cars. But he also had a large family. And some of his family members were reasonably well off. So I suggested that he found it difficult to ask for help 'From your family. It's something you don't like to do, isn't it?' At that point he just walked off and refused to discuss his presentation any further. Would it have helped therefore to have discussed our interpretation of his cell in the middle of the road? Probably not. But with more time, we might have been able to dramatise this room in a road, and play with that image, and through that playing, articulate a challenge to him which wasn't threatening, but merely questioning – much as Boal's (1979, 1992) techniques often prompt questions rather than define answers. And this way we might have effected a shift in this prisoner about himself and his vulnerability.

Back at the bench, we were looking at the box. Here, the image of bully, victim and rescuer could be looked at in several different ways. Which was the sculptor? On the next table along, a similar question might be asked, and here perhaps, a more obvious answer given. Another sculptor was strapping a boxing glove to a spring. The idea was that the spring would be levered back, and with it the bright red boxing glove. Then the lever was released and the boxing glove let fly. Just as the lever and the glove were pulled back, at the very same time, a little man (in fact an action figure sold as a child's toy) was moving towards the glove. Pow! The glove hit the man and the man fell down. Splat! The big fella got knocked down by a force even bigger than him. A heroic, glorious failure. And what did the boxing glove represent? 'Fate' said the sculptor. Such is life. You're going along and Splat! You get knocked down. Such is life. Fate rules, and I'm really an unlucky guy. Wrong place, wrong time, and here the clichés come marching like Orcs towards Helmsdeep. But what many spectators to the sculpture did not know is this – that the creator was himself responsible, by his own admission, for a series of violent thefts against pedestrians. Which might possibly incline them to think that the boxing glove more effectively represented him – the sculptor – than any idea of Fate. Well, whichever way you looked at it, the image was a key one – working with this offender, this image – and the view that it expressed of the world – that seemed like a pretty good place to start.

This group of prisoners was the third we had worked with. The first were in an adult male prison, the second in a women's gaol. For the final stretch we were in a YOI. Everyone in each group had been through the same process. Everyone – bar two prisoners who'd dropped out, one for personal reasons – had produced a piece of kinetic sculpture good enough to exhibit in a gallery. So far no one, absolutely no one, had 'fucked off' their machine, broken it, smashed it, reduced it to splintered wood and twisted metal. So I was pretty anxious it wasn't going to happen now. In fact if he punched it, I would stand in the way. I would defend it to my last, I would leap...Wait a minute, what was I saying? It's crude, it's rough, it still doesn't work... Isn't this all getting a bit personal? As I was thinking this, I became aware once more of what our not-quite-star-material pupil was saying. He was saying that the reason he'd got so left behind, the reason he was pissed off, the reason he had lost faith in the whole fucking project was because he'd been prevented. Prevented from working, prevented from developing his own ideas, prevented from expressing himself. Someone else had prevented him. This person had fucked with his head, interfered with his machine, destroyed his creativity. Christ, who's that? I'll get the bastard. That explains everything... Then I realise who he's talking about.

With each of the three groups, the process had started with drama games and exercises, geared towards getting the prisoners to externalise their feelings, ideas and reflections on certain key themes. The principal theme was crime (inevitably) and in this context, personal stories. Within those stories there were, again, key features that we wanted to identify; certain dynamic elements which if identified would start to lay bare the behaviour patterns and belief systems of the participants – such as triggers to action, repetition, and significant relationships. In every case this moved on to further examination of family, issues of grievance and self-identity – essential patches within the tapestry of personal mythology. We included some short teaching modules on image, metaphor and story. This was to encourage the participants to consciously select imagery for their sculptures that would either reveal or conceal vital episodes in their personal histories. Reveal, because we wanted them to use metaphor imaginatively (one woman chose a series of pictures of a large fish being accidentally killed by a ship), but also conceal, because we would rather them use a concealing metaphor than make no reference to the incident at all. The aim was to give everyone a similar vocabulary for tackling the later stages of the project. Once this more formal teaching section was completed, we issued body-sized pieces of paper for the creation of the body maps. Here, we adapted a popular exercise in which the participant lies down on the paper and a partner draws a body outline around them. Next, we asked each participant to draw a dotted line down the centre of the figure. We asked that everyone identify the left hand side, as a map of the past and the right, as map of the future. Then we asked that each participant searched for images, words or drawings to place on the map, either to mark an event that had happened (on the left), or one that was desired (on the right). Images were to be placed near a chosen part of the body – if you ran away from a childrens' home, an image of flight might be placed near the feet. If the escape left you with loneliness, that image might go near the heart, and connecting lines/arteries would link these two images. Participants could write or draw or cut out images or words from a large range of magazines which we provided, everything from cartoons to home furnishing to music to rock climbing. (Far more of the budget went on these we expected, and still we discovered how hard it is to find images either of black families, or of black and white figures together – outside the fashion pages).

The project proved a fascinating study of gender differences. At this stage, where visual sensibility and spatial awareness was called for, the women's' work on body maps was more sophisticated and involved more complex visual imagery. Metaphors were employed more widely. One woman had a 'shed in her head', another used those photographs of a ship colliding with a whale, and the whale carcass turning the water red. A third found an image of a cigarette stuck in a cake, and the image was later used as a design template for her sculpture. The men moved more predictably to pictures of guns, cars, drugs and drink (sorry, guys) although it is true to say that some were quite specific about their need for a certain gun, a certain car or a certain drug. ('Which bastard nicked my cocaine?') And working with images in relation to each other, as in image drama work, the creators did often give themselves away, usually without meaning to. This would include the man who gave himself a beer bottle for a head, the man with an empty 'right hand side', and the man whose spine was a joint.

With the body maps completed, each prisoner made a presentation of their work, explaining the imagery where they wanted to – there was always the option of not doing so – and talking about the experiences represented. The only rule we insisted on was that each participant should make some reference to offences or how they came to be in prison. And we made plain we would ask about these incidents. The women were more ready to own up to their own stupidity and gullibility. They admitted mistakes and named the men who had tricked them. They talked about letting down their children. Several admitted to carrying drugs into the country, often at the behest of men whom they'd scarcely met. The men, on the other hand, talked about 'fate' or 'being in the wrong place at the wrong time' or 'being grassed up' (and occasionally a dark inference of unfinished business in that quarter). The men were less transparent and more often than not you had to dig for the truth. The claims of one man to be starting 'a new life' and 'putting it all behind him' were somewhat undermined by his own defiant boasting, which could possibly be interpreted that he was planning to go on the run. But not all the guys were so cloaked in their contributions. Others couldn't be shut up, and at those times, the sessions became educational. One prisoner was prepared to tell us exactly how to get rich quick, using a tried and tested, almost foolproof system which he'd perfected over a number of years. You select a successful business with a large office block, and once most of the office workers had gone home, you walk in like you belong there and park yourself at an empty desk. You take off your jacket and pop it on the back of the chair. Then you get chatting with the tea lady, accept the offer of tea, pretend to do a bit of work and hang around until the cleaners come in. While they're in another office, you load up as many laptops as you can and walk out of the fire escape door into your waiting van. Make a few trips if you can. It's good to have some small talk about the weather or the state of the stock market. Unfortunately for this particular confidence trickster, progress in forensics caught up with him, and one day, without realising it, he left his DNA on a cup of tea.

After the body maps came exercises which tightened our focus down on to issues of trigger, impulse and offence. We encouraged the prisoners to see each offence as a story. How often did that story repeat itself? Where was the dreaming? What was the trigger? The long fuse and the short fuse. The simmering family wars in the background. The adrenaline rush, the bolted escape, the unexpected mistake, the knock on the door. The hiding in the attic and the long, slow falling into resentment. Then the dream re-written until, finally, the comfort of friends in the same shit-hole.

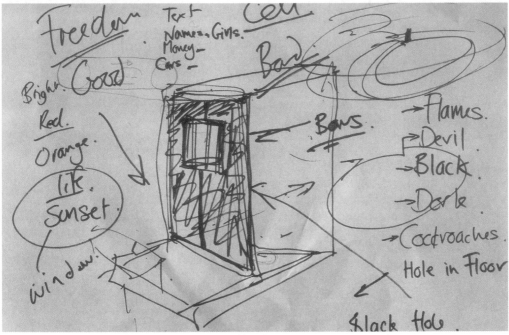

Photos by Jack Webb

Photos by Jack Webb

Photos by Jack Webb

Photos by Jack Webb

Then the designs. We had explained at the outset – 'what you build, we'll exhibit. You'll build an automata, a sculpture that moves, that's kinetic'. And we showed how it could be done. Jon, our sculptor, demonstrated with objects. With a kitchen whisk, an egg timer, a piece of clockwork, a rattle, a doll that moved. He showed the principle of the camshaft – one turn and several things move – interconnecting cogs and wheels, levers, pulleys, weights. There's a trigger – perhaps a push or a turn or something is dropped – and a knock-on effect, there's movement, and the sculpture comes alive. So then they sat down and drew their designs. Starting simply with a shape, a sense of movement, not thinking yet about mechanics, but dreaming something onto the page. Then, later, much later, thinking scientifically. How would what make what move? Will it work? Can it be built with the materials we have – wood, metal, plastic, nails, screws, tubes, ball-bearings? Designs were shared, discussed, refined, redrawn.

The prisoners were almost ready to start work. But first, the tools induction. Again, the gender differences kicked in. We were obliged for reasons of health and safety to induct all individuals in the use of the tools we'd carefully and successfully negotiated to bring into the prisons. But for the men, this wasn't necessary, was it? Obviously not. They didn't need to be told how to use a drill or a dremmel, an electric saw or a riveter, did they? Because they knew already, didn't they? Standard, standard. The great male conspiracy signed everyone up. No one admitted to ignorance, not with tools. If you did, well, it made you look like a muppet, obvious. The women on the other hand, all wanted to know. Not only that, they wanted a trial on every difficult piece of equipment. They all did, obviously. How else were they supposed to learn? We were stupid if we thought any different.

John built two mountains out of wood and MDF. On the first mountain there's a man, climbing. On the second is a drug, the heroin. Two handles. One handle powers the man up the mountain, the other the heroin. Easier by far for the heroin to travel to the man than it is for the man to climb the mountain.

Kathy built a scale with the figure of a woman poised between drugs and her baby. Turn the handle and push her one way or the other.

Marvin created two cubes which sat on each other, connected by a spring. If you lifted the handle on the top box, you needed to hold down the lower box or it would come with you. As he wrote 'The box represents me as a person. It's been split in the middle to represent what I want to do in the future and what I want to leave in the past. You could say the top section represents good and the bottom one represents bad. When you pull the box up it will separate but it will be a strong pull (hard to pull) and the bottom section will be pulling down. This means sometimes it's hard to leave the lifestyle you're accustomed to, i.e. a life of crime, and when you try to leave that lifestyle, certain things try to pull you back – peer pressure, temptation, fast money, fast women. There will be a strong pull on the way up and a crashing effect when you let go, meaning if I don't keep hold of my life and my eyes on the ball, I will come crashing back to a life of crime'.

Kevin built a high wooden structure with a wooden lift at the side, like a ski lift on the side of a mountain. The spectator places a ball into the lift, releases a spring and the lift shoots up. At the top, the lift opens to release the ball. The ball can then fall one of several ways down. He wrote about his machine 'The lift represents a hit off drugs when you shoot it up. The steps are when you're up there committing crime and taking more drugs. Then you come down, and the ball could land anywhere – back where you started, or you could end up in jail. It's not inevitable because it could also take me to a new life, unchartered territory. Take a chance!'

Jane built a cake made of foam and material, full of layers. Above it is a cigarette suspended by wires. A handle on the side moves the cigarette. The cake represents the maker's acknowledged tendency to 'fuck it all off' once something goes wrong – to throw the good in her life out with the bad, to jeopardise everything – home, child, future – when something goes wrong.

Layla placed a pair of arms and hands made from wire, on top of a large mirror. Just out of reach is a pile of stuff, the detritus of heroin. A syringe, silver paper, a spoon, a match. Turn a handle at the side and the hand reaches out towards the drugs while a second hand follows, trying to reach and stop the first.[2]

Now another member of our team was working with our not-quite-star-pupil. I'd decided to move on. It hadn't helped being blamed as the guy who was messing with his head and preventing him completing the work. He'd been telling me to fuck off, that I was a waster. He said he could understand why the rest of the team was there – Saul, Kerrie, Jon – they all had obvious roles – but he couldn't understand why I was there. Unless it was to piss him off and stop him making his sculpture. So I moved along, on my own track. Feeling bullied. Then, later, I watched the arrival of the rescuer. Jon, our sculptor, was now in that role. Elastic bands were tightened, string was re-measured and the figures started to crank along their tracks. He did it by ignoring the backchat of the sculptor and concentrating on the job in hand – getting the bloody machine working. From my vantage point over the other side of the room, I felt encouraged, if a little vanquished. Thought I'd stay away from the bully. Later, when I returned, the machine had been painted in a heavy coat of white emulsion and had stopped working again. Needless to say, the last thing that Jon had said was 'It's probably better left unpainted – the paint may clog the mechanism.' The dream however, was of a white machine. So that was what it was going to be. And in turn that meant that later, in the evening, after the prisoners had gone back in the cells, it was a sandpapering job for someone, just to get thing running again.

The next day was my last on the project, and I was Tools Monitor, stuck behind a desk. It was clear that there were some strong pieces being finished; and all the major themes had been touched on; drugs, loyalties, temptation, loss, addiction. In contrast to the intricacies and colourful details of the women's' machines, here there were solid blocks of wood and metal, stark, defiant, deliberately unfinished. It was near the end and a rush as usual. But our future porn star did have time to come over. Pretending he wanted a tool. And we chatted for a moment. And he came as close to apologizing as a prisoner can, without actually apologizing. Apparently I was 'a good bloke really' and it was a shame we had to go. 'When are you coming back?'

The kinetic sculptures from the three prisons in the West Midlands were exhibited at Birmingham Repertory Theatre and Burslem School of Art in September and October 2002. The team was Saul Hewish and Chris Johnston (project leaders), Jon Ford (sculptor) and Kerrie Williams (New Vic Borderlines, Newcastle-under-Lyme). Rideout (creative arts for rehabilitation) is based in Stoke-on-Trent.

Notes

1. The Cognitive Skills course developed by Ross and Fabiano (T3 Associates) is entitled Reasoning and Rehabilitation. The Prison Service has also developed their own course, largely based on Ross and Fabiano's work, which is the Enhanced Thinking Skills course. Rideout work with prisoners who have completed either of these courses.
2. The names of the prisoners have been changed to protect their identity.

References

Boal, A., *Theatre of the Oppressed*, (London, Pluto Press, 1979).
Boal, A., *Games for Actors and Non-Actors* (London, Routledge, 1992).
Campbell J., *The Hero With A Thousand Faces*, (London, Paladin, 1998).
Mindell, A., *Dreambody: The Body's Role in Revealing the Self* (Arkana,1990).

Dealing with Drugs

Kate McCoy and Imogen Blood

HMP Manchester 1991

A drama session. One of the group is missing. I ask where he is. There is some mumbling and someone says 'we don't want him in our group anyway – he's a fucking smack-head'. No one in the group speaks up for him and it is generally accepted that heroin users are the lowest of the low.

Various Prisons, North West of England 1993-6

Whatever the theme or subject of the workshop, heroin is mentioned more and more often as a real part of people's lives and not as something that is looked down on or frowned upon. I come to expect that in groups of adult prisoners more than half will have a connection with heroin or cocaine. I become surprised when prisoners tell me they don't take drugs.

Through the 1980s and 1990s the use of heroin in Britain increased dramatically (Edgar and O'Donnell 1998; Millar, 1999). This chapter traces the evolution of a drama based project with drug users, which was created as a reaction to this increase in use. What we believe to be interesting about this project is the partnership between a drugs agency and an arts organisation and the organic development of the work. Drug users are a unique community and this chapter will focus on how we chose to work with them and create new challenging interventions. It is also a record of what we feel we learnt from the process about both drug use and drama.

Background

The TiPP (Theatre in Prisons and Probation) Centre was set up in 1992, with direct input from the Prison and Probation Services, to create a national focus for drama and theatre-based work within the criminal justice system. TiPP's work is based on the premise that arts activities have the power to transform lives. Through its work in prisons, probation centres and hostels, TiPP encountered increasing numbers of workshop participants for whom drugs were an issue, both in relation to their offending behaviour and their lives in general. By the mid-1990s, TiPP workers began to articulate the need for a discrete project that could focus on drugs issues in all their complexity. In 1996, with a grant from Comic Relief and the input of a multi-agency and service user steering committee, TiPP developed a programme of drama-based interventions which were piloted with drug users from 1996 onwards.

Between 1996 and 2000, the private security firm Group 4 was contracted to run HMP Buckley Hall, a male training prison accommodating approximately four hundred, predominantly Category C (medium security) prisoners, in Rochdale, Greater Manchester. Private sector management brought a relatively informal regime to the prison. Prisoners were referred to by their names, officers had been newly appointed and came from a range of work backgrounds and the director and prison management board were keen to establish the prison's reputation for innovation.

From early 1997, Group 4 sub-contracted Turning Point, a large voluntary sector service provider working in the drug, alcohol, mental health and learning disability fields, to provide information, advice and counselling to drug and alcohol users within the prison. As the Turning Point project developed at Buckley Hall, a range of different services were offered including informal drop-in surgeries, relapse prevention groups and one-to-one counselling.

In January 1997, Dealing with Drugs was launched at HMP Buckley Hall as an exploratory project run in partnership by TiPP, Group 4 and Turning Point. The project aimed initially to provide twelve one-day sessions in which prisoners, facilitated by workers from TiPP, would explore drug issues through drama. Group 4 secured the initial funding for this work through the Rochdale Drug Action Team. The Turning Point Drugs Worker organised the workshops, which were held in the prison chapel.

Prison officers attended part of the first session and this was felt to have had an adverse effect on the willingness of prisoners to talk openly about drug-related issues. Subsequently, Group 4 agreed that, providing the drugs worker was present, officers would not interrupt the sessions unless there was an emergency. The TiPP and Turning Point workers liaised closely throughout the project in order to plan the most effective use of the twelve initial sessions. The success of this first phase led to the project becoming a regular part of the prison regime.

Prisoners who participated in a one-day workshop had the opportunity to explore issues in more depth through follow-up workshops. These continued to focus on drug-related topics such as user-dealer dynamics and the concept of addiction. However, as the project progressed and became increasingly user-led, the agenda broadened to include wider issues such as fatherhood, power and feelings about release. In the winter of 1998, TiPP secured funding from the Lloyds TSB Foundation to undertake the first of several longer performance projects, providing an opportunity for more committed and experienced participants to further develop their ideas and skills.

Introducing Drama: 'It's Better than Drugs, Miss!'

Every individual who became involved in the project had their own motivations for attending, but as there had been minimal arts based activity in the prison prior to 1997, participants' expectations were focused specifically on looking at drugs issues. Session titles included 'Drugs and Society', 'Pressures' and 'Starting to Change'. The aim of these initial sessions was to examine real life scenarios and explore characters' motivations and decisions in order to discuss possible change. One of the key aims of the project was to create a safe space in which the men felt happy to share these experiences and to provide sufficient drama skills training to enable these to be expressed. Most of the time we worked at one step removed, i.e. issues were explored through fictional characters, but sometimes we did work at a personal level with participants exploring their own experiences through drama.

Despite having no dramatic vocabulary, the group members with their shared experience of drug use, found this work easy to understand and relate to. The group also experienced the well-documented benefits of working through drama to explore issues and encourage change. A participant who was involved in the project for fourteen months said:

> I've been in a drug rehab twice, and have been seeing numerous drug counsellors. But have failed to express my true feelings on the issue. So I thought I would give drama a go, to see if I could express them. Now, since I've been doing these courses for twelve months, my whole attitude has changed towards drugs. This is due to not only acting out scenes on the issues, but that I've put myself in someone's shoes who is watching the play – and by doing that I've come to the conclusion that actually seeing a life of a drug addict through drama is the best way for the actors to be heard and understood. Therefore, it is my opinion that when I'm acting out the scenes in the play, I'm not only showing normal people from society how an addict lives, I'm actually showing myself, and that's been more effective than anything I've been involved with in the past.

Opening Doors: New Rooms? From Drama to Counselling and Back

The drama workshops were neither intended nor prescribed as treatment. Prisoners referred themselves. There were no eligibility criteria such as a positive drugs test, a conviction for a drugs-related offence or the completion of a detoxification programme. This meant that the group members varied considerably in their experience of and attitudes to drugs. This made the workshops accessible to people who did not wish to identify themselves as having a problem. It meant that doing drama was neither a privilege nor a punishment and, it brought a wide range of perspectives to the sessions.

The men who participated at the early stages had already done some work with Turning Point and were clear that they were attending the drama workshops in order to look at drug use, be that their own or other peoples. However, as the work progressed and the project's reputation spread through the prison, an increasing number of prisoners who were not Turning Point clients asked if they could participate.

A number of these new participants subsequently asked if they could have one-to-one counselling. There seemed to be several explanations for this. Firstly, the drama sessions raised issues for individuals that some wanted to talk about in private. Acting out scenes involving children, partners and parents often elicited feelings of guilt and loss and practical dilemmas about whether, how and when to try to re-build relationships. Looking at the challenges of newly-released prisoners helped people to talk honestly of their fears about what lay beyond the gates instead of using the usual tactics of humour and bravado to avoid confronting the real issues. Secondly, the TIPP workshops had given prisoners an opportunity to test out the drugs worker's attitudes and develop the trust necessary for disclosure in a prison environment. For those without any previous experience of counselling, group work or drug treatment, the drama sessions, though not specifically therapeutic in their aims, gave participants an introduction to sharing personal experiences with professionals and fellow prisoners. Those who were uncertain of whether, what, how and to whom they wanted to 'open up' could practise expressing their feelings and experiences without a commitment to self-disclosure.

Very few Afro-Caribbean prisoners referred themselves directly for Turning Point's counselling but TIPP sessions were very popular with black prisoners and a considerable number of those who participated subsequently requested counselling. Although a detailed discussion of Afro-Caribbean male attitudes to counselling and drug use is beyond the scope of this piece, there seemed to be several explanations for this. Voluntarily discussing personal emotional matters with a worker (especially a white female worker) seemed to be particularly alien to the culture of many of these young black men. Given widespread institutional racism within the criminal justice system, black prisoners may be more reluctant to disclose their drug use than their white counterparts. Some black prisoners also seemed anxious not to be identified with white heroin-using prisoners. Others seemed to resist the problematising of their drug use – perhaps at least partly because of different cultural attitudes towards the use of drugs, particularly Cannabis and Cocaine. That the drama workshops allowed participants to test out the culture of drug services within the prison without needing to label themselves as addicts or even as users seemed to be particularly significant for Afro-Caribbean prisoners.

A number of prisoners participated in counselling, drama sessions and group work. The cynic could point out that prisoners will do anything to get out of their cells, however we believe that these men got quite different therapeutic benefits from each of these activities. Their concurrent experience of several types of intervention can illuminate differences in these approaches and suggest ways in which they enhance each other.

One of the challenges of prison drug counselling is avoiding getting stuck in a rut with individuals. It is sometimes helpful for people to talk through particularly painful experiences repeatedly. Some people find it motivating to have ongoing meetings to review their progress; others appreciate a regular opportunity to let off steam. However, where the same issues are constantly being reviewed or where a client who is motivated to stop using continually lapses and feels stuck in the cycle of change (Prochaska et al., 1992), both parties can become disheartened.

In a drama session, however, new perspectives to old problems are generated and acting out scenarios can prompt individuals to re-frame their own feelings and review their memories of experiences. A participant who is also receiving counselling can continue this process in their one-to-one appointments. Issues raised in a drama session can also offer a way of broaching previously undisclosed topics in counselling. One workshop looked at the relationship between fathers and sons and how drug use might affect these relationships. During the drama workshop, discussion remained focused on the fictional characters that the group had created. However during the following two weeks, three of the eight participants discussed their relationships with their children in counselling sessions, for the first time.

Furthermore, in counselling and, to a slightly lesser extent, in group work programmes, there is a danger that drug users feel they must problematise their lives and themselves. Terry (not his real name), for example, used to come regularly into the Turning Point office and sit there, staring at his feet and talking about how helpless he felt in the face of his addiction. He would explain that he couldn't imagine himself ever being good at anything apart from crime. The counsellor would try to help him unravel his feelings of worthlessness and gain more control over his urges to use heroin. Yet, in drama workshops Terry emerged as sharp-witted, sensitive and adept at solving problems. He laughed, he expressed things that were painful and personal and he touched a cord with others in doing this.

During the first six months, the project remained clearly focused on drug related issues and the relationship between the drama sessions and other Turning Point input developed. A core and committed group ensured that the project would become increasingly participant led.

Starting to Change: a Natural Progression?

Often at the start of the project, the group questioned the relevance of drama exercises that did not seem to relate directly to drug use. However, six months into the project, the original participants began to express frustration about regularly doing drama work around drugs issues. Some argued that it was hard enough to stop using without having to talk about it all the time. Increasingly, the group began to enjoy the creative exercises that they had questioned at the start of the project.

Most of those attending the drama groups had direct or indirect experience of heroin use. The events related were thus often similar to each other; the scenarios depicted many of the same narratives. While some learnt, reflected and took comfort from this, after much repetition, it was possible to become immune to these stories. Friends and family of users recognise that there often comes a time when they can no longer offer a user support or even tolerance until he or she wishes to change. Similarly, through drama, there comes a time when naturalistic representations have served their usefulness; something else is needed.

At the same time a new wave of prisoners began to join the project, in response to positive feedback on the drama elements of the course. Many said they simply wanted to do some drama. At this point the project was reassessed and adapted. There were two main motivating factors for this shift. Firstly the move away from naturalism felt like a natural progression and secondly workers began to feel that there was something missing from the process, a lack of depth in the exploration of drug issues that could be found by working in other ways. More sessions were developed using non-naturalistic and creative techniques. As the groups' performance skills improved, the artistic quality of the work improved, as did its capacity to move an audience. At this point the line between the issues and the art became blurred.

The Cycle of Creativity

For many of the groups creativity had become the prime motivating force. As people became more confident in different dramatic styles, art became more important than drugs. This was a circular process, a cycle of creativity and can be seen as an opposing force to the more familiar addictive cycle, a way of explaining how people get more and more involved with drug use. As Nakken (1988, p. 23) states:

> The true start of any addictive relationship is when the person repeatedly seeks the illusion of relief to avoid unpleasant feelings or situations...This is the beginning of the addictive cycle. If one were to diagram addiction there would be a downward spiralling motion with many valleys and plateaus.

At the point of frustration and dissatisfaction in an addictive cycle, people turn increasingly to drugs. In the cycle of creativity these points generate growth and change. Through changing the way that we view a situation and the frame of our experience, we discover new ways of working to stimulate our creativity further. In the cycle of addiction, our feelings of frustration and hopelessness are accepted as inevitable with further drug use as the only escape. The addictive cycle encourages the idea that it is impossible to behave in any other way.

Conversely, the cycle of creativity gave the group opportunities to change and develop their ideas as they hit barriers. At the start of the cycle, the project looked at drug issues through drama; the issues were the prime motivating force as participants got used to the unfamiliar methodology of theatricality. As the group progressed they became comfortable with and began to understand the possibilities of drama and creativity in general. At this point, saturated with issues they choose to focus on that creative drive. The workshops continued with a primarily creative focus with limited references to drugs issues and then, through their creativity and increased skill base, the group created artistic work. This somehow encapsulated the drug-related issues in a deeper, more resonant way than ever before. Suddenly the issue became fascinating again and focus shifted away from creativity and back to drugs. And so the cycle continued through the project.

Looking Glass Worlds: Different Ways of Seeing

As the project developed, the limits of drama-based group work focussing exclusively on cognitive behavioural and forum theatre approaches became increasingly evident. These approaches seemed to presuppose that the world is a logical, rational place where to look for and encourage changes in behaviour were the only way to unravel the drama of addiction. In contrast to the common perception of drug addiction as an escape from reality, Zoja (1989) interprets it as an attempt to find a clear role in an insecure world. The user thus becomes a 'negative hero', placed at the centre of his or her universe, fighting 'enemies' and attracting attention. Both Cognitive Behavioural approaches and forum theatre techniques feed into this idea by focusing on the individual and their internal dialogue as they battle against the outside world, perhaps further entrenching users in the drama of their own addiction.

The Cognitive Behavioural model of substance use and addiction (Beck, 1991) asserts that internal cues interact with external cues to activate an individual's beliefs about their addiction, which in turn trigger automatic thoughts and cravings. Cognitive Behavioural Therapy (CBT), which has become the prevalent approach in work with drug users, thus focuses on increasing the addict's awareness of and hence control over this internal dialogue. Whilst valuable and easily realised through drama, this is not a particularly creative process.

In the experience of TiPP and Turning Point workers, the creativity of drug users is a powerful and vibrant force, stronger than encountered in any other defined group. Drug users inhabit another world; a world of different perceptions, feelings, rules and logic. They often complain that only those who have used can understand their world. The group of people who have the potential to 'understand' can, however, become increasingly esoteric: only those who have 'been addicts' or who have been 'addicted for years' can 'really' understand. Whilst this can be used as a means of defence from challenge by non-users or former addicts, it does also suggest a need to find a way of expressing the inexpressible. Maybe, in order to meet drug users' needs both to convey a sense of this world to others and to explore and understand it themselves, it is vital to go beyond rationality and reality and experiment with the fantastical, the surreal and the irrational.

Perhaps this is why drug users seem generally to be so good at drama: they are used to travelling between different worlds. In many drama processes, a facilitator will run exercises designed to release creativity, to stop people behaving and reacting on the rational and reasonable level. Participants perform actions in order to go to a deeper place where they do not edit themselves. Similarly with drugs work, when people have done all they can for themselves on a rational and cognitive level, it is time to move to another expressive place that can not be so easily described in verbal language; a place to which drug users arguably have easier access than most other groups.

Forum Theatre (Boal, 1992) gives participants opportunities to rehearse change and acknowledge alternative solutions, but these must be realistic and practically achievable. It is very clear that magic is not allowed. Although forum makes the familiar unfamiliar, it does so within the constraints and parameters of an everyday reality. It makes us see our environment and our interactions afresh but still within the frame of that everyday life. The strategies are offered on a behavioural or attitudinal level and participants are asked to solve problems within a presented framework of real life which has conventions and shared values.

Drug users often use drugs as a way of escaping from the pressures of reality – they want to 'get out of it' – this is a strategy that is used as a way of dealing with situations that become too much in the real world. However the place that they go to is not easily represented in a naturalistic format. Naturalism highlights how the drug or alcohol user is at odds with that rational logical plane of every day reality.

A strategy that was used by one group member in response to a particularly challenging situation was to sing 'Hey Big Spender' in the style of Shirley Bassey. This, according to the rules of forum, could be dismissed as a solution. 'The piece can be of any genre...except 'surrealism' or the 'irrational'' (Boal, 1992, p. 19). But perhaps surrealism and irrationality are the places we need to go to with drug users to look outside the accepted frame of reality.

Even when forum theatre is not presented naturalistically, different styles and techniques are used to reinforce the reality of the situation being discussed. The aim is to 'find images which however symbolic or surreal, can concretise the subject in a theatrical form, at the same time enriching it' (Boal, 1992, p. 228.). There was a desire to move away from the notion of reality and look at issues in a different framework.

It is difficult to represent the relationship between a user and a drug in a forum piece. The problems to be solved, the strategies to be found, do not necessarily exist between the user and the other characters. Through forum theatre, a drug user's problems with his or her family could be explored. There will be value in exploring strategies from both the user's and the family's perspective. However the user's primary and most intimate relationship is with heroin. It is hard to explore this relationship meaningfully using forum theatre techniques without taking the work into potentially psycho-therapeutic territory.

Looking Back: Stuck in Addiction

It might be argued that doing cognitive-based, naturalistic work with drug users over a period of time can actually be a form of nostalgia and may embed some deeper into patterns of behaviour. It serves as a constant reminder of the physical activity and environment of drug use and although the aim is to find alternative strategies, these may be untested in real life or have been attempted with limited success. So while these strategies may act as a rehearsal for real life, it can be hard work to put them into practice and over a longer period of time they seem unfamiliar and less compelling than the familiar, comforting drug use scenarios.

> If I had to offer up a one sentence definition of addiction, I'd call it a form of mourning for the irrecoverable glories of the first time. This means that addiction is essentially nostalgic...
>
> Addiction can show us what is deeply suspect about nostalgia. The drive to return to the past isn't an innocent one. It's about stopping your passage to the future, it's a symptom of fear of death, and the love of predictable experience. (Marlowe 1999, p. 9)

As narratives are built around the nostalgia of the first time, the drama of addiction is created. The group develops a rational and simplified universe that gives logical reasons for drug use through a dramatisation of their own explanations for their lives. When people are asked why they do things, there is a danger that their answers will be viewed as scientific fact, when they are personal responses created to make sense of complex issues and perhaps avoid self-blame and justify actions. Attribution theorist, Booth Davies (1997, p. 2) argues that:

We sometimes lose sight of the distinction between causal accounts that are socially functional, and those which are scientifically functional and the two become intermingled. Thus we may try to shed light on the causes of theft among drug users by asking them to tell us their reasons for stealing.

In a drama workshop, constant naturalistic representation of drug use portrayed as addiction can be disempowering as the social construct of addiction places the addict in a hopeless position.

It would be useful to know if the explanation of heavy drug use in terms of 'addiction' and all that is implied by that term, has its basis in attribution, rather than being scientifically derived...the possibility arises that such beliefs might have attributional implications for drug taking behaviour. In other words, the very act of explaining drug use in certain habitual ways might help to maintain and develop a drug problem in those terms (Booth Davies, 1997, p. 15).

So, as naturalistic drama may feed the myth of addiction, working with comedy and other non-naturalistic forms can encourage drug users to see their drug use within a different framework and set of beliefs, by a slight shift in perceptions. The project used many techniques to explore drug issues and creativity. The following sections will discuss examples of comedy and ritual used in a piece of work which culminated in a performance of The Mark Reynolds Rehabaret for an audience of prisoners and guests. The starting point of the project was to take the idea of variety shows, music hall and cabaret as a form through which to explore the issues of drug use. The idea behind this was a simple connection between routines and rituals which are common both to these art forms and drug use. It would also provide a framework which could encompass many styles of performance without the need for a linear narrative.

From Ritual to Routine

One of the workshops within the performance project began to explore drug use rituals. Harding and Zinberg (1977, p. 112) define a drug use ritual as:

> ...the stylized, prescribed behaviour surrounding the use of a drug. This behaviour may include methods of procuring and administering the drug, selection of physical and social settings for use, activities after the drug has been administered, and methods of preventing untoward drug effects.

In the session, each small group selected a different drug administration ritual, such as injecting heroin, and practised a synchronized mime of the ritual to perform. This exercise proved to be extremely powerful. As group members rehearsed and performed these mimed rituals, they entered into a common physical language, an unspoken bond. Yet from the audience's perspective, the silent routines conjured up images of factory operators working at a conveyor belt. The actors in the mime were in tune with each other yet also detached.

Why do these rituals have such power? On the surface of it, the act of preparing a syringe for injection is a means to an end, namely administering the drug. The actions necessary to do this in the quickest and most efficient way become routine and part of the unspoken behaviour of the group.

Cognitive behavioural approaches recognize the power of drug paraphernalia and settings to trigger cravings in users. The concept of 'needle fixation' describes the way in which some ex-drug users seem to remain addicted to the injection ritual and apparatus themselves, long after they have ceased to be functional. Yet Grund (1993, p. 7) points out that:

> ...such [i.e. behavioural] approaches have often omitted the social dimensions of the rituals of drug users. The functions rituals fulfil in the given social space and their effects on the collective consciousness of the community of users are frequently not considered.

Drug use is primarily a subjective experience. The use of drugs, perhaps particularly Heroin and Cocaine, which have been described by Cleckner (1977) as respectively providing internal and external detachment, is not inherently social. When we focus exclusively on the individual's experience of and relationship with the drug, there is a danger of overlooking the intense bonding power of the shared drug experience.

Drug literature debates whether or not this group bonding through ritual can be described as sacred (Agar, 1977) or archetypal (Zoja, 1989). For Grund (1993), rituals are a functional response to the political climate of the 'war against drugs'. They maximize the effects of scarce drugs and minimize the risks of detection. Probably, particular rituals will have different meanings for different users – functional, social and perhaps sacred.

Drama based on CBT techniques can illuminate the internal dialogue in the user's mind: 'peer pressure', paraphernalia, drug sharing rules and social settings can all be seen as triggers and influences to be balanced within this conflict. Yet, as the simple act of silently miming the act of drug-taking seemed to demonstrate, drama can also go beyond this. As a physical, group process, drama can begin to explore the power of ritual, group identity and the sharing of an indescribable experience. It can bring real insight into the drug user's simultaneous experience of isolation and group cohesion. It can enable exploration of the multi-dimensional dynamics between a group of users as well as the dialectic between conflicting voices in the user's head.

Ritual, in its purest form, is also elaborate and theatrical. 'It also gives a sense of show or play – Lights, Camera: Action!' (Grund, 1993, p. 2). From the exercises involving mimed rituals, the group developed a 'Spliff-Rolling Line Dance' as an act within the show. The silent and secretive ritual, the binding mechanism of a subculture, flamboyantly seized centre stage as a mainstream variety routine, to great comic effect.

Laughing at Ourselves: Why are There no Comedy Smack-Heads?

Addiction is a serious business. Lives are ruined, families ripped apart, men end up in prison. The job was to effect change, this was a serious task. If the project funders could see a dozen prisoners rolling around in fits of laughter on the floor of the chapel on a Friday afternoon, what would they think? Generally prisons are not places filled with laughter and the narrative of Heroin use is rarely amusing. So at the simplest level, working through comedy was a way of bringing laughter to a prison and offering some release from the stresses placed on individuals. It also proved a valuable counterpoint and balance to some of the naturalistic work, which could be harrowing in its effect for both performers and audience.

It could be argued that the fact that a group mainly made up of heroin users should be engaged in a communal activity that involved laughing together, quite often at their own experiences and attitudes, was a massive step from the more commonly perceived view of heroin users injecting in corners, nodding, scratching and drifting in and out of consciousness. Bringing heroin and laughter together not only acted as a release for participants but enabled them to look at their drug use metaphorically and creatively, contributing to an empowering experience.

Comedy and Metaphor

Comedy gives a perfect opportunity to work through metaphor. The majority of people can relate to comedy and appreciate its value without necessarily being able to articulate why they find certain things funny. One of the aims of working through comedy and metaphor was to expand and explore participants' views on drug use in a non-threatening and accessible way.

In a therapeutic setting, metaphor may be used to look at issues in people's lives when they struggle to discuss them directly. If I am unhappy with my life but find it difficult to articulate what my problems are, a therapist may ask me to imagine my life in terms of the physical world and talk about it in those terms. So I may say 'my life is a second hand shop because it is full of old dusty objects' and the therapist will help me explore the metaphor of this shop through a series of questions. For this particular client group, who may be resistant to therapeutic approaches, it may have been difficult to overtly run a session on the metaphors of drug use. This resistance may be based on a reluctance to be therapised, a suspicion of people 'trying to get inside my head' and a level of paranoia that may be high due to the effects of imprisonment and indeed drugs. By working through comedy this process becomes less threatening. The purpose was neither therapy nor treatment and it was the workers' responsibility to ensure that workshops did not stray too far into these areas.

Symbolism is readily attached to drugs and the temptation to view them metaphorically is strong. This can either be a useful or destructive process. 'Saying a thing is or is not like something-it-is-not is a mental operation as old as philosophy and poetry, and the spawning ground of most kinds of understanding, including scientific understanding, and expressiveness...But that does not mean there aren't some metaphors we might well abstain from or try to retire' (Sontag, 1990, p. 5).

There are many established metaphoric ways of looking at heroin that users regularly employ. Heroin is a warm blanket that embraces you or a dark lady that seduces you. The old metaphors may either feed negative states or be so worn and tired from repetition that they cease to have real meaning for the individual. A new metaphor may stimulate thought processes in new directions. Working from the belief that how you choose to perceive something can directly affect how you experience it, the group explored how they perceived heroin metaphorically in order to create and explore new and more useful metaphors.

Through comedy the men were constantly using metaphor and as comedy was the vehicle for it, they felt comfortable in doing so. At times these metaphors were used in purposeful ways, almost as parables to illuminate concrete issues and were explicitly discussed. Boal (1992, p. 228) calls this 'the metaphoric ritual'. 'The Make or Break Juggling Act' used the structure of a magic act to look at the difficulties of release from prison for heroin users. The magician juggled with imaginary balls then invited the prisoners anticipating release to choose a ball which would determine their future. This highlighted the sense of uncertainty and lack of control that drug-using prisoners often feel. This use of metaphor was still strongly linked to ideas of CBT and forum theatre.

Later work moved into the realms of the surreal. In one exercise participants personified different drugs as childhood ambitions and created performances portraying ecstasy as a ballerina dancing the dying swan and heroin as an astronaut who can't cope with space travel. The results were highly surreal. More time was spent interpreting the metaphors and their resonances than the preparation and creation of the performance. It was also acknowledged how difficult it was to verbalise the impact of both performing and watching. At other times performances were appreciated and applauded without analysis. This was because they defied interpretation at a rational, logical level and reduced the audience to helpless laughter. Working through metaphor defied single meanings and allowed participants to find their own resonances and personal meanings.

It can be argued that a heroin user cannot help but view his or her drug use metaphorically. As stressed earlier it is difficult to explain heroin use and when users try to do so they are feeding a widely held belief that individuals possess self knowledge and understanding of the reasons behind their behaviour and that this knowledge even exists. According to Booth Davies (1998, p. 62)

> The statement that 'I cannot stop' is not a statement of fact, but an inference based on the self-observation that I reliably fail to do so. The statement 'I cannot stop' is thus primarily a metaphor; and no other linguistic device adequately captures the moral and behavioural dilemma in which the 'addict' finds him/ herself.

If we accept that metaphor is an integral part of heroin use, engaging users on this level may help to create connections that illuminate the addict's 'moral and behavioural dilemma'. The aim is not to problematise or find universal solutions, but genuinely to explore.

'This is Just How Things are, and I Didn't Know it': Empowerment and Recognition

As mentioned earlier, much of the work came from the idea of rituals and routines. One of the comic moments in the show was a version of a strip search performed as a striptease by two police officers played by prisoners. A strip search is a regular part of a prisoner's life, especially if he is recognized by the authorities of having involvement in drug-related activity. The striptease strip search, however, was performed with relish. Through the performance of two police officers wearing pink rubber gloves strip searching the main character and dancing to stripper music, the actors and audience removed the power from their own humiliating experience of being strip-searched. This made the audience question the whole idea of a strip search from a 'civilised' perspective. They saw something that was essentially familiar to them but the performance of it helped them see it with fresh eyes.

> Comedy is born from the Komai – that is, from the peasant villages – as a joyous celebration after a meal or a feast. Comedy does not tell of famous and powerful men, but of base and ridiculous creatures, though not wicked; and it does not end with the death of the protagonists (this is why the monks find it so offensive). It achieves the effect of the ridiculous by showing the defects and vices of ordinary men. Here Aristotle sees the tendency to laughter as a force for good, which can also have an instructive value: through witty riddles and unexpected metaphors, though it tells us things differently from the way they are, as if it were lying, it actually obliges us to examine them more closely, and it makes us say: Ah, this is just how things are, and I didn't know it.
> (Eco, 1984, p. 472)

During discussions and debates in drama sessions, the idea of 'Prison Promises' appeared. When the phrase was first coined, there was laughter of recognition. For the uninitiated, a prison promise is a statement that a prisoner will make when incarcerated stating that he intends to complete some kind of positive action in the future. This action will almost never be completed. The only variables are around the awareness of the speaker and listener. At one extreme, the speaker will be convinced that he is going to get a job or give up drugs when he gets out, it will only be those listening who can recognise this prison promise and the gap between intention and action, the space between inside and outside. At the other extreme, both the speaker and the listener are simultaneously aware that the promise will never be kept. This is particularly true of drug-related promises. They serve a ritualistic surface purpose, almost a form of social etiquette. It is polite to signal your intention to change or improve, even if all those present know that fruition is unlikely.

Prison Promises were to form a recurrent part of the show, fitting in with our ideas of routines and turns. The promises were presented in between larger scenes. At the start of the show they were highly theatricalised, with the actors portraying a stylised version of knowing self-deception. Through the ridiculousness of the performance that provoked knowing laughter, it was possible to see a truth both about the speaker and his environment. Promises such as 'It'll be much easier to give up when I'm out' and 'I'm seeing a drugs counsellor' were uproariously received, portraying the actor's attitude of 'I know I won't do it, you know I won't do it, even the audience know I won't do it, but I'm still going to say it'. The exaggerated performances showed us in Eco's words, 'this is just how things are and I didn't know it'. This is borne out by a piece of participant feed-back. 'What I felt on the night and afterwards gave me an insight into the soul of the prison, the amount of times that I've had people say a prison promise to me is spooky, as before I'd never listened. Now they stick out like a sore thumb.' Thus the prison promises revealed a buried truth and provided a new common vocabulary to help understand something not previously articulated.

Throughout the play, the style of the prison promises changed. From a stylised, exaggerated start, the performances changed from comic to serious, almost without the audience noticing a progression, until the final line 'I'm going straight' was delivered with a seriousness that was greeted with a perfect silence. The audience who had laughed at the earlier prison promises that seemed to show the futility of attempting change was suddenly confronted by a real desire for change. Without the comedy that had preceded there would have been less impact in this simple and sincere statement.

Conclusion

Cognitive behavioural approaches and Forum theatre techniques can be useful in work with this client group. Where drug counselling and drama work are offered alongside each other on a flexible and voluntary basis, each can provide a way in to the other for prisoners who may be suspicious of 'treatment' or reluctant to problematise their own drug use. While drama is a useful tool for dissecting and rehearsing everyday reality, it also has the potential to go beyond the rational realms of reality. We believe that this can be particularly significant for drug users. Through metaphor, surrealism, comedy and the use of physical language such as rituals, drama can explore the places that drug users go, both individually and as groups, and can offer new perspectives and ways of expressing complex motivations.

Working through the arts with drug users is very powerful. Many of the participants of this project seemed to experience what we have described as a cycle of creativity, as they began to harness their creative energy in purposeful and challenging activity. As the Prison Director, Stuart Mitson, said in a speech after the performance of the 'Mark Reynolds Rehaberet': 'The Arts are healing this place.'

References

Agar, M. H., 'Into that whole ritual thing: ritualistic drug use among urban American Heroin addicts' in DuToit, B. M. (ed.), *Drugs, rituals and altered states of consciousness* (Rotterdam, Balkena, 1977), pp. 137-148.

Beck, A. T., Wright, F. D. et al., *Cognitive Therapy of Substance Abuse*, (New York, The Guildford Press, 1993).

Boal, A., *Games for Actors and Non-Actors*, (London, Routledge, 1992).

Booth Davies, J., *The Myth of Addiction*, 2nd edn, (Amsterdam, Harwood Academic Publishers, 1997).

Cleckner, P. J., 'Cognitive and ritual aspects of drug use among young black urban males' in DuToit, B. M. (ed.), *Drugs, rituals and altered states of consciousness* (Rotterdam, Balkena, 1997), pp. 149-168.

Eco, U., *The Name of the Rose*, (London, Picador, 1984).

Edgar, K., & O'Donnell, I., *Mandatory drug testing in prisons: The relationship between MDT and the level and nature of drug misuse*, (London, Home Office, 1998).

Grund, J-P.C., *Drug use as a Social Ritual: Functionality, Symbolism and Determinants of Self-Regulation*, (Rotterdam, Instituut voor Verslavingsonderzoek, 1993).

Harding, W. M. & Zinberg, M. D., 'The effectiveness of the subculture in developing rituals and social sanctions for controlled drug use' in DuToit, B. M. (ed.), *Drugs, rituals and altered states of consciousness* (Rotterdam, Balkena, 1977), pp. 111-133.

Marlowe, A., *How to Stop Time: Heroin from A to Z*, (London, Virago Press, 1999).

Millar, T., *Is it getting worse? Trends in drug problems in Greater Manchester – a review of multi-agency data*, (University of Manchester Drug Misuse Research Unit, 1999).

Nakken, C., *The Addictive Personality*, (Minnesota, Hazelden Foundation, 1988).

Prochaska, J. O., DiClemente, C. C. and Norcross, J. C., 'In search of how people change: Applications to addictive behavior', *American Psychologist*, 47 (1992), pp. 1102-14.

Sontag, S., *Aids and its Metaphors*, (London, Penguin, 1988).

Zoja, L., *Drugs, Addiction and Initiation: The Modern Search for Ritual*, (Boston, Sigo Press, 1989).

'If All the World's a Stage, Why Did I Get the Worst Parts?'

Psychodrama with Violent and Sexually Abusive Men

Clark Baim

> *The scene:*   A UK prison, psychodrama group therapy session
> 1st inmate: *I can't play the role of my victim. If I could see his point of view, I wouldn't have abused him in the first place.*
> 2nd inmate: *Isn't that the point?*

This chapter describes my thoughts and experiences about the use of psychodrama with men who have committed sexually abusive and violent offences. It explores how role theory provides an underlying framework for drama-based interventions and contributes to an understanding of the roots of violence. The chapter includes a case example, several practical techniques and some suggestions about engaging participants in personal work.

Introduction: a Personal Journey from Theatre to Psychodrama

When I first arrived in England in 1987 to establish Geese Theatre UK, a company devoted to work in the criminal justice system, I was full of questions about the work we were doing. I wanted to know more about the potential impact of our work and what other drama-based methods we might draw upon. We were performing interactive, improvised plays about life-or-death issues for inmate audiences. Characters on the stage, played by actors in half mask, would face a critical decision, lift their mask and turn to the audience for advice: 'What should I do?' Or, 'What should I say to her?' The inmates would call back to the stage: 'Do the robbery!' or 'Don't be a fool! You'll just end up in jail again!' 'Stop making the same mistakes! Tell her you love her and don't go out and get pissed. And be a real father to your son. He needs you!' (Baim, Brookes and Mountford, 2002).

By calling out advice, and sometimes coming onto the stage, the inmate audiences actively developed a stake in the characters and their stories. Our main measure of success was how involved the people in the audience were in the co-creation – how relevant and meaningful the drama was in that given hour, with that audience and their ideas. It was a proven method, started in 1980 by John Bergman and the original USA Geese Theatre, touring to hundreds of penitentiaries across North America. I had set up the UK company after a successful tour to Britain and Ireland by the US company in 1986. The essential theatre techniques used then continue to work just as well in the UK to this day, with the Geese Theatre UK – now under the directorship of Andrew Watson[1] – continuing its unparalleled success in criminal justice settings throughout the UK and Ireland.

After the performance came the workshop, where twenty or so inmates explored the themes of the show through experiential exercises that worked at varying levels of personal disclosure. For the most part, we kept things pretty metaphorical, working on the fictional/hypothetical level. We were there only for the day, or at most a week. In most institutions, where there was little follow-up for a therapeutic process, it would be irresponsible and anti-therapeutic to open up directly personal issues and leave the inmates raw and uncontained.

Even so, I was curious to know how I might be able to take the work deeper and to know more about where the path might lead. What would happen if the workshop didn't end after just a week, if the prison regime would support the use of drama as it can be used in a directly therapeutic way? What would such dramas look and feel like? What if the dramas we created were not performed by professional actors about fictional characters, but by the inmates themselves, about their own personal life histories and anticipated futures? How much training would I need to work responsibly and ethically on this therapeutic level?

The answers came during a week spent near Newcastle in the north of England, in May 1988. I was part of a five-day psychodrama workshop, and for the first time saw all of my best hopes about drama's potential for healing realised in the life-enhancing dramas of that week. Here, in a workshop of twenty-five or so people, we all participated in dramas enacting the life events of the people present. The dramas enacted were universal but highly personal dramas addressing themes such as bereavement, lost love, someone who was unprotected as a child finally being protected, a mother struggling to let go of a child who is growing up and wanting to leave home, a man trying to manage and resolve traumatic early life experiences, a woman wanting to spread her wings and strike out on her own in defiance of her stifling parents. There were ten or more psychodramas during the five days, and we all enacted the roles in each other's dramas. The psychodramatist directing the workshop, Elaine Sachnoff from my native Chicago, recognised my fascination with the method, and encouraged me to learn more.

The story jumps nine years to 1997, to the time when I was nearing completion of my training as a psychodramatist. By this time, Geese Theatre UK had grown into a company of eleven full time actors and groupworkers, on permanent contracts, presenting performances, workshops and residencies all over the UK. Meanwhile, I was training as a psychodramatist, and began my clinical placement at HM Prison Grendon, at that time the country's only adult prison designed and run along therapeutic community principles. It is a truly therapeutic prison, one of the most inspiring places one could hope to work. I was there to direct psychodramas, under the supervision of Jinnie Jefferies, who had already been the director of psychodrama there for more than fifteen years.

Psychodrama in Prison – Taking Back 'No'

At its most basic, psychodrama provides an opportunity for one person – the protagonist – to depict scenes, relationships and perceptions from his own life. This is normally done in a group setting, with other members of the group playing the roles of significant other people in the protagonist's life, or sometimes representing his internal roles. In psychodrama sessions with men who have committed sexual abuse or violence, the psychodramas often reflect extreme trauma and life threatening danger. For example:

• The psychodrama of the man who was forced at the age of seven to crawl through windows of houses in order to let his father in to burgle the house. In a later scene, the same boy, now a young man of twenty-one and imprisoned for burglary, violence and drugs offences, shakes in fear and anger as he tries to tell his father that he does not want to burgle houses anymore, but wants to live a decent life.

• The psychodrama of a man who, as a boy, had been raped and strangled nearly to death by a neighbour who had 'befriended' him. In the session, the man finally manages to summon up his rage about the abuse and takes back the ability to say 'No!'

• The psychodrama of a man who is still trying, twenty years after the event, to regain some control over the terror he felt when his own mother held a knife to his throat, threatening to kill him while she argued violently with his father.

These are the psychodramas that I have come to think about as dramas where the protagonist reclaims his right and ability to say 'no.' In the many hundreds of psychodramas that I directed at Grendon Prison, what I saw demonstrated over and over again in the life histories of the inmates was how their own rights and feelings had been overridden, their own dignity smashed. What so many of the dramas enacted, at the most basic level, was a man simply taking back the right to say 'no' to his abusers, his parents, his siblings, his supposed carers or his peers. After being granted this 'no,' with his pain being heard and understood for the first time and in a safe and contained environment, he can begin to practice a new strategy for meeting his needs through compassion, co-operation and communication, rather than using the coercion and force he used to commit his crimes.

One way of looking at the roots of violence and sexual abuse is how they derive from early experiences where the basic right to have boundaries and to say 'no' have been overridden by more powerful figures. When we lose the ability to say 'no' and have these boundaries respected, the anger we feel may eventually become intolerable and emerge through a similar coercion or forcing of others, overriding their boundaries and their ability to say 'no.' And so the cycle continues. It is not mysterious, or even particularly secret or difficult to see. What the violent perpetrator does is something that we all do to one extent or another when we project out onto others the bad and painful feelings that we find intolerable. What are these feelings? At their root, they are the most basic ones of all: fear, anger and the desire for comfort and safety (Crittenden, 2000, 2002). Most of us find a way of communicating these feelings and meeting our needs through non-criminal means. Men who are in prison for violent and sexually abusive offences have tried to meet the same basic needs; the difference is that they have used force, violence, threats, weapons and even murder to cope with their intolerable feelings and meet their needs.

Role Theory and the Development of the 'Offender' Role

Psychodrama is intrinsically rooted in role theory, which has also informed many innovative uses of drama, particularly applications in education and therapy (Blatner, 1997). Given that role theory has such underlying importance, and bearing in mind that no single model provides all of the answers (see for example Baim, 2000, for a discussion of attachment theory and neurobiological issues related to violence and sexual offending), it may be useful to consider role theory in some detail for the insights and theoretical framework that it provides.

Thinking about the importance of role theory in relation to drama-based work with offenders, we can use the concept of roles and the language of drama to help us understand the factors influencing who becomes a habitual offender and how he might, if so inclined, leave behind such a destructive role. Such an understanding, using dramatic frames of reference, seems particularly appropriate when developing a rationale for using interventions based on drama.

In the language of drama and roles, we might usefully ask, How does someone learn the role of offender? Are they cast in the role, or is the role self-taught? Why might someone prefer such a role? Once in the role, can the role ever be discarded? Are some people doomed to play out a pre-determined story?

Much of human interaction can be understood by considering the roles and scripts we perform as we go about our daily lives. The idea of society as theatre – with men as actors and society like a stage – is an ancient one in Western thought, dating back to the tradition of *theatrum mundi* (Sennett, 1976, p. 40). In the twentieth century, this ancient idea was incorporated into role theory by J. L. and Zerka Moreno and others (1972, 1975).

One of the principles of role theory is the observation that in the course of our lives we carry out many roles, such as parent, son, daughter, sibling, employee, friend, carer, customer, teacher, driver, neighbour, pedestrian, passenger and innumerable others, each role designating a constellation of behaviours generally associated with that role in a given cultural context. When we know how to perform a given role, it can be said to be in our *role repertoire*. In general, the greater the number of roles in our repertoire, the better able we are to meet our basic needs and function successfully because we have a wide variety of strategies from which to choose.

Roles are strongly influenced by the context in which they occur; our behaviour may alter radically when we move from one social context to another. So, for example, while Prisoner A may one moment be walking along the landing in the role of anonymous inmate, a moment later he may be in the visiting room and in the role of loving father, son, brother or partner.

We will also be more comfortable in some roles than others. Some roles may be maladaptive, meaning that at one point in our life they may have been necessary for survival, but now the role is leading to highly destructive or self-defeating behaviour. We may also have no experience of some essential roles, which is one way of explaining why, for example, unemployed young people often have such difficulty learning how to be an employee for the first time, or why habitual offenders find it so difficult to go straight. Where are the role models for such roles, or indeed the chance to practise them?

To take this concept of roles further, we can see that when we are young, a wide variety of roles are open to us. Surely, isn't every infant a potential partner, parent, worker, trusted friend, esteemed colleague, artist or leader? Given a sufficiently stable and conducive environment, every child may evolve to their highest potential, taking on and developing appropriate and effective roles that help them survive and that best suit them, their abilities and their goals. Even taking into account the reality that, in vast populations of the world, basic survival is still the overwhelming priority and therefore the range of life opportunities is severely limited, no one is born already cast by nature as bad, evil or as an offender.

Summarising the relationship between roles and the development of our sense of who we are, J. L. Moreno had the notion that *roles do not emerge from the self, but the self may emerge from roles* (Moreno, 1972). In other words, the person that we are – our deepest sense of what constitutes our self – develops out of all the roles we are encouraged and permitted to carry out. This idea runs counter to what is generally our more instinctive view of the self, which is that there is some irreducible core self from which our roles and abilities develop. Moreno states exactly the opposite, that the roles come first, and then – possibly – a sense of self.

This description of the formation of self-identity has disturbing implications when we consider what sort of self emerges from mainly negative, anti-social or victim-like roles. In contrast to the optimistic view of the child developing to his full potential, we know that for many children – many of whom later become offenders – the range of roles open to them is severely restricted from the start. The plot is narrowed, and they are typecast in negative and destructive roles. These are the children who, through no fault of their own, are cast by parents, family and surrounding communities into the role of 'stupid bastard,' 'nothing but trouble,' punch bag or sexual plaything. The forces constricting the child's range of roles originate with parents and family, and move outward to the wider community, the school, and society as a whole. Racism and other forms of prejudice can of course worsen the situation.

The result is that the child never learns that he is part of an inter-dependent social network, never learns the role of co-operator. The child learns, rather, that in order to survive he must not express his feelings authentically and he must not trust other people to be there for him when he needs them. He learns that it is safer to suppress painful feelings and to emotionally detach from others, or he learns that the only way to meet his needs is to exaggerate his feelings and use coercion, deception, manipulation or force. By no coincidence, these are the two dominant strategies used by inmates in order to survive in mainstream prisons.

Just as family and social forces constrict the child into anti-social roles, so too may they cut off potential outside rescuers and the development of roles that might offer the child some hope of withstanding the onslaught of neglect and abuse. The abused, neglected and denigrated child is often reduced to a narrow range of roles and behaviours, most of which cause alarm, distress, disgust and anger in others. Thus a negative feedback loop is created, with each transgression further reinforcing the child's anti-social role and sense of grievance. For a child needing attention and nurture, often any attention, even if punishing, is preferable to no attention. And thus the cycle is reinforced, and the roles further ingrained. The child's developing role of anti-social delinquent or victim-with-a-grudge may be further reinforced by stays in secure units, residential care and young offender institutions, living with others like him and being forced away from society. As many studies and writers on criminology have observed, this early institutionalisation often serves to further restrict the range of roles, behaviours, attitudes and thought patterns of the young person.

This is where the description of prison as a university of crime derives from. For which roles are being reinforced in such a place? Usually, by the time he is in a prison, young offender institution or other setting, the offender's destructive roles may be a decade old or more, and this (now grown) child is well practised at treating the world as a hostile place, where threats are ever present, where those with power will abuse it, where everyone is looking out for number one, and where those whom he most trusts will betray him.

By the time he is a teenager, his core beliefs about the world may be that that the world is a place where you take what you can get, and don't make yourself vulnerable. He will often hold a deep-seated mistrust of anyone 'straight' who can upset this view of his world and his role in it. Anyone working in a prison or young offender institution has seen countless examples of inmates 'walking the walk,' putting on a tough street persona as a protective front, playing out the role, hiding their fear and sense of inadequacy, not knowing how to break out of the role, and ultimately getting stuck within the narrow range of roles open to the prisoner. So many of them become walking, talking clichés. It is desperately sad to see so many young people stuck and typecast as villains, and it is an enormous waste of human potential, of human life.

All too often, criminal justice interventions do to offenders the same thing that the offenders have done to their victims: silence them and deny their needs. Confinement or punishment alone cannot teach personal responsibility and concern for others. Without clear, focused interventions that aim to help repair the damage and rewrite the script, to cast the young person in new roles, he may proceed to spend another decade or more, and often his entire life, locked in the role of prisoner, criminal, outcast, and menace to society. He will never move beyond the earliest draft of the script, the earliest roles he played out.

This is why, when offenders do engage in change-oriented work and gain a sense of critical consciousness about their life, they often feel such sadness and anger, even desolation, at the realisation of the waste and hurt they have caused by adhering to the typecast roles. During sessions, I have often heard offenders say phrases such as 'what a waste' when their realisation comes. Is it any wonder they put up so many defences protecting themselves from such an insight, given that recognition brings such pain and regret?

Of course, there are some offenders who do not fit this description. Some have had a fully adequate upbringing and have a large repertoire of socially competent roles, but commit crime under the influence of peer pressure or in reaction to severe economic hardship. There are others who have had every advantage in life, yet allow themselves to be taken in by greed, jealousy, revenge or pure selfish disregard of others. (Witness the personal devastation wrought by the recent Enron and Worldcom scandals). Finally, there are mentally ill or neurologically impaired offenders, for whom special considerations of course apply.

Yet these are a minority. For the vast majority of offenders, the early chapters in their life script foreshadow all too clearly the acts to come. They are following the script, and need help reinventing that script and the roles they choose to play in it. Drama, psychodrama and all of the related techniques offer just such a medium for rewriting and rehearsing new behaviours.

Dramatic Intervention

To begin redrafting the script, we can use the dramatic process to help participants feel empowered to change their future life script and the roles they play. We can work in a spirit of optimism and hope, in the belief that we are all capable of personal change when we are motivated, given the chance to express ourselves differently and able to test out different ways of relating with others. We must also be mindful of the tremendous personal strength of so many of the young people and offenders with whom we work – the strength they have needed simply to survive.

The task is to harness some of that inner strength and put it to work developing positive life skills. We can help offenders look at scenes and situations they have been in, are in now, or want to be in. We can hold up the mirror to their behaviour and encourage them to look at their own reflection, and from there accept responsibility for their own actions and the need for change. By seeing life choices as being part of their own personal story, the people with whom we work may come to see that, although they have indeed written their own life script, they have done so with limited self-awareness or social consciousness, and with a severely restricted range of roles. Perhaps most importantly, if people are serious enough about change, we can use the dramatic process to help them discover which roles they have never developed and to rehearse new roles for the future.

In the most rewarding circumstances, it may even be that people who have habitually committed crime may grow to recognise that they have the power to play a role on the world's stage, to influence society for the better. They may take, for example, a central role in the debates surrounding crime and punishment. Many ex-offenders have overcome the obstacles to change and made important contributions to criminal justice and other social concerns. They offer perhaps the clearest example of people making active and fully conscious choices about their place – their role – in the world, and acting upon these choices by writing a new script.

Psychodrama as it used in Working with Trauma and the Roots of Violence

Adding to the insights gained from considering role theory, we can consider more of the psychological impact issues associated with early trauma and how psychodrama may be helpful.

The offending behaviour of inmates who have been imprisoned for acts of violence or sexual abuse may be partially understood as a distortion of early traumatic experience that remains unprocessed in the mind of the offender, too painful to look at or work through (Greenberg and Paivio, 1998; Jefferies, 1996; de Zulueta, 1998; Schwartz et al., 1993). This distortion has an insidious power to infiltrate all aspects of human function, creating distorted views of self and other and disabling the ability to regulate affect and tolerate painful feelings. Even with the passage of time, the toxicity of the abuse remains (van der Kolk, 1989; Tedeschi and Calhoun, 1995). It will not fade without deliberate attention and working through which allows the trauma victim to add symbolic meaning to the trauma and achieve relief through catharsis, grieving, new understanding and adaptation (Winn, 1994; Goldman and Morrison, 1984; Briere, 1996; Scheff, 1979; Langs, 1999; Whitfield, 1995; Webb and Leehan, 1996).

When one is working with a prisoner who has committed violence or sexual abuse, one is usually working with someone whose core experience of being alive is that of being unvalued, disempowered, excluded, detested, exploited, dehumanised or shamed – in short, being a victim. This principle applies whether or not the prisoner consciously understands his own trauma as damaging; many in fact will see their abuse as being a good thing, that 'it did me no harm' or 'I deserved it' (Briggs, 1995; Burt, 1980; Marshall and Maric, 1996; Salter, 1988; Bannister, 1991).

Although statistical studies regarding the prevalence of early victimisation among people who later become offenders are widely varied and use differing definitions of abuse, the general consensus shows that the overwhelming majority of people who have committed serious and repeated violence or sexual abuse have experienced significant and debilitating trauma, whether it be from physical/sexual abuse, prolonged neglect or major disruptions in early attachments. (Schwartz et al., 1993 & 1995; Briere, 1996; Skuse et al., 1998; Wallis, 1995; Grubin, 1998).

This experience of damage that occurs early in the life of offenders is worthy of high priority in offender treatment, despite common reservations about approaching such issues out of fear of being seen as collusive (Samenow, 1984; Salter, 1995). The mainstream literature on offender treatment (see Chapman and Hough, 1998; Vennard et al., 1997; Barker and Morgan, 1993; Simpson, 1994; Beckett, 1994; Clark and Erooga, 1994; Hanson, 1999) has in general failed to incorporate more than four decades of research into the effects of trauma, post-traumatic stress reactions and the resulting effect on self-regulation.

Yet focusing on offending behaviour while denying historical links with early trauma can damage the therapeutic relationship and treatment prognosis. Indeed, in many cases, ignoring or down-playing the offender's trauma history is to bypass the key factor influencing his offending and the development of his distorted, pro-offending ideas (Schwartz et al., 1993). With any other client group, a therapist would be considered negligent for ignoring or dismissing the relevance of early severe trauma in a client's life history, or insisting that the debilitating emotional effects of that trauma are not relevant to the modification of the client's current behaviour. Such an approach carries with it the high risk of re-abusing the offender by re-silencing him.

It is sobering but unfortunately true that the abuse committed against these individuals when they were young is often far worse than that which they later perpetrate. For the sceptic who may dismiss such an approach as collusive or 'soft' on offenders, it is important to point out the degree of trauma being referred to, which is far beyond the everyday trauma of infancy and childhood. These are the traumas of, for example:

• the boy of eight who is forced by his stepfather to repeatedly rape his infant sister while the stepfather and his friends look on;
• the boy who, throughout his childhood, witnesses his father brutally raping his mother while in a drunken rage;
• the boy who is repeatedly raped by a group of men and then forced to watch as the men inject other boys with muscle relaxants prior to raping them; or
• the trauma of the boy who is strangled and nearly drowned by his father's girlfriend, a woman who he thinks is his mother.

These horrors are committed in secret and behind closed doors against silenced children. As long as they remain unspoken, they retain their debilitating power. The fact that these boys later grow into men who commit further offences makes it all the more crucial to acknowledge their pain and begin the process of healing in the hope of helping them develop and practice safe behaviour. But we must be willing to hear the pain, sadness and loss, and we must also have the training, the skills and the proper context in which to help these stories come into the healing light.

This is where psychodrama – in its clinical form as a method of psychotherapy – can be uniquely effective. It provides a highly accessible, concrete and effective method for moving back and forth through time, simultaneously addressing the individual's offending behaviour as well as its origins (Kipper, 1986; Corsini, 1967; Yablonsky, 1976). Underpinning the work is the belief that sexual and violent offending is most often a learned behaviour and is in most cases a symptom of the perpetrator's maladaptive thinking, feeling and behaviour patterns developed largely in response to earlier trauma (Baim, 2000; Schwartz and Masters, 1993; Bowlby, 1984 and 1988; Crittenden, 2000).

In order for maximum healing to occur, it is necessary that the victim of abuse have his suffering acknowledged and respected by others. Beyond acknowledgment, however, there must also be resolution, by revisiting the scene of the trauma in a structured way and providing a comforting and empowering new experience. Such a new experience can help the protagonist repair some of the developmental damage done to him by providing a powerful alternative memory of the traumatic events: the way it happened the first time, and the way it should have happened. The protagonist can then draw on the empowering experience of his psychodrama in order to manage his fear and grief and to make adaptations that make the memory more tolerable.

Going back in time also serves as an opportunity for directly addressing and modifying the destructive urge to abuse. The role of the perpetrator is tracked back to its precipitating source (Moreno, 1972; Bustos, 1994) and addressed and modified at that source. Both the perpetrator and victim roles derive from the same originating event(s), which is why it is so crucial to track back the damaging role to its point of origin and promote a freeing of the log jam of emotional repression that has contributed so greatly to the offending behaviour (Corsini, 1951a and b, 1952).

Ideally, offence-focused work and post-trauma work should co-exist within a single psychodrama session. When psychodrama is conducted in this manner, the role of offender and the role of victim can be given equal credence. This strategy also addresses the general misgivings about trauma work with sex offenders, namely that they will be allowed to focus on their own abuse to the exclusion of work on taking responsibility for their crimes. In this format, they are asked to hold both roles in mind at the same time.

Post trauma work with offenders does not differ significantly from trauma work done with any group of trauma victims. The key differences are in the context of the trauma work, the risk factors involved which impact on public protection and confidentiality, and finally, the timing of the trauma work. Bearing in mind the exigencies of working within criminal justice and, by extension, within the broader framework of public protection, it is crucial that work on the offender's own trauma history is never undertaken when there is a risk that the offender will use his traumatic experience to justify his crimes or absolve himself of culpability. Balancing these two therapeutic imperatives demands enormous resources of human tolerance and the considered application of evidence from the fields of psychobiology, psychology, trauma counselling, sociology and criminology (Baim, 1999; van der Kolk, 1994 a and b; Kipper, 1998; Hunter, 1995; Jenkins, 1997).

Clinical Example

The following clinical example is typical of psychodramas directed by the author with adult men convicted of violent or sexual offences. These psychodramas relate the effects of the offender's core trauma experience to his later offending, taking precautions to ensure the offender does not reinforce his victim stance but rather removes it entirely by allowing him to emotionally work through his victim experience. The psychodramas trace back the roles of victim and perpetrator to their point of origin in order to provide a psychodramatic modification of the events precipitating the two roles. The psychodrama below was directed by the author according to the principles and methods of 'classical' psychodrama (Moreno, 1972; Moreno and Moreno, 1975; Hollander, 1978), the psychodrama spiral (Goldman and Morrison, 1984) and the Therapeutic Spiral (Hudgins, 2000 and 2002; Hudgins and

Drucker, 1998), a model designed specifically for psychodramatic work with survivors of trauma. The inclusion of a scene of self-forgiveness, found here toward the end of the drama, has been discussed by Sachnoff (1999). Names and identifying details have been altered for reasons of confidentiality.

Jack's Psychodrama

Jack is a thirty-two year old man who is serving a fifteen-year sentence for aggravated armed robbery and attempted murder. He has been in prison for six years and is, at the time of this psychodrama, in group therapy. He has joined the psychodrama group in order to better understand what drives his offending behaviour and how to better express his feelings. He recognises that he usually presents a false front to the world of being a brave, tough, macho man – a 'gangster' – but he says that inside feels like a little, fearful boy, who is sensitive and wants to be caring to other people.

In today's session, Jack wants to express and resolve some of the feelings he has buried deep inside for almost twenty years, about the time he was sexually abused by a neighbour. Jack explains at the start of his psychodrama that, 'It's really about my anger at the man who did that to me, when I was thirteen. I think that a lot of the drugs and drinking and violence and gang violence and beating up sex offenders was me trying to get out my anger on other people, when I really wanted to get back at him. I brushed it off, and said to myself that it wasn't important, but it's stayed with me. I am still angry about it.'

Jack then narrates us forward, describing a man in his thirties who was friendly to the boys in the neighbourhood. Jack had spoken to him and the man gave him sweets and money. Then one day Jack went to the man's flat and saw an ornamental sword on the wall and asked the man for it. The man gave the sword to Jack, and Jack felt like he was actually taking advantage of the man, unaware that he was being groomed for abuse.

Jack then narrates how the man invited him back some weeks later, and tricked Jack by play-wrestling him into a position where he was on his hands and knees. The man took Jack by surprise and began to masturbate him, and Jack, totally confused by what was happening, became frozen still. The only words Jack remembers the man saying are, 'Look how much you've come.' He then remembers leaving the flat, going home and keeping quiet about the abuse. He felt like no one would understand.

Jack then chooses another inmate as his main inner strength: caring. He also speaks about other strengths, and they are represented in the room. This focus on strengths is intended to provide Jack with a solid base from which to move forward into the traumatic terrain of his abuse. He then casts two other group members in the role of himself at age thirteen and of the man who abused him. The psychodrama is then played out in a highly structured format of steps using increasing intensity and realism, the director checking with Jack at each stage about how he is feeling and whether he feels able to move to the next level of realism.

The two group members representing the roles of thirteen year old Jack and the man who abused him now stand in the scene, which represents the room in the man's house where Jack was abused. The scene is not enacted, but rather is played out with voices only, as in a radio play. This is all that Jack can bear at this point, and he begins to sob as he hears and re-experiences the sense of fear, dread, shame, confusion, anger, shock and sadness that he felt at the time. As he weeps, he says his mother and uncle Terry should have been there and would have helped him if they'd known. What should have happened at the time, but did not, is that Jack should have been protected from this man, by alert and assertive adults. Instead he was neglected, abandoned and ignored. So in the psychodrama, after Jack's cathartic release of emotion, comes a scene of repair in which Jack does get protected as he should have been. A second, similar scene of abuse is staged, and Jack watches intently as his mother and uncle, played by two other group members, go in with fury, remove the man from the scene and then comfort thirteen year old Jack. The two adults tell young Jack that he is not responsible for what the man did, and they tell him that they love him and are very sorry about what has happened. Jack cries again as he witnesses this scene, which for twenty years he had longed for.

The director then offers Jack the opportunity to experience this rescue scene himself, rather than observing it from the outside. After checking out with the director what boundaries are in place to make sure he is not re-abused or that he does not end up exploding with anger and killing someone in the psychodrama (a real fear), Jack enters the scene as if he were thirteen years old again and allows himself to be rescued, protected and comforted by his mother and uncle. His relief is palpable, and he soaks up the words of reassurance. He also explains to his mother how disappointed he is that she never seems to listen to him or notice him because she is always busy doing something else. In the psychodrama, his mother listens and acknowledges his disappointment.

After Jack has thoroughly taken in the protection and comforting that he should have received at the time but did not, the director suggests that this might be a time for Jack himself to take back some of his own power and use it in a focused and appropriate way (rather than through the displaced violence he used during his crimes). In other words, Jack is invited to reclaim his ability to say 'no'.

To do this, Jack leaves the role of himself at age thirteen and returns to his own adult role. The scene of abuse is re-staged, with the other group member representing young Jack once again in the scene. As Jack watches the scene re-played, this time he feels strong enough and spontaneous enough to enter the scene and *rescue himself* from the abuse. The scene is constructed to allow Jack to use great, directed force to remove the man from the flat. Four group members hold cushions in front of themselves, representing the man trying to abuse Jack. Jack himself now pushes back the four men, using the strength of ten. Jack pushes against the cushions and screams, 'Get out, you pervert! How dare you do that to me! To a kid!' There is no question that Jack has truly taken back his power from this abuser.

Jack then goes over to his thirteen year old self, still played by another group member. He takes his younger self out of the flat and back to his own home. In an important scene of self-forgiveness, Jack tells his younger self that it was not his fault, that he didn't know what was happening, and that he doesn't need to be ashamed. Jack then reverses roles and hears this for himself as his younger self.

Jack ends the psychodrama by returning to his own role and re-connecting with the strengths he identified at the start of the psychodrama, such as being caring. Jack then considers how the anger he felt about his abuser had been misdirected for so many years against anyone and everyone. He spoke about how he wanted revenge, but didn't know how or where to express his feelings. He said that now he didn't feel the need to punish other people as much. The director reminded him that he now had experienced two versions of the same event: the one that should not have happened and the one that should have happened. When he remembered the traumatic version, he could also remember the other to help himself feel stronger. The purpose of this psychodrama had been not to make Jack's pain go away, but rather to change his perception of his own power to manage his thoughts and feelings. Jack recognised that he had taken back this power, and that he no longer would be terrified of this memory.

As the session nears its end, all of the group members de-role, with special care given to the group members who played the roles of abuser and abused. The whole group then has a sharing session, in which each man shares a personal connection to Jack's psychodrama. This is an essential part of every psychodrama session, and aids the connectedness and healing among all of the group members.

Several weeks later, Jack told his main therapy group that he felt much better after having done his psychodrama. Although it was difficult and felt risky at the time, he now felt relieved that he had finally expressed his anger where it should have gone. Most of all, he felt understood by the other inmates and staff.

More than a year after this session, Jack was continuing to do therapeutic work, and showed many indications that he was making successful progress toward release. He no longer felt the need to strut around the wing in a macho pose. Additionally, he no longer had angry outbursts on the wing, and was generally seen to be far more tolerant and caring toward other inmates.

Techniques

This section explains several drama-based and psychodramatic techniques that practitioners may find useful. As with all therapeutic procedures, such techniques should only be used by properly trained and supervised practitioners.

There are many well-documented warm-ups and structured experiential learning techniques. Those outlined here are offered merely as a starting place. Readers who are interested in the use of warm-ups, drama games and experiential learning techniques may wish to read Baim, Brookes and Mountford (2002), Dayton (1990) or White (2002).

Warm-up: Safe and Unsafe Families

In order to begin a module on relationships, attachment strategies or post-trauma work in a group for adult male offenders, you can begin by asking the group members to create sculpts, or frozen pictures, of hypothetical families. The group members can be divided into small groups and asked to create images of 'A family that communicates well and supports each other – a safe family,' and 'A family where anger and fear are always present – an unsafe family.' These sculpts can then be processed to look at issues regarding what helps and what damages the children. The images can be moved forward and backward through time, to gain an awareness of how behaviour and attitudes are passed down generation to generation.

Inevitably, the group members will make connections with their own upbringing. These sculpts can also be used to demonstrate the principles of functional and maladaptive attachment, e.g. 'Looking at this father and son, what happens to their relationship if father is abusing his son, but the son can't tell his mother?' Or, 'What are this boy's basic needs? What strategies does he use to meet these needs?' Where appropriate, encourage the group members to make links with their own behaviour as an adult as well as their behaviour as a child.

The Offender and Victim Psychodrama Sequence

This is a sequence of four psychodramatic encounters. They need not be undertaken in the exact sequence shown, but should instead inform an underlying structure for all psychodramatic work with offenders who have committed violence and sexual abuse. In other words, at some point in his therapy, each offender should have the opportunity to have each of the following conversations (Taylor, 1999):

• A conversation between me as a perpetrator of abuse, and those who perpetrated against me. ('I am like you in this way...')
• A conversation between me as a victim of abuse, and those who perpetrated against me. ('You hurt me in this way...')
• A conversation between me as a perpetrator of abuse and the victims I have abused. ('I hurt you in this way ...')
• A conversation between me as a victim of abuse, and the victims I have perpetrated against. ('I am like you in this way...')

The above conversations are facilitated with the emphasis on allowing the offender's own best self and own best critic to emerge. Regardless of the sequence, the conversations must be facilitated in such a way as to allow the offender to feel that he is being heard and not judged.

It is suggested that at some point each conversation be viewed by the client/ protagonist using the technique of 'mirroring,' where he stands back and observes the dialogue as an onlooker. This will allow him a more objective understanding of how the various roles fit together and how they have influenced each other over time.

Internal Dialogues

In the context of the above sequence of four conversations, this would be three additional dialogues:

• A conversation between the part of me that wants to offend and the part of me that does not;
• A conversation between myself as a victim of abuse and myself as a perpetrator of abuse; and
• A conversation between me as an adult and me as a child.

These internal dialogues may encourage motivation and the sense of self-determination and choice. For example, you could ask the person to place himself along a continuum between the part that wants to offend and the part that doesn't. Which part holds more power now? What about a year ago? What about in a year's time? What influences one part to get stronger or weaker? What is the offending voice saying? What needs is it trying to meet (e.g. for comfort, protection, safety)? What other ways can these needs be met?

Confronting the Perpetrator Role

When facilitating a psychodrama in which the offender is in role as his perpetrator self, the director can engage with the perpetrator as with any maladaptive role. That is to say, the facilitator can allow the protagonist to feel safe in portraying this side of himself, without fear of judgment and without fear that this role will be targeted for elimination. After all, aspects of the role were once necessary for the protagonist's survival, so the threat of eliminating this role may create an understandable resistance (Metcalf, 1997). By bringing this role into the light of day, exploring its origins, and allowing safe role completion, the energy and heat are diminished, the role loses its power and ultimately dissipates (Kipper, 1998).

There is, however, a real risk of re-traumatising the offender when he enacts his own perpetrator role. Many offenders are terrified that they will over-identify with their perpetrator role, and somehow get stuck again in the role. Others carry profound shame in relation to the role. Therefore a structured progression should be followed which will minimise the likelihood of such traumatisation by allowing the protagonist to control the degree of identification with the role. The following stages are a useful guide:

• After the protagonist identifies his intrapsychic, interpersonal and transpersonal strengths (Hudgins, 2000 and 2002), have him *describe* the perpetrator role.
• The protagonist *places the role* in the space (e.g. scene of the offence) by identifying and describing his physical position and actions at the time.
• The protagonist *anchors the role with object(s)*, placing the object(s) in the space.
• Continuing to stand out of the scene, the protagonist provides a *voice-over*, repeating the words he used at the time. Where appropriate, this may be done using auxiliaries (other group members in role).
• The protagonist enters the scene and takes his own role, enacting his perpetrator role and certain key moments of the offence. Through the use of role reversals with his own current self, with his victim, and with other internal and external roles, the protagonist is helped to diminish the strength of his own perpetrator role and achieve a healthier internal role balance.

Skills Practice Role-Plays

Psychodrama is more than a method for addressing trauma; it also offers techniques to help practice new interpersonal skills. The principle of *expanding the role repertoire* can be put into practice by using skills-practise role-plays (Baim, Brookes and Mountford,

2002). For example, an offender who has recently been involved in heated arguments with staff at his hostel regarding what he considers to be unfair rules can be helped to role-play alternative ways of dealing with his grievances. He can practise interpersonal skills such as listening, making an assertive but polite request, finding a compromise, and/ or dealing with frustration or disappointment.

Perspective Taking

Drama-based methods and psychodrama are particularly effective methods for encouraging perspective taking skills. By taking on the first person portrayal of other characters – real or fictional – and speaking with imagination, authenticity and respect from differing perspectives, the client/group member will naturally broaden his perspective and his thinking about other people and their rights and needs.

For example, in a group of men who have been convicted of violent offences against their partners, members of the group may benefit from enacting the various roles in a hypothetical family where a) There is no violence; and b) Where there is violence. Members of the group can alternate the roles and explore the perspectives of different family members and surrounding people, for example mother, father, two children, a neighbour, an arresting officer, a probation officer, a worker at the shelter, another woman resident at the shelter, a man who has already been through treatment. All of these people will have a different perspective. The challenge for the group members is to play these roles with respect and authenticity and thereby move beyond the bounds of their own egocentric view.[2]

Role Training

After the offence-focused work and post-trauma work has been successfully addressed, it may be useful, as part of the role training aims of the offender programme, to ask the group members to take on the role of 'Mister Self-Aware.' This is the role of a hypothetical man who has committed violent or sexual offences in the past, but has now undergone a full treatment programme. He is as self-aware as he possibly can be. He knows his high-risk situations, he has his coping strategies rehearsed, and he is able to make appropriate friendships in the community. Crucially, he is not a 'Mr. Goody-two-shoes.' Rather, he is more like an older, life sentence prisoner who has played all the games in the past, thinking he was tough enough and clever enough to get past the system, or beat it. Now, Mr. Self-aware has devoted his energies to being low risk, and maintaining a balanced, healthy lifestyle free of offending. Allow the group members to take on this role and practice being Mr. Self-aware for long periods of time. I have occasionally asked group members to stay in role as Mr Self-aware all week, until the next session. This has, for some participants, been a profound learning experience.

Conclusion

As the field of drama-based work with offenders develops, it is increasingly the case that people practicing in the field are moving into therapeutic contexts. In this chapter, I have drawn what I hope are some useful distinctions and offered some guidance for practitioners who wish to train and develop their practice across the entire spectrum of drama-based approaches. Many practitioners may wish to remain strictly focused on one aspect, for instance theatre workshops for personal growth. Others may wish to focus solely on psychodrama and psychotherapeutic contexts. What I have found most rewarding personally and professionally is the ability to work along the entire spectrum of drama-based possibilities, tailoring my approach to the individual, the group and the context.

Although it is not appropriate for all offenders, psychodrama is relevant for a large percentage of people who have committed violence and sexual abuse. Psychodrama can provide a powerfully corrective emotional experience and can help offenders by addressing themes such as victim stance, external locus of control, the effects of early abuse, traumatic sexualisation, maladaptive learning and functioning and poor attachment history. Psychodramatic trauma work also complements the goals of standard cognitive-behavioural approaches by directly addressing cognitive distortions, victim empathy and relapse prevention (Baim et al., 1999; Robson and Lambie, 1995).

To work truly therapeutically with offenders means that we must be willing to work with the neediness and fear behind the angry mask or beneath the cool, macho front. It means being willing to hear and not judge the raging child who escaped annihilation and now inhabits a destructive adult body, so that the responsible adult self can emerge and take full control of himself, his emotions, his thinking and behaviour. A very basic quality of human nature is that we find it hard to feel sorry for others who are in pain when it seems that no one feels sorry for our pain. We need that acknowledgment in order to free us up and satisfy a fundamental demand of the ego: to be heard, seen and respected (Miller, 1995; Sanford, 1993).

Some people may criticise such an approach as being 'soft' on offenders. Yet acknowledging wider factors, and seeking explanations, is not the same as looking for excuses. The offender's search for an explanation, when in proper perspective, can be a genuine search for insight and self-understanding. Indeed it is often an essential step toward helping the offender take charge of his life choices and break the cycle of handed-down legacies. We are all too aware of the pattern of criminal behaviour running through whole communities or being passed down through generations of a family.

There is a constant balance – a constant dialogue back and forth – between individual responsibility and external causes. This is the paradox at the centre of all work with offenders and youth at risk: while on the one hand we must insist that each offender take full responsibility for his own actions, we must also recognise that his behaviour exists within a wider cultural and historical context and within the context of his own life. This paradox is always present, so any explanation must be framed appropriately so that it can be of some use. Just as it would be a terrible disservice to an offender to encourage him to see himself as a powerless victim of circumstance, it is equally wrong-headed to chime on about individual responsibility while ignoring the realities of the offender's personal history, social environment and the wider influence of societal values, all of which contribute to the roles he plays out in society.

Notes

1. Other directors of Geese Theatre UK have been Saul Hewish, Simon Ruding and Sally Brookes. John Bergman, Director of Geese Theatre USA, was Artistic Consultant to the UK company until 1997. For more of the history of the two organisations, see Baim, Brookes and Mountford (2002).

2. The form of role-play described is *whole group role-play* (Baim, Brookes and Mountford, 2002)

Further Information

www.psychodrama.org.uk
Website of the British Psychodrama Association

www.asgpp.org
Website of the American Society of Group Psychotherapy and Psychodrama

www.blatner.com/adam/
A treasure trove of information about psychodrama

www.badth.co.uk or www.dryw.freeserve.co.uk/BADTh.htm
Website of the British Association of Dramatherapists

www.geese.co.uk
Geese Theatre UK's website

References

Baim, C., 'Techniques in Supervision for those working with sexual abusers', in Deacon, L. and Gocke, B. (eds.) *Understanding Perpetrators, Protecting Children: A practitioner's guide to working effectively with child sexual abusers*, (London Whiting and Birch, 1999).

Baim, C., 'Time's Distorted Mirror: Trauma Work with Adult Male Sex Offenders', In Kellerman, P. F. and Hudgins, M. K. (eds.), *Psychodrama with Trauma Survivors: Acting Out Your Pain*, (London, Jessica Kingsley, 2000).

Baim, C., Allam, J., Eames, T., Dunford, S., Hunt, S., 'The use of psychodrama to enhance victim empathy in sex offenders: An evaluation', *The Journal of Sexual Aggression*, 4 (1), (1999), pp. 4-14.

Baim, C., Brookes, S. and Mountford, A. (eds.), *The Geese Theatre Handbook: Drama with offenders and people at risk*, (Winchester, Waterside Press, 2002).

Bannister, A., 'Learning to Live Again: Psychodramatic Techniques with Sexually Abused Young People', in P. Holmes and M. Karp (eds.), *Psychodrama: Inspiration and Technique*, (London, Tavistock/ Routledge, 1991).

Barker, M. & Morgan, R., *Sex Offenders: A Framework for the Evaluation of Community Based Treatment*, (Report to the Home Office. Bristol University, Faculty of Law, 1993).

Beckett, R., 'Cognitive-behavioural Treatment of Sex Offenders', in Morrison, T.,

Erooga, M., Beckett, R. (eds.), *Sexual Offending Against Children: Assessment and Treatment of Male Abusers*, (London, Routledge, 1994).

Blatner, A., *Acting-in: Practical Applications of Psychodramatic Methods* (3rd edition). (London, Free Association Books, 1997) or (New York, Springer, 1996).

Bowlby, J., 'Violence in the family as a disorder of the attachment and care-giving systems', *The American Journal of Psychoanalysis* 44, (1984) pp. 9-27.

Bowlby, J., *A Secure Base – Clinical Applications of Attachment Theory*, (London, Routledge, 1988).

Briere, J., 'A Self-Trauma Model for Treating Adult Survivors of Severe Child Abuse', in Briere, J., Berliner, L., Bulkley, J. A., Jenny, C., and Reid, T. (eds.), *The APSAC Handbook on child maltreatment*, (Thousand Oaks, CA., Sage Publications, 1996) pp. 140-57.

Briggs, F. (ed.), *From Victim to Offender: How Child Sexual Abuse Victims Become Offenders*, (St Leonards, New South Wales, Allen and Unwin, 1995).

Burt, M. R., Cultural Myths and Supports for Rape. *Journal of Personality and Social Psychology*, 38(2), (1980), pp. 217-230.

Bustos, D., 'Wings and roots: locus, matrix, status nascendi and the concept of clusters', in P. Holmes, M. Karp & M. Watson (eds.), *Psychodrama Since Moreno: Innovations in Theory and Practice*, (London, Routledge, 1994).

Chapman, T. and Hough, M., *Evidence Based Practice: A Guide to Effective Practice*, (London, HM Inspectorate of Probation, 1998).

Clark, P. and Erooga, M., 'Groupwork with men who sexually abuse children', in Morrison, T., Erooga, M., Beckett, R. (eds.), *Sexual Offending Against Children: Assessment and Treatment of Male Abusers*, (London, Routledge, 1994).

Corsini, R. J., 'Psychodramatic Treatment of a Paedophile', *Group Psychotherapy, Journal of Sociopsychopathology and Sociatry*, 4 (3), (1951a), pp. 66-171.

- , 'The Method of Psychodrama in Prison', *Group Psychotherapy*, 3 (4), (1951b) pp. 321-326.

- , Immediate Therapy. *Group Psychotherapy*, 4, (1952), pp. 322-330.

- , *Role-playing in Psychotherapy*, (Chicago, Aldine 1967).

Crittenden, P., 'A Dynamic-Maturational Approach to Continuity and Change in Pattern of Attachment', in Crittenden, P. and Claussen, A. (eds.), *The Organisation of Attachment Relationships: Maturation, Culture and Context*. (Cambridge University Press, 2000).

- , 'Attachment and Psychopathology,' Presentation in Broadstairs, Kent (2002).

Dayton, T., *Drama Games*, (Deerfield Beach, Fl., Health Communications, Inc. 1990).

de Zulueta, F., *From Pain to Violence: The Traumatic Roots of Destructiveness*, (London, Whurr Publishers, 1998).

Goldman, E. and Morrison, D., *Psychodrama: Experience and Process*, (Dubuque, Iowa, Kendall/Hunt 1984).

Greenberg, L. S. and Paivio, S. C., 'Allowing and accepting painful emotional experiences', *The International Journal of Action Methods: Psychodrama, Skill Training and Role-playing*, 51 (3), (1998) pp. 47-61.

Grubin, D., 'Sexual Offending Against Children: Understanding the risk', *Police*

Research Series, Paper 99, (London: Policing and Reducing Crime Unit – Research, Development and Statistics Directorate, 1998).

Hanson, K., 'Working with sex offenders: A Personal View', *The Journal of Sexual Aggression*, 4 (2), (1999), pp. 81-93.

Hollander, C. E., 'A process for psychodrama training: the Hollander psychodrama curve' (revised ed.), (Denver, Snow Lion Press, 1978).

Hudgins, M. K., 'The Therapeutic Spiral Model: Treating PTSD in Action', in Kellerman, P. F. and Hudgins, M. K. (eds.), *Psychodrama with Trauma Survivors: Acting Out Your Pain*, (London, Jessica Kingsley, 2000).

- , *Experiential Treatment for PTSD: The Therapeutic Spiral Model*, (New York, Springer, 2002).

Hudgins, M. K. and Drucker, K., 'The Containing Double as Part of the Therapeutic Spiral Model for Treating Trauma Survivors', *The International Journal of Action Methods: Psychodrama, Skill Training, and Role-playing*, 51 (2), (1998), pp. 63-74.

Hunter, M., *Child Survivors and Perpetrators of Sexual Abuse – Treatment Innovations*, (London, Sage, 1995).

Jefferies, J., 'A Psychodrama Perspective', in Cordess, C. & Cox, M. (eds.), *Forensic Psychotherapy*, (London, Jessica Kingsley Publishers, 1996).

Jenkins, A., *Invitations to Responsibility – the therapeutic engagement of men who are violent and abusive*, (Adelaide, S. Australia, Dulwich Centre Publications, 1997).

Kipper, D., *Psychotherapy Through Clincal Role-playing*, (New York, Brunner/ Mazel, 1986).

- , 'Psychodrama and Trauma: Implications for Future Interventions of Psychodramatic Role-Playing Modalities', *The International Journal of Action Methods: Psychodrama, Skill Training and Role-playing*, 51 (3), (1998), pp. 113-121.

Langs, R., *Psychotherapy and Science*, (London, Sage, 1999).

Marshall, W. L. & Maric, A., 'Cognitive and Emotional Components of Generalized Empathy Deficits in Child Molesters', *Journal of Child Sexual Abuse*, 5 (2), (1996), pp. 101-110.

Miller, A., *The drama of being a child*, (London, Virago, 1995).

Metcalf, K., 'Role Theory and Eating Disorders', *Psychodrama Network News, newsletter of the American Society of Group Psychotherapy and Psychodrama*, (January, 1997).

Moreno, J. L., *Psychodrama First Volume*. (Ambler, Pennsylvania, Beacon Press, Inc., 1972) (First published 1946).

Moreno, J. L. and Moreno, Z. T., *Psychodrama Volume Two*, (Beacon, New York, Beacon House, 1975).

Robson, M. & Lambie, I., 'Using Psychodrama to Facilitate Victim Empathy in Adolescent Sexual Offenders', *Journal of the Australian and New Zealand Psychodrama Association*, 4, (1995), pp. 13-19.

Sachnoff, E., 'Letter to the Editor', *The International Journal of Action Methods: Psychodrama, Skill Training and Role-playing*, 51 (4), (1999), pp. 165.

Salter, A., *Treating Child Sex Offenders and Victims*, (London, Sage, 1988).

Salter, A., *Transforming Trauma – a guide to understanding and treating adult survivors of child sexual abuse*, (London, Sage, 1995).

Samenow, S., *Inside the Criminal Mind*, (New York, Times Books/Random House, 1984).

Sanford, L. T., *Strong at the broken places – overcoming the trauma of child abuse.* (London, Virago, 1993).

Scheff, T. J., *Catharsis in Healing, Ritual and Drama*, (London, Univ. of California Press, 1979).

Schwartz, M. F., Galperin, L. D. and Masters, W. H., 'Dissociation and Treatment of compulsive re-enactment of trauma: Sexual compulsivity', in Hunter, M. (ed.), *The Sexually Abused Male*, Vol. 3., (Lexington, MA., Lexington Books, 1993).

Schwartz, M. F., Galperin, L. D. and Masters, W. H., 'Sexual Trauma Within the Context of Traumatic and Inescapable Stress, Neglect, and Poisonous Pedagogy', in Hunter, M. (ed.), *Adult Survivors of Sexual Abuse*, (London, Sage, 1995).

Schwartz, M. F. and Masters, W. H., 'Integration of Trauma-based, Cognitive Behavioural, Systemic and Addiction Approaches for Treatment of Hypersexual Pair-Bonding Disorder', in Carnes, P. J. (ed.), *Sexual Addiction and Compulsivity, Vol. 1*, (London, Brunner Mazel, 1993).

Sennett, R., *The Fall of Public Man*, (London, Cambridge University Press, 1976).

Simpson, L., *Evaluation of Treatment Methods in Child Sexual Abuse: A Literature Review*, (University of Bath and Dorset Area Child Protection Committee, 1994).

Skuse D., Bentovim A., Hodges J., Stevenson J., Andreou C., Lanyado M., New M., Williams B. and McMillan D., 'Risk factors for development of sexually abusive behaviour in sexually victimised adolescent boys: cross sectional study', *British Medical Journal*, 317(7152), (1998), pp. 175-9.

Taylor, S., Personal communication, (1999).

Tedeschi, R. G. and Calhoun, L. G., *Trauma and Transformation – Growing in the Aftermath of Suffering*, (London, Sage Publications, 1995).

Van der Kolk, B., 'The compulsion to repeat the trauma: re-enactment, revictimisation and masochism', *Psychiatric Clinics of North America*, 12, (1989), pp. 389-411.

Van der Kolk, B., 'Childhood Abuse and Neglect and Loss of Self-Regulation', *The Bulletin of the Menninger Clinic*, 58 (2), (1994a), pp. 1-14.

Van der Kolk, B.A., 'The body keeps the score – Memory and the evolving psychobiology of post traumatic stress', *Harvard Review of Psychiatry*, 1(3), (1994b), pp. 253-65.

Van Mentz, M., *The Effective Use of Role-play*, (London, Kogan Page, 1983).

Vennard, J., Hedderman, C., Sugg, D., 'Changing Offenders' Attitudes and Behaviour: What Works', *Home Office Research Study 171*, (London, Home Office Research and Statistics Directorate, 1997).

Yablonsky, L., *Psychodrama: Resolving Emotional Problems Through Role-playing*, (New York, Basic Books, 1976).

Wallis, K., 'Perspectives on Offenders', in Briggs, F. (ed.), *From Victim to Offender: How Child Sexual Abuse Victims Become Offenders*, (St Leonards, New South Wales, Allen and Unwin, 1995).

Webb, L. P. and Leehan, J., *Group Treatment for Adult Survivors of Abuse – A Manual for Practitioners*, (London, Sage, 1996).

White, L., *The Action Manual: Techniques to Enliven the Group Process and Individual Counselling*, (Toronto: Self-published, 2002), available from www.lizwhiteinaction.com
Whitfield, C. L., *Memory and Abuse – Remembering and Healing the Effects of Trauma*, (Deerfield Beach, FL., Health Communications, 1995).
Winn, L., *Post Traumatic Stress Disorder and Dramatherapy*, (London, Jessica Kingsley, 1994).
Yardley-Matwiejczuk, K., *Role-play: Theory and Practice*, (London, Sage, 1997).

Author's note

Many thanks to Alyson Coupe for her help with this chapter.

Prison Transformation in South Africa

Centre for Conflict Resolution

This chapter presents a number of different perspectives of the Prisons Transformation Project, run by the Centre for Conflict Resolution (CCR) in Pollsmoor Prison, South Africa. The chapter includes sections written by researchers, trainers, a prison guard and a prisoner who were involved in the project.

The Prison Transformation Project

Chris Giffard, Joanna Flanders-Thomas and Roshila Nair

The Centre for Conflict Resolution (CCR) has, for the past three-and-a-half years, been operating a Prison Transformation Project in Pollsmoor Prison in Cape Town. The programme has succeeded in altering some of the old-style attitudes, and also working against the inertia so often evident in an institution that tends to be inward-looking.

The Problems Facing Pollsmoor Admission Centre

The Pollsmoor Admission Centre (formerly the Maximum Prison) is the largest of the five prisons making up the Pollsmoor Management Area. The vast majority of its 3,200 inmates are un-sentenced awaiting-trial prisoners, or sentenced prisoners facing further charges. As an awaiting-trial prison (or remand centre) its population is constantly changing. On a daily basis, about three hundred prisoners are booked out to appear in various courts around Cape Town. Some return as sentenced prisoners, others do not return at all, but large numbers come back to their cells to await a future court date, sometimes as distant as six months later.

During the mid-1990s conditions in Pollsmoor worsened. High and unprecedented levels of overcrowding meant that in some sections of the prison there were twice as many prisoners as the physical structures allowed for, most of them in large communal cells. The prison management's approach was to maintain a repressive regime in the prison. The dominant method of relating to prisoners was through instruction. The Prison staff did little else but count prisoners, lock and unlock doors, and ensure that food was delivered. Guard dogs were used to control and intimidate prisoners. Prison staff members routinely used physical violence and verbal threats to gain prisoners' compliance with orders. This repressive approach generated extremely high levels of tension in the prison and physical assaults were commonplace.

Gangsterism was – and is – a potent feature of Pollsmoor prison life, and gangs are segregated into three separate sections on a single floor, accommodating a total of between five hundred and seven hundred and fifty. This segregation is in part an attempt to limit the gangs' ongoing recruitment of new members from amongst the recent arrivals. Due to the fact that warders are present in the sections for less than two-thirds of the day, the gangs are enormously powerful in the communal cells. Gang rule involves much violence, including sexual violence. In general, the gangs pose an enormous threat to efforts to transform and demilitarise the prison and to attempts to rehabilitate inmates. All of this, in turn, has a hugely negative impact on the communities to which inmates return on their release from prison.

In 1997 transformation within the Department of Correctional Services saw blacks taking up management positions for the first time at Pollsmoor Prison. These were senior ranking prison staff members who had previously been denied promotion under the apartheid regime, or because of their opposition to apartheid. The new management immediately began to make changes in the prison. Guard dogs were removed from the prison building. Other overt signs of repression, such as the unnecessary stationing of armed guards on the roof when prisoners were exercising, were dispensed with. Prison staff members were instructed to deal with prisoners in a humane fashion. The prison head himself demonstrated this new approach by engaging directly with prisoners, including gang leaders, in the communal cells.

The new management also targeted the source of many of the conflicts and much of the violence in the prison, the gangs. The major gangs in Pollsmoor Prison's Admission Centre are the 26s, 27s and 28s – the numbers gangs. These gangs were segregated into three separate sections on a single floor in an attempt to limit the ongoing recruitment of gang members from amongst new arrivals to the prison. The gangs are extremely powerful in the communal cells during lock-up times. Gang rule involves extensive use of violence, including sexual violence. In general, gangs in South African prisons are a major obstacle to efforts to transform and demilitarize the prison culture. Gang rule impacts negatively on attempts to rehabilitate prisoners, and consequently also on the communities to which prisoners return when released.

This was the context, in 1998, into which CCR was invited by Pollsmoor Prison management to run conflict resolution workshops for staff members working with juveniles in the Admission Centre. Pollsmoor Prison staff identified conflict resolution as an important part of transformation in the prison, especially with regard to reducing the levels of violence and building more positive relationships among prisoners, staff, prisoners and staff, and management and staff – all those who make up the prison community. A sustained effort by CCR to impact on these goals was seen as necessary. Thus, in 1999 CCR launched the Prisons Transformation Project to focus more intensively on all the areas identified for intervention in prisons within a conflict resolution framework, in particular, the reduction of re-offending of prisoners, or recidivism. For demilitarization, reduction of violence, reduction of recidivism and transformation to occur, all sectors of the prison community need to be engaged in the transformation process.

The Work of CCR's Prisons Transformation Project

The focus of CCR's Prisons Transformation Project has been influenced by both the initial work with Pollsmoor Prison in 1998 and national imperatives as set out by the Constitution and the recommendations of the Truth and Reconciliation Commission's (TRC) final report. The primary goal of the project is to contribute to the transformation of prisons from a militaristic organisational culture to a culture of learning, growth and development, where human rights are respected and people are treated with dignity and respect. As well, the aim is to equip and empower management, staff and prisoners to manage conflict more effectively.

The Project is underpinned by two core perspectives. First, what happens to inmates inside prison has a significant impact on what they do and how they behave on their release. If society wants to reduce the likelihood that they return to crime and violence, then it has to engage seriously in rehabilitation programmes. The rehabilitation of prisoners is a critical *security* and *crime prevention* strategy, contributing to the creation of safer cities and the protection of citizens and visitors from harm.

Second, in providing that 'everyone has inherent dignity and the right to have their dignity respected and protected' (Section 10), our Constitution does not exclude prisoners. On the contrary, it provides explicitly and specifically that everyone who is detained, including every sentenced prisoner, has the right to conditions of detention that are consistent with human dignity (Section 35(2)(e)).

A prison is not a closed system; most offenders are eventually released from prison into the community. Therefore, what happens to prisoners inside prison has a direct impact on the community. Sometimes, an individual entering prison to await trial for a minor offence might return to the community a 'hardened criminal' (more aggressive and prone to violence and crime), having been affected by the violence associated with gang rule in prison. It is often said that South African prisons are a breeding ground for criminals because of the inhumane conditions and violence rife in prisons. CCR's Prisons Transformation Project differs from most other prison programmes aimed at rehabilitation of prisoners for this very reason. While most other programmes target sentenced prisoners, CCR's training programmes target mainly awaiting-trial prisoners. The facilities and services available to awaiting-trial prisoners are very limited: they have no access to social workers, psychologists, or training programmes. Instead, health care is limited and there is massive overcrowding in cells. Awaiting-trial prisoners are housed in extremely confined conditions (sometimes up to sixty to a cell designed to hold fifteen to twenty prisoners) twenty-three out of twenty-four hours a day. CCR has therefore concentrated its prisoner training programmes on this neglected population in prison. This is a key intervention sector to reduce recidivism as many awaiting-trial prisoners are never sentenced. More often than not, they re-emerge in communities as 'hardened criminals' and are more likely to embark on a path of criminal behaviour and return to prison sooner or later.

CCR has experienced some successes in running pilot programmes for awaiting-trial prisoners at Pollsmoor Prison. The long-term aim is to train and equip prison staff members with the skills needed to run programmes with prisoners. Prisons would thus be staffed with on-site conflict resolution trainers with the capacity to implement and run programmes to reduce levels of violence and build more constructive relationships in the prison community. The Department of Correctional Services would thus attain a level of self sufficiency in transforming prisons from militarized institutions to institutions with a human rights culture as stated in the Constitution (Section 35(2) Act No. 108 of 1996).

In terms of the Constitution, transformation of institutions in South Africa has a political emphasis on demilitarization and on creating a civilian culture where human rights are respected and all people treated with dignity. In its final report to the State President, the TRC discusses the training of prison personnel and recommends that:

• Prison officers receive human rights training as a basic guide for treatment of prisoners and the management of the prison systems.
• Prison staff be adequately trained in prison law, their duties and responsibilities, ethics and conflict resolution.
• Prison staff receive training in creative and humane ways of motivating prisoners to regain their human dignity and co-operate with the rehabilitation programmes in prisons. (Truth and Reconciliation Commission Final Report 1998, p. 314, paragraph 26).
• With regard to the rehabilitation of prisoners, the TRC recommends that: skills training for prisoners become a priority.
• All prison warders receive training, which will enable them to recognise the basic needs in this regard.
• Prisoners receive training in human rights and non-violent ways of conflict resolution.
• Counselling should be made available to all prisoners.
• Prisoners have access to literacy classes and skills training. Work sessions should be designed to promote rehabilitation, rather than simply being punitive hard labour (Truth and Reconciliation Commission Final Report 1998, p. 314, paragraph 27).

The training provided by CCR targets these national goals directly. In South Africa most of the current prison staff have been trained under the old apartheid system, which taught correctional services staff to treat prisoners as second-class citizens. Prison staff members therefore need the tools to create the culture of human rights and co-operation among prisoners that our democratic government wants to nurture. Prisoners who are involved in conflict resolution programmes are provided with an opportunity in prison never offered to them before to reflect on the personal benefits of non-violent behaviour. They are treated with dignity and encouraged to use the programme's opportunity to examine their personal responses to the world.

CCR's programme consists of four-day conflict resolution workshops. Training is aimed at providing participants with an understanding of the basic nature of conflict, and provides them with tools to handle conflict constructively.

Interacting in Prisons to Make Change Possible

Stan Henkeman

Training within the prison context brings with it unique challenges. Participants, whether prison staff or prisoners, are often traumatised individuals, given the stressful environment within which they find themselves. Because the prison environment is aggressive, regimented and dangerous, participants are often reluctant to attend workshops that are clinical and strictly factual. At the Centre for Conflict Resolution (CCR) our experience has shown that a fun, interactive approach has a much stronger impact on participants than a conventional one where the facilitator dominates the workshop and 'lectures' to them. An interactive approach is an opportunity to challenge the militaristic prison culture, which is a legacy of apartheid. A strong feature of this culture is the lack of adherence to human rights and constitutional values in the practices of most of the prison staff towards prisoners. The incessant, negative peer pressure prisoners subject each other to also contributes to the aggressive prison environment with conflict rife at all levels. Most of the workshops conducted by CCR take place over four days, during which time we witness in the process real shifts in the way participants make sense of their realities and begin to leave behind their old social masks. What follows is a discussion of some key aspects of the interactive approach that add value to our workshops in prisons.

Facilitation

Our facilitation is based on the action-learning model where:

• Every participant is encouraged to reflect on all activities;
• Learnings to inform future actions are then identified. In other words, a space is created in the training session and environment for experiential learning, where through a series of interactions and reflections a participant comes to the learning or 'lesson' by himself;
• Activities are mostly in the form of interactive exercises, games and discussions. The emphasis is on enjoyment, creativity and full participation. For example, an exercise enjoyed by most participants is the 'trust walk.' Participants are given blindfolds and work in pairs. Each participant gets an opportunity to lead or guide his blindfolded partner through a course determined by the facilitator, using just his voice. The course is normally outside the training room. Once back in the training room, participants reflect on their experiences in plenary, which is often very meaningful for them, as most of them struggle with the issue of trust.
• Learnings are extracted from various exercises and participants discuss possibilities for acting differently in future.

The Training Space

The training environment plays an important role in facilitating positive outcomes for participants. It is very useful to create different spaces to achieve different outcomes. For obvious reasons, prisoners enjoy environment changes. In CCR's training we generally distinguish between three types of training spaces:
• The primary, formal training space must lend itself to interaction. Participants should be able to see each other. For example, a circle or horse-shoe arrangement is most conducive to this;
• Secondly, it is useful to choose activities that can be done outdoors. It has been our experience that outdoor games and activities allow participants the opportunity to make as much noise as they want to and relax;
• The third type of space we create is known as the sacred circle. Some exercises are done in the sacred circle, but this is primarily a space for reflection. It is used as a check-in space in the morning, for reflection on learnings and sharing of feelings throughout the workshop. Participants are discouraged from challenging what someone says in this safe space, as the emphasis is on affirming self and others. For a participant, it is often a highlight in the workshop to be invited to share in the sacred circle. One of the key features of the sacred circle is that confidentiality is respected.

Creating a Common Thread or Focus

The greatest reward for any facilitator working in the prison environment is witnessing those profound moments when participants gain insights into their lives as they share deeply of lessons learnt and how future actions will be influenced by the new skills acquired during the workshop. It has been our experience at CCR that running a workshop along a particular theme that participants can fully identify with works well to facilitate shifts from negative to positive attitudes regarding conflict management. For example, CCR uses the theme 'Change is possible. Change begins with me' in our prison workshops. This catchy refrain has proved to be very popular among the prisoners who have participated in the workshops, has become the subject of poems and dramas and is often quoted in conversations. The theme 'Searching for opportunities to manage conflict creatively' encourages participants to reflect on their habits and practices in new, more constructive ways. Instead of dwelling on the dangers of conflict, many participants actively pursue the opportunities conflict provides to restore the relationships damaged by aggressive communication, threats and violence, which constitute the more common forms of interaction in the militaristic prison environment.

Conclusion

At CCR we believe that our training in conflict resolution should contribute meaningfully to the process of transformation occurring in the Department of Correctional Services, both at organisational and personal levels. It is, however, at the personal level that we target our contribution mostly towards change and empowerment of prison staff seeking to see themselves as service providers rather than as security force personnel. As far as working with prisoners is concerned, we see ourselves as part of a broader network of service providers contributing to their rehabilitation and restoration. Our workshops are designed to help prepare prisoners for their eventual release and reintegration into society. It is therefore important that we challenge our participants, whether prisoners or staff members, to dig deep within themselves to reconnect with their humanity. Only then can the prison as an institution change from its present militaristic culture to a human rights one. An interactive approach, in our view, can facilitate engagement with what for many is a very frightening endeavour.

Journey to Nouveau Pollsmoor Prison

A Correctional Officer's Story

By Christopher Glen Malgas

The Prisons Transformation Project run by the Centre for Conflict Resolution (CCR) illustrates some measure of how prisoners and gangsters can change. But prison staff members need to change too. The changes that have taken place at Pollsmoor Prison since 1997 have taught me a lot. They have made me realise how important it is to change the nature of the prison itself. But to accomplish that we need to show prison staff that change is in their interest too.

I have worked in the prison system for a long time. I arrived from Mossel Bay in the Eastern Cape to join the Department of Correctional Services in 1977. I joined the Department because my cousin was a prison warder at the time and recommended it as a good, stable job, even though being coloured meant limited career prospects in the prison system. I had worked a few months in the prison in Mossel Bay as an untrained probation warder. It was only when I was sent to the Westlake Training College, near Pollsmoor Prison, that I received basic training as a prison warder. All coloured staff of the Department of Correctional Services went to this college for training during the apartheid era.

The basic course for warders lasted six months and constituted purely military training. In fact, the army trained the course instructors. Training consisted of military drill, saluting, showing respect to senior officers and handling a range of firearms. We even had a course on 'ethics' to teach us what cutlery to use at dinner and how to behave at formal dances! But there was nothing in the course about working with prisoners.

After I completed the basic training course, I became a senior instructor. I too was now a 'military man' and spent my days getting my trainees fit and drilling them over and over in military etiquette. On weekends I worked at Pollsmoor Prison in what is now known as the Admissions Centre. I remained an instructor at Westlake Training College for many years. When it closed in 1989, I was manager of the physical training department.

In 1989 the Police and Prisons Civil Rights Union (POPCRU) was formed. I was one of its founder members, as were many warders then based at Westlake Training College. At the time, I was transferred to 'Maximum' (now the Admission Centre) at Pollsmoor Prison. Working full-time at Pollsmoor Prison came as a big shock to me. I was posted in a section popularly known as 'Boipatong' (the name of a conflict-ridden township on the Eastrand in the former Transvaal province), which held sentenced prisoners still awaiting further trials. Almost daily, stabbings and fights took place among the prisoners, but I handled myself with confidence because of my self-defence training. Prisoners and staff respected my physical strength, which made me feel on top of the world.

That feeling did not last long though. I found myself constantly challenging the white warders in the section. I did not like the inhumane way they treated the prisoners. They locked the gates and unlocked them again when required. They counted the prisoners regularly. They did not even bother to open the cell gates to pass food to prisoners but just pushed the plates under the gate. There were seldom opportunities for prisoners to take exercise; when prisoners were let out into the courtyard, fights usually broke out. Guard dogs were kept in sections where prisoners slept, which created enormous fear and tension.

Coloured warders were not allowed to enter the staff offices or to sit on chairs in the prison. I challenged white warders about this too. Because of my attitude and the fact that I outranked some of them, white warders in the section were reluctant to work with me. Eventually I, together with a few other warders, was asked to leave the section on a trumped-up charge.

I then spent brief periods in the prison visitors' section and the library. In 1992 I was posted as head of the juvenile prison in Section B4, which although physically attached to the women's prison had a separate entrance. Legislation had just been passed to separate children from adults in prison. Section B4 held juveniles aged fourteen to seventeen. I had twelve staff and a full-time social worker in the section. It was the first time in Pollsmoor Prison that a coloured warder was placed in charge of white staff.

It was here that I began to work more closely with individuals and civil society groups from outside the prison, particularly the National Institute for the Care and Rehabilitation of Offenders (NICRO). By then, experience had taught me that the way one treats a prisoner affects his behaviour both inside prison and outside when released. My staff and I tried to develop caring relationships with the children in our charge. We made contact with their families and ran a literacy programme. We also received support from some of the local schools and a number of the children were able to write exams, thus pursuing an education in prison.

I had recently become a father. The experience and emotions stirred by fatherhood helped me to develop nurturing relationships with the children in Section B4. We treated them with the care that any child deserves – after all they were children with the same needs of children elsewhere. We tried to improve their nutrition and organised games as best we could. We did all this despite having few available resources. And it worked. The behaviour of the children in Section B4 improved; their response to us improved. The prison itself was now kept neat and clean. Both prison staff and the children slowly learned the importance of respecting, rather than fearing, each other.

Mr. Johnny Jansen was appointed head of Pollsmoor Prison's Admission Centre in 1997. It was the first time a black person was appointed to this senior post in the prison. Soon after he arrived, a departmental task force raided the prison without his knowledge and assaulted a number of prisoners. A huge crisis ensued, as black prison staff believed that the whole thing was a set-up to get rid off Mr. Jansen. I, together with some other prison staff, supported him through the crisis, as we believed that the prison could improve under a more sensitive, black leadership.

With Mr. Jansen as head of the prison, the institution has become a very different place to work in. It is no longer dominated by whites desperate to retain power. Mr. Jansen's approach is to tackle difficult problems head on. Gangs are one of the biggest threats to transformation in the prison, as they control almost every aspect of prison life – distribution of food and clothes, sexual relationships and so forth. They are also responsible for much of the violence and corruption in the prison. At the time, CCR had already been working at Pollsmoor Prison for a couple of years, mostly with the juveniles in the Medium A prison. Mr. Jansen requested CCR to target one of the gang floors, Section D3. I was asked to work in this section, which has been the biggest challenge I have had to face in my life so far. I called on the experience I had gained working with the children in Section B4. There, I had learned the importance of a daily structured programme for prisoners, especially for the awaiting-trial prisoners who have little else to do but wait for a court date.

CCR staff assisted me with putting together this daily programme. Not only did we begin a series of workshops with CCR, but we also set up an initiative for volunteers to hold monthly workshops after hours in the cells. After a year and a half of working in Section D3 (at the time of writing), we have made giant strides. The section is far safer than it used to be. There are very few assaults, even though members of different gangs are held in the same cells. We have managed to create a more co-operative environment by teaching the prisoners in this section how to relate to and respect each other and how to deal with conflict constructively. I myself have learnt a tremendous amount about these issues. For example, I can now go into a tense situation and defuse it by talking to prisoners constructively rather than threatening them.

But this change has happened in just one small section of Pollsmoor Prison. There are two other gangs and numerous other sections. The lessons learnt in Section D3 need to be spread more widely throughout the prison. Other prison staff members need to learn these lessons and skills too. Although South African prisons have been formally demilitarized, this has not been the case in practice. A military culture is still rife in our prisons. Some prison staff still believe that all their job entails is keeping prisoners behind bars and continue to misuse the power and authority that comes with their uniform – a sad legacy of apartheid. Most likely, their training has been just like mine when I started my career in prison services, which teaches nothing about building human relationships in the prison.

Prison staff need to be made aware that it is not just the prisoners' but their own lives that will improve if they embrace transformation and move from a military to a human rights culture in prison. They can accomplish this by acquiring the necessary skills to relate differently to prisoners and each other, but first they must want to change. Rather than merely waiting for retirement, it is possible to feel fulfilled working in prison services. It is unfortunate that most prison staff have been working within a militaristic culture for so long that they cannot even imagine that things can be done differently to change the prison environment.

All staff members need exposure to training programmes that teach respect for diversity and celebrate cultural and individual differences. We must all undergo courses in conflict resolution and mediation, as conflict is part and parcel of any environment, including prisons. Basic training for prison staff needs to change too. While in-service training is important for older staff members, it would help if basic training taught incoming staff how to relate to prisoners within a human rights framework. Slowly but surely a humane culture will take root in our prisons.

The Department of Correctional Services and its prisons were very badly impacted on by apartheid. Prison services were turned into a military force. Most staff members have not been re-trained to meet the demands of prison under a democratic order. We continue in our old ways mostly out of sheer ignorance of the benefits of change. Without being taught how to change, it is difficult for us to see that there is another, more constructive way to work in prisons. With the small miracle in Section D3 at Pollsmoor Prison, we have caught a glimpse that things can change, if we ourselves change and are prepared to change. By engaging with our own change, we surely will be able to inspire the prisoners in our care to change too. It is a basic truth that regardless of our different roles as staff members and prisoners, we are all human beings engaging with each other and making up the prison community. As such, we need each other so that we can be the best we can, like in any other community.

If we all believe in and really want it, nouveau (new) Pollsmoor Prison, a place of peace and constructive human relations, could just be over the horizon. After all, we hardly believed that South Africa would become a democracy before the millennium was out. And now we live in the miracle of a democratic South Africa! What further proof do we need that change for the better is possible?

Doing Time. From punishment to Rehabilitation and Restoration

By Paul

> 'In this great future don't forget your past'
> (Lyrics from 'No woman, no cry', Bob Marley)

It can generally be said about life that we learn from our mistakes. Although, this may seem a negative concept on the face of it, in reality making mistakes is humankind's frame of reference for problem-solving. Mistakes become opportunities for learning, which decrease our steep learning curve. This process facilitates our social evolution and leads to progress.

History is a record of our mistakes and is a crucial part of any rehabilitation, restoration and development process. Therefore, to understand the needs of the present and future, it is important to remember, analyse and understand the past. So while the history of South African prisons may present an extremely dark and negative picture, we must use it to create something positive.

A History of Punishment and Violence in our Prisons

The many phases through which our prisons have progressed mirror, by and large, South African society's history and politics. When I first entered prison in the early 1970s, I found the institution to be an extension of the racist apartheid ideology, systemically entrenched throughout society. I will never forget the thoughts that ran through my head as I was being admitted to Pollsmoor Prison. A notice ordered in big, bold Afrikaans: 'Alle waardevolle artikels, geld, ringe en horlosies moet by hierdie toonbank ingehandig word.' (All valuable articles, money, rings and watches must be handed in at this counter.) I thought, 'Would they regard my soul as being valuable?' This silent question was soon answered with an unequivocal NO.

I was eighteen-years-old at the time and my experiences in prison have left an indelible impression on my mind. Constantly subjected to horrendous human rights abuses by warders and other prisoners, I soon resolved to harden my attitude. Any sacrosanct value I held for life, I stored away deep in my sub-conscious to preserve my sanity in the brutal environment I found myself.

The brutality of the apartheid system manifested itself with full force in prison. Warders constantly physically and mentally assaulted prisoners. Medical attention was often withheld as a form of punishment. Food was used as a weapon against prisoners; it was often withheld to weaken the resolve of rebellious prisoners. Any attempt at revolt was squashed as soon as it started. Teargas and attack dogs were used regularly to 'soften up' prisoners. Those who stood up for their rights were identified as culprits and were severely beaten. Then, in their bloodied, broken state, they were thrown into solitary confinement. They were refused medical attention and had their food rations severely limited. Reduced to helpless nothingness, many often ended up in straitjackets.

Many prisoners were complaining of brutal assaults and had wounds and scars consistent with severe physical abuse. The prison authorities simply turned a blind eye to the stream of complaints and refused to investigate the charges being made. Often, prisoners were denied the right to legal representation until their wounds had sufficiently healed and the physical evidence of abuse disappeared on the victims' bodies. Thus, prisoners were forced to endure a wide spectrum of human rights abuses and remained in a precarious and helpless position.

Some prisoners realised that they had to take the initiative and do something to tilt the scales of justice in their favour. They decided to use the brutal apartheid system against itself. They organised themselves and began to introduce into court hearings information about their ordeals in prison, information that was unrelated to their cases. This brilliant move was accompanied by the writing of hundreds of letters about the abusive conditions they had to endure. These letters were smuggled out to friends, families and lawyers, and eventually their efforts had the desired effect. Knowledge about the abusive conditions in prison attracted the attention of the liberal press. The courts hesitatingly confirmed that prisoners are human and that they are indeed part of society.

During this turbulent time in the apartheid prisons, some self-defence efforts by the notorious prison gangs (whose histories go back to the 1800s) had a negative result. In the 1960s and 1970s the prison gangs undertook to wreak havoc as a means of resistance. Frequent clashes between warders and organised groups of prisoners occurred. At first the structure and discipline of the prison gangs served as a catalyst for more prisoners joining.

Unfortunately, the 'total onslaught' approach of the prison gangs proved to be a double-edged sword. In our haste to use this approach to resist the oppression and violence of the warders, everything else became unimportant. Non-conformation was not tolerated and a moral and emotional vacuum was created. We ourselves became increasingly guilty of perpetrating the same human rights abuses we were fighting against and a culture of increased violence began to flourish among prisoners.

In the 1980s and 1990s outside gangs began to infiltrate the prison and the prison gangs' hierarchies and activities changed increasingly. We lost any focus of resistance and assimilated an Africanised version of American gangland culture. The prison gangs descended into the moral abyss and prisoner-on-prisoner violence reached an all time high.

Towards a Future of Hope – What We Can Learn From History

The violence and many mistakes made in prison did not happen in isolation. It was not just prison authorities and prisoners who were culpable, but the state and society in general. Buy-in by all members of society is necessary to ensure that a culture of human rights is respected in any community, including prison. At the very least, there should be an expectation that rights are respected and that the necessary efforts are made and resources allocated by those responsible for creating the conditions for this happen. For a safer society, for safer communities (including prison), the state and society must be involved in transformation efforts. The previous system of brutal punishment only succeeded in hardening attitudes among prisoners, warders and members of the community. With apartheid as its rich cousin, the abusive prison system bred contempt for respect among human beings. In marginalising prisoners, it created a class of people with a destructive identity, no purpose in life and therefore no future. This has merely served to perpetuate the current vicious cycle of crime in South Africa.

It is only through an inclusive (which means including the prisoner and everybody else concerned), properly structured process of restoration, rehabilitation and development that we will be able to ensure positive, long-term sustainability of the corrections process.

Rehabilitation, Restoration and Development in Action

More than eighty per cent of prisoners return to Pollsmoor Prison after being released. They return to the 'college of knowledge' as it is popularly known amongst inmates, persisting in a life of crime. It is all too clear that the system is terminally deficient – for the prisoner, the justice system and society in general. This, frightening though it is, is a fact. The vicious cycle of crime in South Africa affects everyone. The causes for the high rate of recidivism may be debatable, but it is most certainly closely linked to the severe lack of viable alternatives for newly released prisoners. This, combined with low self-esteem, negative self-identity and morally bankrupt role models, is the perfect recipe for a prisoner's failure to lead a constructive life upon release.

The solution should therefore lie in restoring the prisoner's sense of positive identity and enhancing self-esteem – in other words, promoting restoration, rehabilitation and development. This will sow the seeds to develop a sense of pride, create purpose in life and build belief in a positive future worth living for and working towards. Achieving this, even on a very small scale, will create the positive role models so desperately needed to inspire and sustain the rehabilitation process among prisoners.

What better place than prison itself to provide the classroom needed to end the cycle of crime our country is caught in. The audience is captive and one of the most crucial resources – time – is in abundance. Because of our country's violent and unjust past, our current democratic society still has many scarred and broken people living in it. Many souls have been injured and it is they who tend to end up in our jails. These injured souls are in urgent need of restoration. The healing process for them must include:

• Trauma counselling to teach prisoners how to deal with painful memories of the past. Such counselling will enable them to come to terms with their hidden fears and to confront the unresolved issues that influence their negative choices and aggressive behaviour. In some instances sustained psychological intervention will be required to heal the deeper emotional scars;
• Drug rehabilitation in the form of medical intervention and intensive counselling must be provided to counter the deep-rooted problem of substance abuse among prisoners. The majority of prisoners are drug dependent. Their continued criminal activities are often driven by a hunger to satisfy their drug habit. If the drug problem in South African prisons is not aggressively combated, the cycle of crime will not be broken;
• Family support in the process of prisoner restoration is essential. Where possible, families of prisoners must be regularly involved in a prisoner's healing process. This will encourage the prisoner by sending the message that he or she does not have to stand alone and has the support of loved ones in the difficult journey ahead. At the same time, this process will help to develop the necessary support structure for the prisoner's return to a functional life upon release.

In the past prisoners were given the opportunity to pursue careers by learning work skills. Trade training and certification is important in providing the basics for future employment and viable work opportunities upon release. It is imperative that these efforts be intensified. However, without simultaneously nurturing the necessary life skills for living, released prisoners will not be able to reach their full potential as functional human beings. These life skills could be taught in workshop format, which encourages participation. Workshops should focus on:

• Social skills to deal with dynamic changes in society, and which encourage acceptance of the 'social contract' of rights and responsibilities in society, such as those encouraged in our Constitution;
• Communication skills to teach verbal and writing competence, which will encourage effective communication; this is important for clearly expressing feelings and needs;
• Conflict resolution skills to nurture constructive methods to deal with inner and inter-personal conflicts; a conflict resolution approach teaches skills in problem-solving and solution-finding, thereby building capacity in the individual and creating the necessary platform to resolve conflicts in a peaceful, non-violent way.

I believe that the issue of handling conflict is central to a prisoner's learning curve to facilitate his or her change and restoration. Most of the problems faced by prisoners arise from an inability to deal with unresolved inner conflict, which gives rise to feelings of anger, fear and pain. These feelings in turn manifest outwardly in aggressive behaviour, which generates conflict with others and often leads to violence. Learning the necessary skills to resolve conflict non-violently will go a long way in empowering prisoners with the confidence to create their own socially acceptable path in life. Conflict resolution skills also facilitate the learning of some of the other skills mentioned above, such as communication and social skills.

Conclusion

To ensure a solution that will be sustainable in the long-term we need to plan proactively. The efforts of different role-players – prisoners, prison staff, government, members of prisoners' families, members of the community, the media, members of civil society from non-governmental and religious organisations, and so forth – must be combined to achieve our goal. This goal is the restoration, rehabilitation and development of prisoners to break the cycle of crime, recidivism and violence in our country.

All role-players must accept that there will be setbacks from time to time. We in South Africa are new to change and democracy. There are many hurdles to be crossed, but we must not allow negativity and despondency to cloud our focus. Our past must guide our progress. The culture of injustice and human rights abuses must never again be allowed to take root or persist in our communities, including prisons. Our common engagement in building a better life for all and our constant evaluation of the processes we undertake will ensure that the successes we achieve, bit by bit, will serve to further motivate us and provide the momentum needed to reach our goal. We must never lose sight of our common goal – complete rehabilitation of prisoners to crush the cycle of crime in order to build a better and safer South Africa – together.

Further Reading

http://ccrweb.ccr.uct.ac.za/
Excellent web site for further information about CCR, and conflict resolution work in Africa.

References

Office of the Inspecting Judge, *Annual Report 2000*, pp. 10-11.
Truth and Reconciliation Commission Final Report, Vol. 5, (Cape Town, Juta and Co., 1998).

The True Prison

Ken Saro-Wiwa
Nigeria, 1993

It is not the leaking roof
Nor the singing mosquitoes
In the damp, wretched cell
It is not the clank of the key
As the warden locks you in
It is not the measly rations
Unfit for beast or man
Nor yet the emptiness of day
Dipping into the blankness of night
It is not
It is not
It is not

It is the lies that have been drummed
Into your ears for a generation
It is the security agent running amok
Exciting callous calamitous orders
In exchange for a wretched meal a day
The magistrate writing into her book
A punishment she knows is undeserved
The moral decrepitude
The mental ineptitude
The meat of dictators
Cowardice masking as obedience
Lurking in our denigrated souls
It is fear damping trousers
That we dare not wash
It is this
It is this
It is this
Dear friend, turns our free world
Into a dreary prison

Theatre and Eclecticism:
The 'Tandari' Experience

Emman Frank Idoko

Introduction

Community Theatre-for-Development is gradually becoming a dominant genre in Africa, especially for practitioners of theatre who are concerned with development of the underprivileged, and concerned with grinding poverty, resulting from appalling corruption and bad governance. This practice spans Africa – the work of Ngugi wa Thiongo in Kenya, for example, who has done a lot of work on Theatre for Development there, notably in an experiment at the Kamiriithu theatre. His inclinations generally focus on language use, and that was practically demonstrated by his 'epistemological break with the English language' in favour of Kikuyu. Zakes Mda's experiments were conducted with a group called The Maratholi Travelling Theatre. He experimented on the democratisation of communication in the practice of theatre, and most of his work is based in Lesotho. Also notable is the work of David Kerr in Botswana, and the foundation laid at the Ahmadu Bello University, Zaria, Nigeria, by Michael Etherton who has worked in Zambia. At the Ahmadu Bello University, he experimented with the possibilities of evolving development communication that begins at the base of society. He left a legacy that is carried further by the ABU Collective; Oga Abah, Salihu Bappa, John Illah; the practice at the University of Jos, Nigeria: the formation of the Nigerian Popular Theatre Alliance (NPTA) and several foundations laid down by donor organizations, NGOs and GOs throughout Nigeria. The intention generally is to create in the practice of theatre, openness for participation, and a shift away from conventional theatre practice, with a structure that involves its recipients, and whose social reality constitutes the subject matter discussed in the drama.

Realising the potential that theatre has in enabling development, I embarked upon a project at a reformation centre in Maiduguri, the capital of Borno State, Nigeria. During a preliminary investigation, I discovered that, due to funding problems, there were very few inmates in the centre, and the number of young people was usually not more than twenty. The duration of their stay is limited to six months and can be extended when the welfare officers feel that reformation and a likely future for the child has not been guaranteed. Several of the young people were also awaiting trial. This number was adequate to attempt a theatre experiment. The project had the follow objectives:

179

• To identify strategies of development through the theatre that begins at the base of society and specifically in the process of reforming a child;

• To establish a potential strategy for education through theatre, thus widening the horizon of the children in the reformation centre. This strategy would involve their participation in the creative process.

Background

The economic, socio-cultural and political problems experienced since independence in Nigeria, have created a situation of anxiety, apathy and poverty, which has had a dislocating effect on the social and cultural infrastructures. This was generally blamed on the continuous dictatorial rule of the military, which had an adverse effect on the citizens. Young people were also affected, through the consequent destruction of school systems and marriage breakdown. Families could no longer cater for their children largely due to low wages, and an inability to settle education bills. Consequently, the young people seek ways of fending for themselves. They engage in petty trading, and when this does not satisfy their needs, they resort to stealing. The streets are, therefore, littered with roaming children, who are an easy target for politicians who mobilise them to settle political scores against their perceived political enemies.

The Rehabilitation Centres were established in 1978 to attempt rehabilitation, and correction of erring young people between the ages of eleven and eighteen. Due to the general economic crisis, in addition to the general social dislocation, these institutions found themselves in a difficult situation, making the reform process almost impossible. Instead of coming out reformed, the young people became hardened criminals. It became expedient, therefore, to attempt using Theatre for Development as an alternative strategy that might assist in the reformation process.

Generally, the mode of discourse in theatre for conscientisation entails a practical process. The approach usually starts from understanding the political and social structures that encourage the commission of crimes of these young people, and the reasons that make the reformation process difficult. The following process was used in approaching the project. A conducive atmosphere was created through exercises, to enable a situation of trust and rapport with the participants which facilitated easy discussion, data collection and analysis. All those involved in the reformation process became a source for the data, but the inmates and the welfare officers in the centre were involved directly in the democratic process of creativity. The next stage was prioritising an identified problem. This served as the subject matter of the story that went through an intensive improvisation process and subsequent performance. Post-performance discussions then took place to evaluate the success, failures or limitations of the process, and a follow-up action.

The dialogue at the beginning of the project was a little difficult, because the inmates were not used to discussing freely with older people. Through questions and gradual confidence building, their inhibition weakened. The discussion centred on their lives outside the centre, the 'offence' they had committed, the court process, whether they were satisfied with the judicial process, what they were doing in the centre, and what they had learnt so far. In the process of this discussion, the theatre concept was introduced, to give them an idea of what we intended. With the introduction of the theatre process, the barriers came down, and they became excited. The fact that they had variously watched performances on television and videos also helped a great deal. In these discussions, common problems were identified. As far as most of them were concerned, the judicial process was perjured, and justice had not been done in the handling of their cases. The next common problem was that the food they received in the centre was very poor. On this issue they were a bit cautious and edgy. They had serious health problems, and virtually no medical attention. Several of them had skin infections, and open, untreated sores. This was largely due to poor sanitation as they used a bucket toilet in their cells. The possibility of an epidemic spreading was very high.

After several discussion sessions, we arrived at *injustice (rashin gaskia)*, as our accepted problem. General as it was, it related to the specific problem of reform, their relationship with society, and the process of handling their cases. After identifying our generally agreed problem (note should be taken that the facilitator did not want to insist on any pre-conceived problem), a general discussion took place. The discussion centred on the following question: would we want to consider injustice generally, which is prevalent in the judicial system; or are we to consider only the most extreme cases? They felt that poor people were the only ones perpetually harassed, and, looking very closely at the backgrounds of the young people in the centre, it was clear that they came from poor families. As far as they were concerned, rich people do not allow their children to end up in the centre. They explained that in some instances they were not even called to testify and defend themselves in court. We attributed that to the ruling military regime, which takes decisions without consulting anyone. It was clear that they were not completely ignorant of the societal problems. Serious reservations were expressed about the alleged offences that brought them in as, according to them, they had stolen because they had to survive and were being punished without regard for the social context of such offences. The judges were not concerned about how a street-child survives. The following questions became very crucial:

1. What are the implications of doing theatre based on injustice in an institution that is supposed to administer justice, under the criminal justice system?
2. How are the actors positioned in the whole criminal justice system?
3. Would the theatre activity help or hinder the process of conscientisation?
4. Do the project coordinators have adequate power to mediate in the problem?

Through intensive improvisations and exercises, we evolved a story line.

Story

We created a poor family of four, with two children, Binta and Mamman. Mamman is portrayed as a naughty child who beats his sister at every given opportunity, and does not respect his parents. Everyone in the community knew him as the 'bad guy'. The children assist their father in taking the animals for grazing, but suddenly the father falls ill and dies. Mamman does not change, in spite of advice by his mother. His mother decides to call in the police when she can no longer control him. Mamman is taken into a reform centre. Three months later, he returns from the centre a quiet and changed boy, which surprises everyone in the community. Their neighbour, his mother's friend, is not convinced by this sudden transformation. She advises Hajiya Garuwa, Mamman's mother, to do something about it. Hajiya Garuwa confesses that Mamman is actually not her son, but the son of her late husband's second wife, who is also dead. The neighbour convinces her to consult a Boka (medicine man) to eliminate the boy, so that his evil influence would be erased from the family, and she will receive a bigger share of her husband's assets.

She goes to a Boka and is given a poisoned loaf of bread to give to her son. Unfortunately, Mamman does not come back from grazing the animals until later, and the loaf of bread changes colour. Mamman refuses to eat the bread because he is not hungry. In desperation, Hajiya tries to force him to eat it. When she cannot, she screams for help. The problem is brought to the attention of the police; Mamman is arrested and, because he is now above the age of eighteen is taken to the adult prison, not the reform centre. Without finding out the real cause of the problem, he is taken in. As far as everyone is concerned, Mamman is still the same old 'bad guy'.

The story exposed a three-dimensional crisis: firstly, the crisis of polygamy and its attendant problems as it affects the child; secondly, the role of the criminal justice systems; and thirdly, the stigmatisation of a child, which adversely affects the correction and rehabilitation process and re-integration into society. The child is enmeshed in this knotty dilemma. Most of the inmates are accused of a range of minor offences which generally reflects a larger societal problem. The inmates are exposed to all forms of temptations and dangers. We went through several rehearsals and exercises.

Performance

A series of interruptions due to the unpredictable nature of the inmates' tenure at the centre (those awaiting trial are taken to court and some of them never come back, while some would have completed their sentence, for example) necessitated our fixture of a date for performance. Several parts were re-cast, giving an opportunity for everyone to be part of the process. Several other obstacles made performance impossible. This included the initial refusal by the authorities (which feared exposure) to allow the inmates to perform, and the difficulties posed by the officials in the centre, who expected to be bribed in order to offer any kind of assistance. We decided to evaluate the process itself.

Post-performance Discussion and Evaluation

We started by examining the content of the drama, and how the story touched on the problems of the inmates. One of the inmates said that society was not doing anything to help underprivileged children. He also said that the play talked about how the law punished Mamman, who has been under constant harassment by his stepmother, without trying to find the cause of the problem, a similar situation to his own experience. He said he was incarcerated because he stole his master's money. This resulted from the master's refusal to pay his monthly wage, with which he planned to settle his school fees. The 'deputy head boy' asked whether it was right for him to break the law, to satisfy his interests, and he responded with another question: was it right for master to cheat him? The inmates agreed generally that the judicial process was biased. One of the inmates narrated his ordeal. He said the boy he fought with was not punished because his father, an Alhaji (a rich man), took his child away. They all agreed that the criminal justice system was interested only in protecting its own, and not in reformation. The inmates claimed that they were not aware of anyone who was reformed by their stay in the centre. Rather, they 'graduate' to the main prison, a parlance they use for qualifying for the adult prison. They attributed this partly to the discussions they usually have when they retire at night into their cells, experimenting with strategies to avoid being caught when a crime is committed. The session, according to them, was entertaining, and they looked forward to it as an opportunity to play, an activity which was not part of their normal schedule. They requested that the project co-ordinator ask the officials to introduce recreation to keep them from thinking too much.

Follow-up Action

At the end of the workshop, we felt that simply to discuss the problems and identify their immediate and remote causes was not enough '...if this is not linked with critical analysis and with action on the underlying causes and structures; it is not enough to rehearse struggle if it does not lead to struggle' (Kidd, 1980, p. 11).

The process of attempting a resolution of some of the problems that were within our reach became expedient. This included asking questions and making suggestions towards resolving the problem of discharged inmates who go back into crime. It was suggested that the inmates continue school, and for those who were not in school, that they get into apprenticeship and learn a trade or craft, through a process of skill development. It was also suggested that the facilitator approach members of the criminal justice system to discuss perjured cases. In order to achieve the alternative to schooling, it was suggested that there should be collaboration with welfare workers, to evolve skill development projects within the centres and assist in contacting offices and workshops where the young people could develop some skills after their tenure in the centre. This would make it easier to create openings for them as apprentices with mechanic, ceramic, and carpentry workshops, where they would receive constant supervision, to prevent them from turning to crime. This was the most trying period of the process – recognising the fact that the practitioner of Theatre for Development may not have the 'connections' or power to be able to resolve concretely most of the problems. Empowering the inmates through conscientisation will make the functionaries of government uncomfortable. Paradoxically, the government constitutes the most immediate sector that could aid in the resolution of the problem. In spite of the recorded successes and suggestions of strategies for resolving the problems, there were areas of critical concern. First was the language question.

The Language Problem

Language use would, here, take into consideration what constitutes the whole medium of communicating ideas and values in this particular practice. Ngugi, for instance experimented in this way with his Kamiriithu experience and had problems[1] in spite of insisting on communicating in the language of the people. In a multi-cultural and multi-ethnic society like Nigeria, the choice of language would be a problem. It was not different with the theatre in 'Tandari'. The young people I worked with come from various ethnic backgrounds, and speak different languages. In spite of the location of the community in a predominantly Kanuri speaking ethnic group, Kanuri was not the language of daily communication. Instead, Hausa language is dominant in the Maiduguri metropolis, and this was manifested in the centre. Why Hausa is dominant was not our area of focus. It was the significance of the language and its function in the project that was crucial. The choice of the language to be used was thrown open for discussion, and Hausa was chosen as our medium of communication. For young people, play, song and dance serve as an easy medium for learning subsequently doing theatre. We were not sure about the nature of the songs and dance we would adopt, that would easily transmit such knowledge as should be acquired in this generic process. This was also open for discussion. The inmates were excited about singing songs, and we attempted to create some. Songs and dances became necessary because of their inherent entertaining nature, and their ability to help in the physical growth of the children, which should be, in any case, part and parcel of their reformation process. It was also necessary because it would not be complete to practice theatre in Africa without its accompanying elements: songs, dances, music, masquerading and so on.

Even as we reached the conclusion and went through the process of creating songs, the centre's security officer interrupted us. In the reform process, physical exercises were not permitted because, according to the rule, that would make the inmates prone to criminality, because they would have too much energy. Ridiculous as this may be, it was a reflection of the perception of a society which sees a prison sentence as a punishment. Paradoxically, these young people are taken out to work in the centre's farm, whose production supplements their feeding. In order to guard against the perceived excesses of our work, we had a security officer permanently detailed to watch the process.

Censorship and Government Interference

This takes us to the censorship problem. In most Theatre for Development practice in Africa, the tendency is for governments consistently to interfere with projects, place excessive censorship on them, or ban outright such activity. That is because of their feeling of inadequacy; fear of their excesses being exposed and of losing their grip on power as a result of the possibility of empowering the people. That is why it takes a long time for democracy to thrive and for any meaningful success to occur in Theatre for Development practice. An important reference point is the Kumba Workshop in Cameroon, where the President: '...was in fact demanding self-censorship on the part of the organisers of the workshop. Indeed, the fact that the President of a whole country had to give authorisation for a theatre workshop to take place in some remote village tells its own story' (Mda, 1993, p. 106). Most importantly it is felt that politics should not be discussed. The Kamiriithu experiment in Kenya is another, where the government interfered with such activity, this time violently. Ironically, when the government becomes threatened by the practice and reacts, the elite, who in any case dictate the direction in which the process would go, escape into the safety cocoon of their institution but, 'when government attempts an integration of this structure into mainstream hegemony, the same practitioners provide a blueprint of co-operation'. It is this contradiction that leads Ahab to wonder:

> ...where Popular Theatre animateurs stand in relation to the people? To the government? And ...the divide between those who claim to be engaged in a process of democratisation from within indigenous structures and those who construct a praxis for the poor on paper? Or are we all engaged in using popular forms of statement for purposes of cultural underdevelopment? (Abah, 1993, p. 9).

The involvement of target communities in the theatre production process, as part and parcel of the creativity, encourages a democratic process of decision-making. This creates an enabling situation of self-help and ability to sustain development. But because of the bureaucratic procedures that a facilitator/animateur goes through in the process of popular theatre, coupled with the fact that community leaders and powerful members are usually informed and their consent sought before permission is granted, critical questions must be raised. The 'Tandari' practice was no different, as it also went through several bureaucratic bottlenecks. The State Director for Social Welfare and the supervisor at the centre had to give their permission before the work began. Consistent censorship took place to make sure that whatever happened conformed with the values of the state. Given these circumstances, how would this activity be possible, without negating the focus of the practice?

The difficulty in making the practice a people's theatre also manifests itself in the relationship between the practitioner and the target community. In spite of the commitment of practitioners of Theatre for Development, their ideological articulation influences their approaches. Because of the preconceived structural arrangement, the activity they engage in with the people would be far from democratic. Armed with this ideological weapon, their work would hinder the reception of views that are being expressed by the members of the community. This subordinates the unconscious critical views the people share among themselves. Consequently, they may not be able to articulate, through drama, the full extent and implication of the social contradiction.

These problems of Theatre for Development, especially related to government interference with projects, and constant harassment, were addressed in the Bayreuth Conference.[2] One suggested solution was to make a concerted effort to convince government of the importance of a democratic process in governance and any problem-solving situation. The second is to liaise with government functionaries in development projects to ease suspicion and tension that leads to excessive censorship and in some cases arrests and detentions. Finally, to let the people be at the forefront of the dialoguing process and the creation of the drama when such projects are being executed.

It becomes imperative, therefore, to modify the existing structures/methodology of Theatre for Development (it is instructive to note that the strength of the genre is its openness) in order to involve government. It should be noted that the relationship between government and the people might not necessarily be negative. This consistent alienation of state bureaucracies in such projects, rather than solving problems, creates a more intensive division between the majority of the people who are impoverished, and government, the latter being the custodian of the material ability for sustenance of the society. Rather than turning to donor organisations, which have their own ideological interests and operate from a complex socio-political and economic base, the government functionaries should be made to be aware of the underprivileged nature of the majority of the populace they govern. With the evolving democracy in Nigeria today, it is hoped that this tension and suspicion may ease.

The question that usually arises is how community members, in this case specifically those of the 'Tandari' community, can participate in an activity that is alien to them. Alien in the sense that the form and structural process of such performance is acquired from the conventional 'rules' of theatre practice this genre is negating – structures of actualisation such as characterisation, speech forms, costuming, projection, and so on. It is acceptable that, within the African cultural space, performances play a vital role in the social, political, economic, and cultural ethos, but the 'new' dramatic structures introduced in the process of Theatre for Development do not mediate that cultural backdrop. At best, some of the inmates have watched dramas and performances on television or have been exposed to video. These exposures are not only a mediation of Western cultural perceptions, but constitute only spectacle, because the social and cultural meaning is completely at variance with recipients' socialisation. So, whatever is presented in the process of this practice flows from the coordinator's ideas and is not born out of group work. How could a coordinator, whose socialisation is completely at variance with his target audience, hope to convince the people within a community to trust him, a stranger, and open up to him, in dialoguing that is democratic? The inmates in 'Tandari' knew virtually nothing about the technicalities of theatre, and this had to be introduced at the beginning of the process. How can this genre of theatre achieve its intended change with the claim of participation? Is there, therefore, any difference between this form of theatre and conventional theatre that also utilises the language of the people?

Conclusion

In conclusion, in spite of the problems experienced in the 'Tandari' practice, it adapted to the prevailing socio-cultural circumstances and exposed potential areas of concern for the would-be facilitator in enabling eclecticism to prevail in the practice of Theatre for Development. It is, therefore, important that in doing Theatre for Development and experiencing the inevitable friction between cultural activists and state bureaucracy, the contradictions of form, and the unresolved question of post-conscientisation action, an unflinching commitment to the cause of the underprivileged is required. It is also important to reflect theoretically, in conferences and seminars giving credence to strategies which seek to create a more participatory, more problem-solving Theatre for Development form. It is also important to be adaptable and eclectic in choosing and employing the strategies of participatory theatre, especially when governments seek to appropriate Theatre for Development methodology for their own benefit. This is also in order not to risk reducing the political and artistic opportunities of cultural activists in the quest for liberation pedagogy when confronted by the integration and appropriation processes of governments.

Notes

1. Kenya is a multi-ethnic society, and Ngugi's use of Kikuyu was seen as 'tribal'. This further highlights the stress on the use of language and its problems in such societies, a common phenomenon in Africa, though Ngugi argues that, for them, the use of Kikuyu was not a symptom of tribalism, but a convenient 'channel for expressing a national culture'. David Kerr also argues in defence of Ngugi's position that the struggle to create an African language theatre is important, but the language alone will not create a liberating popular practice. Rather, the political and bureaucratic elite will continue to manipulate the people by integrating popular forms of culture, blinding them 'to the fact that the real goals of popular communication – the empowerment of communities at the cultural, political, and economic levels – are being withheld' (see Kerr, 1991). Kerr may have a strong case in taking this position, but it will be dangerous to brush aside the problem. That the issue is raised in the first place means that there is a problem on the ground, and attempts must be made to address it. If Kiswahili, for instance, is the most acceptable language of communication in Kenya, in spite of Kikuyu being Ngugi's mother tongue, why was it not adopted as the language in the practice to follow a democratic approach? To explain it away quickly as a result of 'a class system which drove people into making ethnic conflict a scapegoat for injustice, and regional patronage for class solidarity' (p. 64) is theoreticising the problem.

2. The Bayreuth Conference took place between 25 October and 2 November 1999, with a title *Cultural Production for Conflict Mediation* organised by the Institute for African Studies, University of Bayreuth, in Germany.

References

Abah, O., 'Perspectives in popular theatre: orality as a definition new realities', in: E. Breitinger (ed.), *Theatre and Performance in Africa*, 31, (Bayreuth, Bayreuth African Studies, 31, 1993), p. 99.

Kerr, D., Popular participatory theatre: the highest stage of cultural underdevelopment? *Research in African Literatures*, 22 (3), (1991), pp. 55-75.

Kidd, R., 'People's theatre, conscientisation and struggle', *Media Development*, 27 (3), (1980), p. 11.

Mda, Z., 'Another theatre of the absurd', in E. Breitinger (ed.), *Theatre and Performance in Africa*, 31, (Bayreuth, Bayreuth African Studies, 1993), pp. 105-106.

Real Social Ties?

The Ins and Outs of Making Theatre in Brazilian Prisons

Paul Heritage

An Entrance

At the American Embassy in London in 2001, I was translating for my partner as he applied for a visa to accompany me on a visit to give a series of lectures at New York University. On the grounds that he has 'no real social ties' in the United Kingdom, the visa application was rejected. Our relationship, the house we own, the joint bank account we have, his studies in Britain were not enough to convince this official that my partner – a Brazilian – would not want to remain permanently in the United States. Indeed, the official perception of the fragility of our relationship was made all too apparent when I was asked if I insisted on taking all my boyfriends to New York. How could our weak and inconstant ties compete with all that the USA would offer to entice him away from the seeming impermanence of what we have created together in London?

The incident forced me to contemplate what are these 'real social ties' that mean so much to the American government that they should be used as factors in determining who shall enter their country. In trying to escape from all that was negative, abusive and degrading in that incident, I began to wonder about the social ties this official so rigorously invoked and the means by which we know if they are real or not. The incident has helped me to think about the social ties that I have been engaged in during the making of theatre that crosses social and community boundaries, in particular the boundaries between where I am in my own social, sexual and national cultures and where I go as an artist. This article will look at those border crossings, with particular reference to my recent work making theatre in Brazilian prisons.

I suspect that anyone who engages in performance work linked to issues of social development has met a version of that embassy official over the years. The borders we have to cross to make the sort of theatre we believe in will always be policed and guarded in some fashion: because of the way in which this work is usually conceived and constructed, there will always be a point of entry made by someone from outside. As the official at the embassy made all too clear, permission to enter is dependent on intention to leave. At the American Embassy my partner and I were naively honest about the social ties that justified our travel together: the reasons for both our entry and our exit. In reflecting on my theatre work, I wonder how honest I have been in my declarations to other guards as I sought permission to make performance beyond the boundaries? I wonder what promises I have made about the time that I would spend across these different borders? What social ties have I created and how real were they? Above all, has it been harder to enter or to exit? In this essay I look at my comings and my goings: the ins and outs of making theatre in Brazilian prisons.

As a Point of Departure, I Begin With an Exit...

There is often a moment at the end of a drama workshop when you try to take the temperature of a project. In those fleeting moments while the group is dispersing, you can often discover the most important things in the casual question and the overheard comment. This is particularly true in prison, as different realities crash into each other with the movement out of the physical and metaphysical space of the drama workshop and back to the prison.

In 2000 I was watching a workshop in a São Paulo prison which formed part of *Projeto Drama*, an education project implemented in forty-three prisons across the state. The programme, which was part of my work in Brazil for over three years, involved a succession of four-day drama-based workshops on AIDS/HIV. As they were leaving, I talked informally with the men about the impact of the drama workshops. When asked if he thought that the project would change his behaviour in the future, one of the young men exploded with emotion. 'I have just taken part in a workshop where I have cried, hugged, laughed, played in ways that I have never done in the past. I have changed totally. Perhaps next week I will have unsafe sex. I don't know. Why are you so obsessed with the future? What has happened now is most important.'

That prisoner's comment brought a sharp realization of how far I have come in looking to make theatre that is tied to other social realities. The justification for making this work – the application for my visa to enter this world – has often been made in terms of the way in which theatre has a social impact beyond the moment of performance. It is not in the now that this work is tested, but in some indeterminate future: it will reduce risk, increase safety, construct citizenship in some other world that is not the one in which the performance or the dramatic activity has taken place. Performance work is thus established that is in some way not bound by time or space, but becomes boundless. Is this what we want? Is this what we are promising?

Securing the Boundaries?

Prison drama is constructed before we as artists seek to re-make it. Played out first as social realism and then as romantic melodrama (or is it the other way round?), life in prison is always seen through the peepholes of our cultural imagination. Latin American prisons are places that inhabit our nightmares. Whether these images come from Hollywood or international human rights agencies, the story is of torture and a denial of human rights. Brazil is a country which is framed by clichés that come as much from stories of crime and street kids as from beaches and Bossa Nova. But since

1993 I have been trying to make theatre with prisoners in Brasília, São Paulo, Recife and Rio de Janeiro.

To experience a city such as Rio de Janeiro or São Paulo is of course a negotiation with its borders and its margins. The shape and form of these cities, like so many others in Brazil and beyond, is one of the key consequences of the modernist revolution. As rural immigrants arrived they were pushed to the margins of the cities, which might paradoxically be close to the centre. Networks of friends and family who followed them were crucial to a sense of survival within an unknown social reality, and thus the survival strategies of the poor were recognized as cultural. The reaction of the State was an inaction that was legitimized by maintaining the illegality of these areas and their assumed peripheral position in relation to the economic life of the city (Tufte, p. 62). The reaction of the middle-classes? A constant assertion of their difference and superiority, often configured in terms of European or North American cultural values, and articulating a predominate sense of danger at these borders. The reaction of those who live on the other side of the border is experienced as victimization to a violence that is as likely to be perpetrated by the State as it is by the criminal forces that have filled the vacuum of civic power and order. But such territories are also subject to a fierce romanticism which variously colours the regional past or the present community, and at times even seeks to tint the crime that devastates all these borderlands.

Luiz Eduardo Soares was, until 17 March 2000, responsible for the political and operational strategies of public security in the State of Rio de Janeiro. He has written of life in the *favelas*[1] as being reminiscent of feudal warfare:

> The masculine hegemony is affirmed in the supremacy of courage and loyalty, which has always been restricted to the arts of war, and to a hierarchized environment exclusive to the group itself which enforces an explosive situation of fratricidal factionalism (Soares, 2000; p. 271).

These values are precisely those that modern society has supposedly abandoned in favour of a world which recognizes at a certain level the equality of human beings, subject only to the laws of their gods (in the religious version) or the laws of their Society. It is a development that has allowed the rise of the individual and the citizen, of a world in which politics, civic administration and psychology govern lives. Even when violent reaction is brought to the fore, such as in the street demonstrations against globalization in London, Montreal and Genoa, the rule of law is supposedly superior to the law of force. In the Brazilian *favelas*, this cannot be assumed. Lest there be any doubt how far these borderlands are removed in fact and imagination from contemporary notions of society, we can look to the system implemented by the administration of a previous governor of Rio de Janeiro. From 1994-8, Marcello Alencar authorized payments to individual police officers that were involved in acts of 'bravery'. The police were encouraged to enter into armed conflicts with bandits, and receive a reward for the number of fatal victims they claimed. The system was referred to by press and politicians as the *premiação faroeste* – the Far West Prize.

The culture of the prison reflects and further exaggerates the lawlessness that we

191

associate with all borderlands. Of course, that is not what we expect of prisons. They are meant to be the place where the law is most rigorously in force, but that is rarely the case. We in Britain should not be surprised or complacent when we remember that it was John Major as prime minister who, in claiming that prison works, remarked that at least when a man is in prison he cannot commit any more crimes. The idea that a prison is so far outside of our social world that it is a place where crime cannot be committed finds its logical and terrifying conclusion in the 1994 massacre of one hundred and eleven prisoners in less that two hours in the São Paulo prison complex of Carandiru, and in the daily assassinations that produce an annual massacre of unimaginable and often unrecorded levels in the prison systems of Rio de Janeiro and São Paulo.

The walls that divide the prison from the rest of society are not the only boundaries that separate those within from those without. Social, economic and racial factors determine global prison populations as much as legal and judicial agencies. In São Paulo, where seventy per cent of the population is white, the incarceration rate per 100,000 is 76.8 for whites and 280.5 for blacks. Black people account for sixty-six per cent of the homicide victims, and the lethality index (number of people killed by the police divided by the number of people wounded in such encounters) is thirty-seven per cent to one hundred per cent higher for blacks as compared to whites.[2] In Rio de Janeiro, sixty per cent of the population is white, while black people make up seventy per cent of those killed by the police and sixty per cent of those killed in prison. Thus black people are over-represented both in the prisons and the morgues. Penal policy reveals itself as a means of social exclusion, and the boundaries of the prison wall can be seen to be as much social and cultural as bricks and mortar, but in every way real.

If the incarceration of the prison population can be seen as based on factors that go beyond the physical and judicial, then the means by which such boundaries are crossed must also go beyond the concrete and the legal. To talk of cultural action in the face of such barbarities is not to underestimate the forces that conserve such a status quo, but to recognize that there are multiple ways in which liberty, justice, and human rights can be achieved. All of us working in the cultural development field are faced with questions about the realities of our work in comparison to that of well-diggers and AIDS nurses. But the complexity and interconnection of issues such as social exclusion, the environment and health care open a space for our interventions.

Going Inside...

The prison gate is a transitional space marked by rituals that seek to distance the world that is left behind from the world that is entered. Visitors, guards and prisoners each in their way are subject to the rites of this particular passage, which operate on both exit and entrance. Drauzio Varella has worked for ten years as a doctor in Carandiru, Brazil's largest prison. Perhaps in his words we can see how the entrance to prison life is controlled as much by ideology as by vigilance:

> No need to knock to go in; as your head approaches the window of the small door, the shadowy face of the porter appears telepathically from inside. The opening of the door

follows the oldest routine of all prisons, which dictates that a door can only open when the last door and the following one have been closed. It's a good lesson that helps you learn to wait without showing any signs of impatience. It won't help. I hear the tapping of the door being unlocked and I'm in the Ratoeira – the mousetrap – an atrium with bars and on the left two ample windows for the visitor to identify himself. Between these windows is a corridor that leads to the Director-General's office, large and full of light. The table is old. On the wall behind is a photograph of the State Governor. But underneath it, one of the directors, a man who has spent his life in the prison, has put up a brass plaque: 'It is easier for a camel to pass through the eye of a needle than for a rich man to be a prisoner in Carandiru.'

I return to the Ratoeira. I wait for the internal gate to open and stand in front of the wall that circles the prison, watched over by military police armed with machine guns. I pass into the Divinéia, a large yard that is shaped like a funnel. At its neck lies the room reserved for body searches, obligatory for everyone who enters, except for directors, lawyers, and doctors. Before gaining access to the pavilions, you have to enter this room and raise your arms in front of one of the guards, who will give you a quick frisk at the waist and a pat on the outside of the thighs.

It's another prison ritual (Varella,1998, p. 9).3

Like the directors, lawyers and doctors, I am rarely searched as I enter Brazilian prisons, which only serves to increase my anxieties. If security is compromised by prejudice, then it is unlikely to be effective. But I wonder, what would the guards be looking for if they were they to search me? And what should I declare? My foreignness is obvious, and my gender and age are reasonably apparent. Class and sexuality are both confused, as gestures, intonations and dress codes that might mean certain things to a British guard are regarded as a part of my nationality in Brazil. My status is in contradiction: I am university professor, theatre director and Englishman. These play out in different ways for me in Brazil and Britain, but my comings and goings bear a curious relationship to the power of all these factors. I have a large wooden key made for me by prisoners in Brasília. It reminds me that the real keys of prison are only half as effective as the cultural and social means by which the doors are locked and unlocked.

I can still remember the first time that I entered a Brazilian prison. It was through the same small door that Dr. Varella describes above. There, in a prison that holds over nine thousand, I was taken to see a samba competition. Of all the images I could have expected, this was the least likely for me to have conjured and the one that vividly remains after the physical horrors have become part of an accustomed – if not familiar – world. The greatest shock was to see how the inmates were organizing cultural activities in a self-sufficient way that I had never seen possible in the British prison system. It was as difficult to interpret such activity as it was for me to judge the sambas, which I was asked to do in the middle of my visit. Perhaps we should not read such manifestations with quite the naïve enthusiasm of my first encounter. Today, I might temper my wonder with the thought that such practices are a means of survival, expected and incorporated into the system. My work in prison inevitably owes a debt to the participatory traditions that are associated with such cultural forms, and is permissible only because the authorities open the doors. But within my work, I have attempted to ask if it is possible to break the ways in which spaces and lives in prison are circumscribed and imagined within constrained possibilities.

In making theatre in prison, we engage in a marginal activity in a marginal space. What is it that performance can offer as it declares its arrival at these different borders of marginalization? When writing previously on a theatre company based in one of Rio de Janeiro's *favelas*, I commented that theatre can operate as a register of individual and collective social histories (Heritage, 1998). It is common for Brazil to be called a country without memory, and the lack of official structures within such a marginalized community as a *favela* makes the act of registering histories all the more difficult and all the more necessary.

> Individual stories of violence or of resistance start to gain a wider resonance in the collective story telling and remembering that forms a part of this process. Without it, individual acts of barbarism are experienced as terrible and chaotic incidents that are out of control because they are a part of no pattern. The physical fabric of the favela is in itself provisional and subject to constant disruption and destruction, unlike the official urban environment which is generally experienced as stable and permanent. While modern and historic cities are integral parts of the national patrimony, the favela is that part which must be removed if all that is deemed wholesome and healthy is to survive. The survival of the lives of the residents in any form of cultural registration is thus at odds with the very environment in which those lives are lived (Ibid, p. 145).

This is all the more apparent when theatre is made in prison, a site that arbitrarily re-structures the subject's experience of place and time. Theatre, in contrast, de-structures our perceptions of where and when. In its very aliveness and immediacy, theatrical performance adheres to spatial and temporal boundaries that declare it is only ever here and now. It has no past and demands no future. It asks only that it exists at this moment, while it simultaneously offers the possibility that all time can be present in that one instance. Augusto Boal, the Brazilian theatre director, reflecting on his incarceration during the military dictatorship, offers a prisoner's perspective on the reconstitution of the boundaries of time and space which resound with an echo of the power of performance:

> In prison, I had a certain kind of freedom. We, who are free in space, are prisoners of time. Those who are prisoners of space, of time become free. Outside, in the daily routine of life, the day to day tasks would not allow me to see myself – I was always in a hurry, always doing, going to do, seeing it done: in my cell, I was obliged to look at myself and see. Outside, schedules, tasks, smiles – the rituals of life gave me no time to reflect. To say 'good morning' to myself in the mirror. We hardly spoke, myself and I. In the huge space, I had no time. Now that I had time, I had no space. In the diffuse disintegration of time in

prison – that time in which now was permanent, no before or afterwards: just the eternal moment existed – and in the concentrated scantiness of the dense space, I thought of myself. There, I heard the sound of silence (Boal, 2000).

Finding the Exits

It is not only on an ontological level that theatre finds its place in prisons, but in the very real possibilities that it offers of new civic relationships that are currently prohibited by the construction of our system of criminal justice. Despite the geographic centrality of many of our Victorian prisons in Britain, they seemingly occupy the Renaissance position of being outside our city walls. Throughout his book on his five hundred days at the forefront of public security in Rio de Janeiro, Luiz Eduardo Soares emphasizes that what is most decisive in the successful policing of any society is the direct involvement of its citizens in the processes of administering the law. 'Above all,' he writes, 'in this field that is so complex and so delicate, the objective and the subjective superimpose themselves in a way that is almost inextricable' (Soares, 2000, p. 47). Thus, demands for vengeance and for mercy mingle with technical and economic considerations about how a person can most effectively be processed, incarcerated and subsequently liberated.

Perhaps here is where theatre finds its function. The special relationship between private and public, individual and collective, psychological and social that are contained in the very act of performance mean that it crosses the borders that normally keep such worlds apart. Perhaps these are the social ties that theatre can offer to a world where so much has been ripped asunder. At the very least, theatre offers the possibility that prisoners who are the objects of the system's vigilance and society's denunciations can begin to look and to speak as subjects in their own lives.

Finding the Entrances

Thus it has often been the making of theatre that has attracted me within the prison context, a search for the means by which performance-based activities can be sustained. In order to find ways in which theatre could become a language and an action that could be incorporated into the daily life of the prison, I have worked closely with the techniques of Theatre of the Oppressed. In recent years Boal and members of his Centre for the Theatre of the Oppressed have become involved in the development of these projects. The basis of *Projeto Drama* and another of my projects, *Staging Human Rights* (2001-02), has been to train prison teachers in the use of theatrical games and exercises that can be used most effectively by non-actors. I have written elsewhere about other approaches, including the use of Shakespeare with juvenile prisoners in Brazil (Heritage, 2002). However, the methodologies of Theatre of the Oppressed offer the possibility that after the artist has left the theatrical activity will remain. In *Staging Human Rights*, teachers are running cycles of workshops and Forum Theatre performances across thirty-seven prisons. No amount of coming and going by artists could match the depth and structural impact of this project. Even if it were possible to hire theatre artists to implement a project on such a scale – even if the aesthetic possibilities might thus be enhanced – no visiting artist could achieve what these prison teachers are doing. They are part of the commitment by the prison system to a way of thinking, talking and doing.

While we hope that the value of the project lies in the insights and discoveries it makes about human rights in prisons, its impact may be most profoundly felt in other ways. Perhaps the strength of the project lies not in what it enables people to say, but rather in the actuality of what they are doing. It is in the staging of human rights that the most fundamental rights are guaranteed. This is not an abdication of the responsibility of content: the location of the project and the nature of the participants determine that the subject matter of these dramas will release visions and explore territories that are absent from the main stages of Brazilian culture. But these projects reach beyond content to make other connections.

A Different Exit

August 2001, and I am with a group of twenty prisoners rehearsing their contribution to the *Staging Human Rights* project. It is a Forum Theatre play about the amorous relationship between an ex-prisoner and his lawyer, and I watch as the new connections we seek are being tentatively forged. I have come to a small town, eight hours' drive from the city of São Paulo, and the prisoners have been invited to perform their Forum Theatre play in the town square the following week. The rehearsal falters. Members of the all-male cast are uncertain about which of them should play the female lawyer; they are tense about rehearsing in front of the guards; they are nervous about how they will be received when they present the play to the general public. The guards shift and smoke, enter and exit unannounced. They too are nervous. Is security the issue here? And if so, whose? We are rehearsing in a space away from the prison, so the guards could be here to protect society from any possible threat by a prisoner. Or perhaps they are here to defend me as a foreigner among high-risk prisoners. Or perhaps the prisoners need defending from each other. Or perhaps it is the guards' own security that is at risk. If so, is that a physical risk, or is it something that is happening through the theatre?

As the rehearsal progresses and the prisoners become more comfortable, the guards seem increasingly restless. By now, the prisoner playing the female lawyer is giving a real show, and there is a sense of enjoyment and achievement in the room. Thoughts of the public who will see the performance have now become an incentive to the group to tell the story as clearly and passionately as possible. They work hard, repeating and refining their original ideas, throwing away, editing, creating as the play grows and the conflict becomes more tightly focused. They accept my directions and enjoy the discipline of rehearsal. When I miss something out or cut something essential, they show me once again that oppression always exists in the detail. A samba is added, making the scene both simpler and more profound. Having found what they were looking for, the rehearsal comes to a close with laughter, dancing, and the eager anticipation of seven more days of rehearsal and the performance to come.

Forum Theatre directly tests its connections with an audience. On the day of this presentation, the town of *Presidente Prudente* made a connection with its maximum-security prison in ways that would usually be unthinkable. Would the audience enter the stage to substitute for the protagonist and seek alternatives to the problem presented? In this rather unconventional version of the Forum model, they could choose to substitute for either the ex-prisoner or the female lawyer. In the event, all the interventions were made on the side of the lawyer. I worried that the prisoners might be upset that no one had wanted to substitute for the ex-prisoner. But they watched in delight while a line-up of valiant audience members fought for the right to love someone regardless of criminal record.

It is not the sort of content that we imagined when we created the project. Indeed, when I arrived for the rehearsal I was uncertain if it was really an appropriate subject for the project. Other workshops during the *Staging Human Rights* programme have covered issues of access to health care and education, conjugal visits, giving birth in handcuffs and the inevitable but nonetheless shocking instances of violence and torture. Was this story of forbidden love really about human rights in prisons? And then I remembered what one of the men had said to me in another prison, about another situation: 'I want the right to serve my sentence as it stands.' Perhaps that is what this scene was about: the right to serve a sentence and finish it, not to carry it with you forever. And perhaps that is what made the guards so nervous when they watched the men rehearsing. The role the guard has come to play in the prison is to extend the boundaries of punishment beyond that of the sentence. To do so they must sever the human connections the men have with each other, with themselves as guards and with society beyond the prison. The theatre we are trying to create seeks to do the opposite.

A Different Entrance

In the scene described above, we can already see theatre's failures emerging along with its successes. Those guards, nervously making comments at the back of the hall, are the same ones that will take the men back to their cells. They are the same ones that will tell the prisoners what fools they made of themselves during the rehearsal, the same ones that will look for the merest hint of a smile or insubordination to make sure that João, Giovanni or Johnny doesn't make it to tomorrow's rehearsal. And they are the same ones who might also take part in their own drama workshops as part of the *Staging Human Rights* programme. Indeed, the guards' programme is the most significant advance on the current project and, wherever possible, takes place away from the prison environment, to remove the guards from the environment and culture of the prison. Based on the same techniques of theatre games and exercises used to work towards Forum Theatre presentation, the only direct connection to the work produced by prisoners comes in the final Legislative Forum Theatre presentation at the end of the project.

Never having worked with guards before, I had no means of predicting the results. I expected resistance, which we were given in abundance. What I could not have predicted was the level of emotion and anger towards the society that discriminates against them for where they work. As one of them said in an early workshop, the three worst jobs in São Paulo are street cleaner, grave digger and prison guard, but the prison guard is the worst because it combines the work of the other two. Nor could I have expected to hear a guard say at the end of one of the workshops that he loved the chance to do the drama games because for the two hours of the workshop he forgot he was in prison. This was most remarkable, as at that moment he was about four hours' drive from his prison, off-duty, out of uniform and in a school building. The guards as much as the prisoners live twenty-four hours a day in their prisons.

Staging Human Rights is not remarkable for anything other than such moments when it unfixes the world and makes new connections and new crossings possible. It draws attention for its scale: thirty-seven prisons across a state the size of Spain, with the involvement of over 10,000 prisoners, guards, prison staff, and families. At a seminar on community, culture and globalisation organized by the Rockefeller Foundation in May 2001, one of the conveners, Don Adams, posed a question: 'Can we preserve our decentralization and still effectively oppose the huge global corporations and quasi-governmental agencies thus far calling the shots? What would it take for this balance to shift?' Reflecting on my own practice, it seemed that I had spent nearly a decade engaged in a process of globalizing my work so that it could grow to the proportions of *Staging Human Rights*. How had this come about, and what are the implications?

My First Entrance

When I finished my first theatre project in a Brazilian prison in 1993, I felt an elation that was rare even within the pleasure zones of this sort of work. At the outset, the guards wouldn't even let me have a room for the workshops, so I was forced to work in whatever outside space was available. We spent the initial weeks exposed to airless heat and the gaze of the entire prison population, as twenty Brazilian prisoners and one English academic began to make images of their worlds on the baked red earth of the exercise yard. Over the eight months of the first project in Brasília, I not only managed to conquer a regular meeting-space inside the prison, but those twenty inmates were also able to take their play to the Ministry of Justice headquarters for a performance to judges, journalists and politicians. As I took my leave of Colonel Flávio Souto, the prison director, I was taken aback by his response, which recognized the benefits of the project while totally demeaning the scale on which it had taken place. He found my energies laudable but laughable. At the end of his day, there is so much that needs to be done for the prison population as a whole that a project which prioritized so much time and money for twenty prisoners was an irrelevance.

Colonel Souto made me more determined than ever to find ways in which I could increase the impact of the work I do. I expanded the project in Brasília so that by 1996 there were five theatre workshops running on a regular basis and the work was seen to benefit those beyond the immediate participants. Some of the original group left the prison and formed a theatre company which in 2001 is still touring schools and colleges in the Federal District of Brasília. With each performance they make their own response to the Colonel. Then in 1996, I began working in São Paulo, which holds twenty-five per cent of the total prison population of Brazil in only twelve per cent of the prisons. The problems there are on a scale that would make a drama workshop with twenty prisoners seem very small indeed.

Uncertain Exits

My work evolved to try to meet this challenge. I started looking at ways in which it might be possible to train existing prison staff to use cultural means to engage prisoners with their lives. That process culminated in *Projeto Drama*, mentioned above. This was followed by *Staging Human Rights*, which is funded by the UK Community Fund and brings together the Centre for the Theatre of the Oppressed with FUNAP, the State Agency for Education and Work in São Paulo. British participating organizations include People's Palace Projects (based at Queen Mary, University of London) and the Centre for Applied Theatre (based at the University of Manchester).

It seems as if I have been working towards a 'globalizing' of cultural work within the warped world of the prison. In São Paulo for the launch of the human rights project in March 2001, I addressed the directors of the forty prisons where the project was due to take place. Standing beside the Secretary of State for Justice, I reflected on how far I had come since the dusty patio to which the workshops were banished in 1993. These directors had recently to cope with prison rebellions that had captured world headlines. While the State can rarely organize anything coherent within the system, the prisoners had managed to take 5,000 hostages across a series of prisons on the same day. Neither human rights nor theatre can have seemed a major priority for many of the people in the room on that Thursday morning, who looked as if they had become hostages to a process that they did not understand.

But I too was confused. And my confusion grows with the projects. While *Staging Human Rights* goes forward, we are now planning a five-year youth project with juvenile prisoners in Rio de Janeiro. Meanwhile, I am discussing with the Ministry of Justice how we can implement the human rights project in another six states across Brazil in 2002. Of course, I hope that every participant will continue to 'write their own page of the story' however big the project becomes. But my focus has been on the ways in which cultural-development work can be multiplied, and its impact extended, rather than on those small and particular experiences which I think we all believe initiate and incite the creative and political process.

And that is why I find in the fabric of my current project echoes of Don Adams' question about how we preserve the decentralization of our own work against the drive towards globalization. How big should we go? What is our responsibility as cultural activists when faced with the need to justify the impact of our work? It surely cannot be a numbers game. What is the balance between quality and quantity? The programme I describe above will not be equally good for 10,000 people. Does that matter? The original drama project in Brasília did not have an equal effect on the twenty people who took part. But is my desire to replicate a theatre project across forty prisons caught up in the imperatives of a capitalist model that gives value only to that which can be reproduced? Is the theatrical experience worth more when it can be packaged in such a way that it can be repeated? That way Disney lies.

I have no answers to these multiplying questions. I know that my fascination with performance is rooted in its unique existence at its moment of utterance, in the impossibility of its reproduction. Yet here I am trying to build ways in which it can be structured and repeated. Perhaps it has something to do with the prison itself. As I have written on another occasion:

> A prison is a world where survival is tested at its limits. Performance is normally thought of as that which does not survive, thus in seeking to ensure a continuity of theatre in the prisons, I seem to have been engaged in a bizarre act of negation: denying something essential in both the institution of prison and the activity of theatre. The survival of performance in prisons has for me become a form of resistance and negation of the system itself. And perhaps that is why replication and reproduction have become important (Delgado and Svich, 2002; in press).

Making theatre in prisons is a means of staging impossible encounters. All the greatest plays seem to be initiated by a meeting that should not or cannot happen: Oedipus with his father; Romeo with Juliet; Estragon and Vladimir with Godot. My memories of the last ten years of making theatre in Brazilian prisons are full of just such impossible encounters. The aim is for prisoners and guards to find new ways of engaging with each other and their world, seeking to restage the seemingly impossible meeting between prisons and society.

On each of my visits to see the work as it progresses, it is as difficult as ever to match the individual experiences of the participants with the conditions in which they are working. The power of a simple theatre game to transform the dehumanized spaces and relationships of a prison never fails to move and excite me, even after fifteen years of making theatre within the criminal justice system in Britain and abroad. As one prisoner reaches across to touch another, you know that a contact is being made that only happens because of this activity we call theatre, and it is in direct contradiction to the ways in which people are meant to relate within that space. Prisoners, teachers and guards have all given moving personal testimony to the impact of the work, reminding me of all that has been achieved in these years.

Of course, if such work is allowed to continue and grow, it probably doesn't represent much of a threat to a system that is in need of a complete revolution. I have written elsewhere about the relationship between prison theatre projects and rebellions (see Thompson,1999; pp. 231-238), and it is as important in Brazil as it is in Britain to question at all times the acceptance of cultural projects by a system that is based on such degrading and inhuman conditions. *Projeto Drama*, dealing with AIDS/HIV and therefore with sex and drugs in prisons, was never likely to trouble the prison authorities. It raised subjects that the authorities would prefer to remain unspoken, but like the prison itself, the programme appeared to address the security of the inmate. However, in announcing the new programme on human rights, I was aware that in both form and content we threatened to challenge the boundaries that hold the prison and the prisoner in place.

For all the quantitative data that has been gathered about the projects – how many workshops run, how many prisoners attended, how many condoms distributed – there remain doubts haunting the qualitative impact of this project. Does it work? As a result of these programmes will we really be able to say that there is less risk of AIDS/HIV in the São Paulo prison system? Will human-rights abuses really be prevented? What is the relationship between the reality of the prisons and the image of them that has been re-made through this work? The answers to these questions don't seem to get any closer as the project expands. Indeed, the 'proof' that is required of the efficacy of the work seems to become more elusive as the demand for it becomes that much more empirical. The Department of Preventative Medicine at the University of São Paulo undertook an independent evaluation of our AIDS/HIV programme that included interviews with four hundred prisoners before and after the project. They concluded that there was a significant change in the level of knowledge and attitudes concerning AIDS by those who participated in the programme and that all the objectives were achieved.

Despite that apparent success, as I have noted elsewhere (Thompson, 1999, pp. 31-41), I have chosen to look for indicators of success away from the notion of individual change. Of course we hope that as a result of the AIDS/HIV project people will make individual choices that do not place themselves at risk. But we cannot show that. What we can show is how the presence of this drama work in the prison changes the institution, and how new relationships come about as a result of the project. This in turn may lead to an environment of respect for self and for the other, and that might make some of the necessary individual changes more possible.

Although successes are important to note, failures are too. For every successful workshop, there is the one that didn't happen because a guard wouldn't open a door or a fight in the yard meant that all activities were stopped for a week. If I remember what theatre has been able to achieve, then I must also remember the young man who wrote the poem on which we based the first play I produced in a Brazilian prison in 1993. Two months later he died of meningitis in the prison because none of the public hospitals would take him. His name was Moisés, and his poem still serves as a reminder of the question that must stand behind all our work in prisons: *Why, Brasil? (Porque o Brasil?* Thompson, 1999, p. 41). It is in the questions and not the answers that these projects seek to make their interventions through encounters that might otherwise be impossible.

I have been a privileged spectator in Brazilian prisons for nearly ten years. My visa to enter this world has been the theatre skills that I teach, and I hope that by passing these on throughout the system, crossings can be made both ways. Our visits to the other worlds that performance offers are by their very nature limited, yet we are constantly embarking on journeys within such projects that seem to offer something more than the transience of the performance itself.

Staging Human Rights is intended to offer a means by which supposedly human connections can stand against the social discord that separates. The ties that currently bind prisoner and guard will be tested, as much as the ones that bind both of them with the society that has placed them inside the prison. As prisoners and guards begin to talk about the hidden worlds they inhabit, they can start to participate in public and urgent debates about crime, violence and prisons in ways that challenge the dominant discourses that condemn us all to live in the ever increasing shadows of the borderlands that we have created.

Notes

1. The *Favelas* are Brazil's shantytowns. I use the Brazilian word as any translation evokes the settlements found in English-speaking countries such as India and South Africa. The use of the Portuguese word reminds me of the cultural specificity of these improvised communities.
2. All statistics from Julita Lemgruber, *Racial bias in the Brazilian Criminal Justice System* Presentation to the World Conference against Racism, Racial Discrimination, Xenophobia and Related Intolerance, Durban, August 2001.
3. The prison complex of Carandiru has subsequently been deactivated, and four of the seven pavilions were symbolically blown up by the state authorities on 8 December 2002. Dr Varella's book, *Estação Carandiru*, has been made into a film by director Hector Babenco for Sony Classics, and received its world premiere on 11 April 2003. The BBC recorded a ninty minute dramatization of *Estação Carandiru* for the Radio 3 seires *Wired*. Broadcast May 2002 and June 2003. Available from www.peoplespalace.org
4. The phrase comes from Azril Bacal during an email group discussion prior to our meeting at Rockefeller Study Centre in Bellagio, May 2001.

References

Boal, A., Keynote speech at *Mundança de Cena II: teatro construindo cidadania*, Recife, September 2000. Published by The British Council (Brazil) in December 2001.

Boon, R. & Plastow, J., *Theatre Matters: Performance and Culture on the World Stage* (Cambridge University Press, 1998).

Delgado, M. & Svich, C., *Theatre in Crisis?: Performance Manifestos for a New Century* (Manchester University Press, 2002).

Heritage, P., 'The Promise of Performance', Boon, R. & Plastow, J., *Theatre Matters: Performance and Culture on the World Stage* (Cambridge University Press, 1998).

Heritage, P., 'Stolen Kisses', in Delgado, M & Svich, C., *Theatre in Crisis? Performance Manifesto for a New Century*, (Manchester University Press, 2002).

Ridenti, Marcelo., *Em busca do povo brasileiro: artistas da revolução, do CPC à era da tv* (Rio de Janeiro, Record, 2000).

Soares, Luiz Eduardo *Meu casaco de general* (Rio de Janeiro, Companhia de Letras, 2000).

Thompson, James (ed.), *Prison Theatre: Practices and Perspectives*, Jessica Kingsley, 1999).

Varella, Drauzio, *Estação Carandiru*, (São Paulo, Companhia das Letras, 1998).

INDEX